Hardy's Landscape Revisited

Hardy's Landscape Revisited

Thomas Hardy's Wessex in the Twenty-First Century

Tony Fincham

ROBERT HALE · LONDON

© Tony Fincham 2010
First published in Great Britain 2010

ISBN 978-0-7090-8699-4

Robert Hale Limited
Clerkenwell House
Clerkenwell Green
London EC1R 0HT

www.halebooks.com

A catalogue record for this book is available from the British Library

2 4 6 8 10 9 7 5 3 1

Typeset in 10/12.5pt Goudy
by e-type, Liverpool
Printed in Thailand

For Elizabeth and Paul, who unwittingly first brought me to Wessex.
And Mary, Rebecca, Guy, Clara and Harriet.

Acknowledgements

Michael Irwin, who initially put me in touch with Robert Hale, and whose example, both as a scholar and Hardy Society Chairman, I shall ever be trying to emulate.

At Robert Hale – Andrew Stilwell, who initially commissioned this work, and to Victoria Lyle, who saw it through to fruition. Many thanks for their guidance and endless patience and understanding.

Bill and Vera Jesty.

Helen Gibson, especially in her role at the DCM.

Dr Elizabeth James at the British Library.

Mavis Pilbeam.

Andrew and Marilyn Leah and all my friends and colleagues at the Thomas Hardy Society. Do contact us at www.hardysociety.org.

Maps 1.1 and 2.1 are reproduced by kind permission of the trustees of the Dorset County Museum.
Maps 4.1 and 7.2 copyright Guy Fincham.
Maps 6.1 and 7.1 are reproduced by permission of David and Charles, Newton Abbot.

All pictures are copyright Tony Fincham except:

2.1 copyright Simon Ellis
2.3, 3.2, 3.4 and 4.4 copyright Guy Fincham
9.1 and 9.2 copyright Helen Gibson
9.3 copyright Becky Fincham

Contents

Introduction

Why another book on Thomas Hardy's landscapes? Time passes, the landscape changes, our attitude towards our environment changes – and our understanding of Hardy changes with those shifting attitudes. 2010 represents 170 years since Hardy was born, eighty-two since he died and thirty-eight since the publication of Denys Kay-Robinson's groundbreaking (and near-definitive) work *Hardy's Wessex Re-appraised*. I have not tried to emulate Kay-Robinson – no one else could cram so many references into a page – but have borrowed where borrowing is due. With twenty-first century emphasis, this is a 'green' book about a 'green' writer. It is composed of a series of walks (or in one case a bicycle ride) through Hardy's landscapes – allowing the reader to appreciate not only the beauty and the wonder of the natural world, but also the unique contribution which Hardy has made to our ability to interpret that world. May I say, at the outset, that this book is very much a work in progress – the landscape changes, we are still gaining in knowledge of Hardy's world, there are new interpretations to be made – our perception of Wessex will never be static.

Hardy's understanding of the natural world arose from the juxtaposition of a childhood spent in the *Egdon* wilderness (at one with nature, but wholly aware of the harsh realities of agricultural life), the deeply penetrating vision of the poet ('the man who used to notice such things'), and his early enthusiastic readings of Darwin. Hardy's consequent comprehension of the equality of all living species and man's dependence upon nature is reflected strongly in his writing as well as in the attitudes of many in the twenty-first century. He is a green writer who uses environments to reflect character and changes in environment to reflect changes in character; ever-conscious also of the influence of man on the most seemingly natural of landscapes and the weathering effects of nature on the most man-made of structures. Hardy's understanding of man's place in the environment, his refusal to idealize the rustic and his unbiased attitude towards the terrible damage man has wrought upon that environment make him a writer with a strong message for this current age of global warming, over-population and rampant consumerism. Hardy, like Shakespeare, has an enduring message which transcends the centuries, with their transient intellectual and popular fashions.

The Wessex Question

Hardy initially wrote out of his own experience, about the areas of Dorset, London and Cornwall which he knew, using some real names and some fictitious and varying them fairly arbitrarily between novels. His first use of the term 'Wessex' was as a passing reference in chapter XLIX of *Far From the Madding Crowd* (1874). The resurrection of such historic terminology was an offshoot of Romanticism; Barnes's Dorset dialect was derived from 'Saxon Wessex' and in 1866 Charles Kingsley wrote of 'Wessex Worthies', an expression which resurfaces in *The Mayor of Casterbridge*. From *The Hand of Ethelberta* (1875) onwards Hardy began to construct 'the part real part dream country' which was to become his brand-name – a process which came to fruition in 1895 with the publication of the first collected edition of his works, complete with a detailed map of Wessex.

Hardy admitted that he 'ventured to adopt the word "Wessex" from the pages of early English history' to give 'fictitious significance' to the name 'of the district once included in that extinct kingdom'. Historically, Saxon Wessex originated in the sixth century in the area which is now modern Hampshire but slowly engulfed surrounding counties so that by Alfred the Great's reign in the late ninth century it included all of southern England; during his reign Mercia was also subsumed, so that the Kingdom of Wessex became the Kingdom of England. Hardy's Wessex therefore has never overlapped exactly with its Saxon progenitor.

The Wessexification of his fiction – and subsequently poetry – served two purposes. Firstly, and most obviously, it defined both his product and his territory. This was a shrewd marketing ploy which continues to pay vast dividends. Romanticism heralded the great age of literary tourism; what better way to maintain interest in your writings, not only during your lifetime but posthumously also, than by creating a semi-fictitious landscape which can forever-after be a place of pilgrimage? If the brand proves successful – and Hardy's Wessex probably outranks all except Goethe and Rousseau's efforts with the Alps – it ultimately has a profound effect upon the real countryside upon which the fiction was projected. Recently English Nature sponsored a five-year Hardy's Egdon Heath Project; this was an attempt to reconstruct Hardy's Great Heath by 'restoring' a 'natural' environment which, from the historical evidence, never existed outside the pages of his fiction. This is a bizarre offshoot of Hardy's literary success, the environmental impact of which must be open to question.

A mere twenty-one years after Hardy first used the word Wessex he noted that his 'dream-country' was well established. It had, 'by degrees solidified into a utilitarian region which people can go to, take a house in, and write to the papers from …' One of Hardy's greatest impacts on the British landscape has been this, almost accidental, creation of a twenty-first century Wessex, headed by a Royal Earl and Countess, where you drink Wessex Water, eat organic Wessex produce, send your children to the Wessex Academy, travel in Wessex Taxis and are eventually laid to rest by the Wessex Funeral Service – pushing 'Dorset' into outmoded insignificance.

The second, and in this study more important, aspect of Wessex is the way in which it acted as a disguise, a smokescreen over Hardy's actual landscapes. He wrote from home and most of his landscapes are to be found within a few miles of his cob-and-thatch cottage in Thorncombe Wood. The territory of a Celtic bard is defined as the distance a man can traverse on foot in one day, go beyond this and you are in the territory of another bard. Such a definition suits Hardy well. John Fowles noted that: 'that jealously preserved and frequently concealed Dorset peasant self that lies somewhere near the heart of his creation springs essentially from a very small landscape'.(1) Whilst I do not welcome the pejorative implication of 'peasant', I'm sure that Fowles is otherwise spot-on in his interpretation. Hardy's natural tendency is centripetal; all his landscapes, all his characters draw back to *Egdon* and the cottage where they were first created. The establishment of a structured, clearly defined Wessex was a balancing centrifugal process which both promoted Hardy as a 'regional' rather than purely 'local' novelist and kept prying eyes and literary critics somewhat away from the cottage where his parents were still living and the heath upon which the heart of the sensitive poet was to be found. Thus *Blooms-End*, which in the first edition of *The Return of the Native* was illustrated as being his birthplace, could safely be moved a mile (two kilometres) away to Bhompston and Tess and Jude and his later creations could be seen to geographically inhabit a harmless, more distant Wessex – even though Tess had to return to the edge of the heath to find happiness at *Talbothays* and Jude's umbilical cord stretched all the way back to *Mellstock*, where he was born.

To gain the most from this book you firstly need a copy of *The Complete Poems of Thomas Hardy* edited by James Gibson. Hardy was first and last a poet, who wrote some fiction in-between his poetry; this book is laced with references to Hardy's poems, designated as 'CP' followed by the Gibson poem number. Secondly, particularly if you plan to follow the walks, you need some Ordnance Survey Explorer maps; Sheet OL 15 'Purbeck and South Dorset' plus Sheet 117 'Cerne Abbas and Bere Regis' will cover the vast majority of Hardy's landscapes. To avoid the confusion caused by widely varying editions, citations from Hardy's fiction are not referenced, although the story to which I am referring is generally readily apparent. Hardy's Wessex places names are in the main italicized and a detailed glossary is included at the end of this book.

When is the best time of year to follow these walks? Probably winter or early spring for then, although the going is likely to be muddy, the views are at their best, the crops minimal, and the trees denuded of foliage allow buildings to be seen more clearly and whole landscape vistas to open before your eyes. And Hardy is, above all, a 'landscape novelist' (2), a great visualizer.

Finally, as you use this book to explore Hardy's Wessex – and, hopefully come to a Hardyan understanding of your place, your role even, in the landscape – think of Clym (Hardy) in 'Aftercourses', the postscript to *The Return of the Native*:

> He frequently walked alone on the heath, when the past seized him with its shadowy hand, and held him there to listen to its tale ... his imagination would then people the spot with its ancient inhabitants ...

CHAPTER ONE

————

Egdon Heath

This severe unwelcoming landscape with its strange beauty and untameable
character became one of the grand metaphors of Thomas Hardy's imagination
– a symbol of Nature's indifference to human frustration and despair … (1)

Origins

As the sun rose over the dewy foxgloves and delicate fern fronds of
Piddletown Heath on the second morning of June 1840, the young wife of a
local builder lay exhausted and groaning in the final stages of a difficult
labour, wholly oblivious to the sounds of the waking heath: the churr of the
dew-fall hawk, the creak of the furzeacker (2), the kiss of the stonechat and
the call of the toads. The baby delivered at 8 a.m., initially cast aside as dead,
was to develop from a precocious toddler into a bright, questioning and obser-
vant young child – 'the man who used to notice such things'. The isolated
cottage at the far end of a narrow track to nowhere, grandly labelled 'New
Bockhampton' was no more than an extension of the surrounding heath for:

> Snakes and efts,
> Swarmed in the summer days and nightly bats
> Would fly about our bedrooms. Heathcroppers
> Lived on the hills, and were our only friends;
> So wild it was when first we settled here. (CP 1)

In *The Return of the Native*, Hardy – at the time himself a returned native –
describes Clym Yeobright as having 'been so interwoven with the heath in
his boyhood that hardly anybody could look upon it without thinking of
him'. For, 'if anyone knew the heath well it was Clym. He was permeated
with its scenes, with its substance, and with its odours. He might be said to

13

be its product. His eyes had first opened thereon; with its appearance all the images of his memory were mingled ... His toys had been the flint knives and arrow-heads which he found there ... his flowers the purple bells and yellow gorse; his animal kingdom the snakes and croppers; his society its human haunters.' For Clym, read Hardy.

After repeated rejections by publishers, Hardy finally found his way into print in the spring of 1871 when William Tinsley published *Desperate Remedies*, a sensation novel in the style of Wilkie Collins written somewhat against Hardy's natural inclinations in order to achieve his ambition of becoming a published writer. Over the ensuing four years Hardy turned out one major novel per annum under the continued pressure of monthly serial publication. In 1875, following this creative outpouring, he paused, took stock of his position, read and researched widely before embarking slowly on the text of *The Return of the Native*; this was a novel in five acts following the classic unities of time and place but with the action occurring over one-year-and-a-day rather than the conventional single day.

The Return of the Native is therefore seminal in his canon, not only because it is his most carefully constructed and researched novel, but also because it was written by the thirty-six-year-old, married Hardy returning from his experiences of metropolitan society to write about the tragedy of existence upon the heath on which he was born and with which he was intimately familiar. It was from this heath that all Hardy's fiction arose. It was upon this heath that he developed his intimate understanding of the tragic struggle for existence, both in the natural world of the heathland flora and fauna and in the artificial world of the heathmen – the heathens – who struggled to extract a meagre existence from its barren surface. In observing these parallel struggles, Hardy was acutely aware of the damage that man was causing to his fellow creatures by the overexploitation of limited resources.

The young Hardy was an early and enthusiastic reader of Darwin's *On the Origin of Species* (1859), a book which was to have a profound impact on both his mature thought and his religious convictions. Darwin revealed that there was 'no difference in principle' between man and all other species of animal and plant. Every species had evolved from the same indifferent life-force, thus invalidating the Christian concept of man as a superior 'knowing' species, in the image of God. To Hardy, Darwin's theories closely matched his own experiences of a childhood spent in the *Egdon* wilderness, during which he was continuously conscious both of the wonders of nature and the harsh realities of life for the agricultural poor. This led to his rejection of the Wordsworthian ideal of a beneficent nature; instead he saw cruelty and futility on both sides of a two-way relationship. There was no grand design, merely self-interest and an instinctive struggle for survival. As Clym walks away from his engagement tryst with Eustacia Vye:

> ... the dead flat of the scenery overpowered him, though he was fully alive to the beauty of that untarnished early summer green which was worn for the nonce by the poorest blade. There was something in its oppressive horizontality which too much reminded him of the arena of life: it gave him a sense of bare equality with and no superiority to a single living thing under the sun.

When writing about the natural world – and most especially of his native heath – Hardy treats both *Egdon* and its human population as one large evolutionary text which requires scientific decoding; through such an analysis, the poet struggles towards an understanding of the purpose of life on earth. Although at times this produced bleak despair – the wish 'to have my life unbe' – or at least, like Peter Pan, to never grow up, it also led to a consciousness of that 'blessed hope, whereof he knew / And I was unaware' (CP 119).

For Hardy, *Egdon* is, 'a place perfectly accordant with man's nature – neither ghastly, hateful nor ugly: neither commonplace, unmeaning nor tame, but like man slighted and enduring'; it is upon *Egdon* therefore that any exploration of his landscape must begin.

History: Domesday

> This obscure, obsolete, superseded country features in Domesday. Its condition is recorded therein as that of heathy, furzy, briary wilderness – 'Bruaria'.

Although Domesday records Hardy's *Egdon* as Bruaria with little land under cultivation, it does indicate that much of the wilderness was being grazed as pasture land. On western *Egdon*, only one farm is recorded, Hethfelton, in an inhospitable position high on the windswept heath of East Stoke Parish; this is subsequently the home of Farmer Lodge in 'The Withered Arm'.

The clearest description of *Egdon* Heath comes from Hermann Lea, the Dorset photographer and Hardy enthusiast, who was supported by Hardy in his illustrated narrative *Thomas Hardy's Wessex*, which was ultimately incorporated into Macmillan's definitive Wessex edition of Hardy's novels as a supplementary volume. Lea describes *Egdon* Heath as:

> That vast expanse of moorland which stretches, practically without a break, from Dorchester to Bournemouth. Its natural, untameable wildness is the charm that makes it so subtly attractive, for it defies all attempts at subjuga-

tion – except in a few isolated spots, and even those efforts to cultivate it have involved an amount of labour and expense which is scarcely justified by the results. It is unconquered and unconquerable by agriculture, and more immutable in character than any other part of the Wessex country. (3)

Hardy states that:

> The untameable, Ishmaelitish thing that Egdon now was it always had been. Civilization was its enemy. Ever since the beginning of vegetation its soil had worn the same antique brown dress. The great inviolate place had an ancient permanence which the sea cannot claim. Who can say of a particular sea that it is old? Distilled by the sun, kneaded by the moon, it is renewed in a year, in a day, or in an hour. The sea changed, the fields changed, the rivers, the villages and the people changed yet Egdon remained.

Civilization Was its Enemy

Yes, but contrary to the impression Hardy gives, heathland is managed land. It is a man-made environment. Pollen analysis of the peat bogs of *Egdon* show that in the distant past, like most of the rest of the British Isles, it was dominated by woodland, albeit a lighter cover than elsewhere, reflecting its thin, inhospitable soil. Mesolithic man – the hunter-gatherer – opened up this light woodland cover whilst Bronze Age man had little difficulty in clearing it altogether hence creating the heath upon which he has left his other permanent memorial, the multiple barrows which dominate the skyline. Once the woodland was lost, human activities perpetuated the change: grazing by heath-croppers, cattle and sheep, furze-cutting for fuel and animal fodder, controlled burning, the taking of clay and sand, and the use of bracken and heather for bedding, thatching and besom-making.

Civilization was its enemy. This has been proved to be especially true over the century since Hardy and Lea described *Egdon*. In 'The Withered Arm', Hardy describes the heath as it was around the time of his birth. Gertrude Lodge is following a secluded route across the heath in an attempt to arrive at *Casterbridge* unobserved:

> Though the date was comparatively recent, Egdon was much less fragmentary in character than now. The attempts – successful and otherwise – at cultivation on the lower slopes, which intrude and break up the original heath into small detached heaths, had not been carried far: Enclosure Acts had not taken effect, and the banks and fences which now exclude the cattle

of those villagers who formerly enjoyed rights of commonage thereon, and the carts of those who had turbary privileges which kept them in firing all the year round were not erected. Gertrude therefore rode along with no other obstacles than the prickly furze-bushes, the mats of heather, the white watercourses, and the natural steeps and declivities of the ground.

The Great Heath extending from Bockhampton to beyond Bournemouth was not just a figment of Hardy's imagination; it was a reality when Hardy's grand-parents settled into their thatched cottage at the eastern extremity of New Bockhampton, and still largely a reality during Hardy's childhood in the 1840–50s. The first edition Ordnance Survey map of 1811 shows heathland starting at the Hardys' cottage and extending continuously and without inter-ruption south-east to the sea at Studland and Bournemouth and with minimal interruption north-east to the New Forest at Ringwood, a distance of thirty miles (fifty kilometres) as the crow flies. The interruptions in continuous heathland were mainly geographical because *Egdon* is – and always has been – broken by river valleys. Firstly, Hardy's 'Valley of the Great Dairies … in which milk and butter grew to rankness', 'the plain so well watered by the River Var or Froom'; next the Piddle, both rivers flowing through Wareham to Poole Harbour; then, further north and east, the great River Stour emptying into Christchurch Bay. History depends on geography; *Egdon* would have been of no use to William I as a hunting ground because it is subdivided by fertile river valleys, unlike the barren New Forest.

Also, unlike the *Great Forest* (New Forest), which still stretches for seven-teen uninterrupted miles (twenty-seven kilometres) from Ringwood to the Solent, there was never one single Great Heath, but rather a continuing series of adjoining heaths, together forming the haggard *Egdon* waste. Thus Piddletown Heath linked to Southover Heath via Islington Wood; Southover led to Affpiddle and Bryantspiddle Heath; and then there were the great and continuous Bere and Wool Heaths which became Hyde and Bloxworth Heaths as the traveller rode eastward. From here Decoy Heath, Gore Heath and Holton Heath, then Lychett Common and the great Canford and Poole Heaths could be followed to the open sandy beach at Bournemouth with not a building in sight. Where is this *Egdon* waste now?

Civilization was its enemy: it has fallen prey to four main human activities:

1. The army
2. Afforestation
3. Enclosure for agriculture
4. House building

I have listed these activities in order of increasing destructiveness.

Lesley Haskins in *Heathlands 'Discover Dorset'* (2003) lists forty-three separate surviving Dorset heaths, of which forty lie between Higher Bockhampton and Hengistbury Head and form the severed remnants of the once great *Egdon*. Many of these remaining heaths are small and irregular, less than fifty acres (twenty hectares) in size, and most are partially afforested. Many of the more southerly components of *Egdon*, which in fact form most of its best preserved stretches, are not listed. This is not because they no longer exist, but because they fall within a military 'danger area', established as a firing range in 1943; these include Highwood, West Holme, Holme and Povington Heaths. North of the Frome, Bovington Heath, Wool Heath and Tonerspuddle Heath were annexed and the public excluded due to the establishment of a tank training ground in 1916, an encroachment subsequently extended to include the Atomic Energy Research Establishment at Winfrith. But, despite this destruction and enclosure, the very act of excluding both the farmer and the public has preserved the heathland habitat in an unspoilt state which would not otherwise have survived. In the valleys around Tyneham the army has preserved an empty natural habitat which would, without the firing range, have suffered the same fate as the west Dorset coastline and been submerged under a sea of caravans, bungalows and other unsightly developments. In a paradox which parallels Hardy's hatred of any form of suffering but his fascination with the mechanics of the Napoleonic wars, the military presence in Purbeck and on southern *Egdon* has been its salvation. Like Hardy, we may abhor warmongers, yet we can see the necessity of allowing soldiers to conserve the countryside.

Afforestation had begun in Hardy's time but accelerated with the establishment of the Forestry Commission in 1919, whose stated aim was to turn 'non-productive' heathland into 'productive' conifer plantations, thus converting 'the heathens'! The core of Hardy's *Egdon* – Piddletown, Bhompston and Duddle Heaths – was fully planted-up whilst the ancient woodland to the east at Islington was decimated by agriculture. From Admiston, just south of Athelhampton, the forest extended all the way to Wareham, apart from the army bases at Bovington Camp and Decoy Heath.

'Wildeve's Patch, as it was called, a plot of land redeemed from the heath, and after long and laborious years brought into cultivation. The man who discovered that it could be broken up died of the labour: the man who succeeded him in possession ruined himself in fertilizing it.' This quote demonstrates how, although the large-scale enclosure of common land was rare in Dorset, a more insidious small-scale 'reclamation' of heath for agriculture occurred during Hardy's lifetime, accelerating in the twentieth century, especially during the world wars. Once heath was destroyed, the farmers – like the army – were reluctant to return the land, however marginal its productivity.

Add in the southward drift of the population, with the consequent demand for building land, and nearly ninety per cent of *Egdon* has been destroyed. Urbanization has wrought the greatest change on east *Egdon* where the desolate Poole and Canford Heaths, lapped only by the tide at the time of Hardy's birth, have been completely engulfed by housing, merging Poole, Bournemouth and Christchurch into one massive conurbation. Bournemouth, which was uninhabited in 1841, had a population of 37,500 when Tess and Alex in *Tess of the D'Urbervilles* took lodgings fifty years later; it was then a 'fashionable watering-place, with its eastern and its western stations, its piers, its groves of pines, its promenades and its covered gardens'. Hardy notes that, 'an outlying eastern tract of the enormous Egdon Waste was close at hand ... within the space of a mile from its outskirts every irregularity of the soil was prehistoric, every channel an undisturbed British trackway; not a sod having been turned since the days of the Caesars.' Sadly, that prehistoric soil has long-since disappeared under the aggressive hand of the developer, so that the population of Bournemouth *alone* now stands at 165,000, and the heath survives in minute, discarded, fenced-off pockets, awaiting the call of the concrete mixer.

Although lowland heathland is internationally recognized as an endangered habitat, it is estimated that one-and-a-half acres (half a hectare) of *Egdon* Heath is still being lost daily, mainly to development. The Domesday Book, which certainly underestimated acreage of wild land, recorded *Egdon* as being around 60,000 acres (24,300 hectares). The first Ordnance Survey map of 1811 shows nearly 80,000 acres (32,400 hectares) of *Egdon* Heath (some authorities put this figure as high as 100,000 acres (40,500 hectares)). Approximately 10,000 acres (4,050 hectares) of unspoilt heathland remain today, of which nearly a quarter is on Ministry of Defence (MOD) property.

Above all, *The Return of the Native* is a book about the landscape and our attitudes towards it. Early in the text, Hardy dismisses the voice of the Age of Reason, as expressed by Hutchins, that *Egdon* was 'of all others the most dreary and unpleasing' of landscapes. Instead he steps beyond the Romanticism of Wordsworth to adopt a neo-Gothic position which points towards early twentieth-century modernism and *The Waste Land* of T.S. Eliot. *Egdon* is both majestic and sublime in a novel and unsettling way:

Fair prospects wed happily with fair times, but alas if times be not fair! Men have oftener suffered from the mockery of a place too smiling for their reason than from the oppression of surroundings over-sadly tinged. Haggard Egdon appealed to a subtler and scarcer instinct, a more recently learnt emotion, than that which responds to the sort of beauty called charming and fair. The time seems near, if it has not actually arrived, when the chastened sublimity of a moor, a sea, or a mountain will be all of nature that is absolutely in keeping with the moods of the more thinking among mankind.

A *Return of the Native* Walk

The Heart of Hardy Country

By foot (three miles/five kilometres)

To fully appreciate the atmosphere, the solitude, of *Egdon* Heath, set out on this walk at daybreak or as dusk is falling; in the latter circumstance, allow for the fact that it will take you 60–90 minutes to complete.

Begin at Thorncombe Wood Car Park, near Hardy's Cottage. Take the path on the left at the far end of the car park and follow it steeply uphill into the trees. Heading for Rushy Pond you soon come into a beautiful glade of tall beeches (plate 1.1). Follow the path straight on and beside an old metal boundary fence to a new wooden gate beside a notice board. This gate was installed as part of Hardy's Egdon Heath Project, an ambitious conservation

1.1 Thorncombe Wood

project designed to return much of *Egdon* Heath to its original state. Trees have been felled and rhododendrons destroyed – cut down in year one, sprayed at the end of year two, to die in year three – with a view to allowing grazing to keep the undergrowth down. Unfortunately, no English domestic animals eat rhododendrons, and local farmers are not keen to invest in cattle which will eat furze and ferns, so the scheme has reached something of a stalemate.

Follow the path uphill from the gate. You are crossing Black Heath, an area which has been extensively cleared but, in the absence of grazing, young trees (mainly silver birch) are creating woodland again. There are plans to reintroduce heath-croppers – the ponies which roamed the heath in Hardy's day – but so far these have not come to fruition and the five-year Hardy's Egdon Heath Project has ended. A family of badgers lives in the dell to your left and in the winter you may be fortunate enough to spot one in the daytime.

Pause for a moment on one of the benches beside Rushy Pond (plate 1.2). It is an idyllic spot. We are only a few hundred yards from Hardy's Cottage. This is an area which he knew intimately as a child. In *The Early Life*, Hardy describes taking the family's 'big brass telescope' to a hill on the heath behind the house to watch an execution nearly three miles (five kilometres)

1.2 Rushy Pond

distant, the roofs of the prison being then clearly visible: 'The whole thing was so sudden that the glass nearly fell from Hardy's hands. He seemed alone on the heath with the hanged man, and crept homeward wishing he had not been so curious.' The spot from which he watched the execution was here beside the pond; Thorncombe was then heath rather than woodland and there was an uninterrupted view towards Dorchester.

This is one of three permanent ponds on the western edge of *Egdon*. The others are Green Hill Pond (p.25) and Heedless Williams Pond, inaccessible and hidden by tall trees just north of the lane midway between Bockhampton Cross and the *Quiet Woman*. Local legend maintains that the unfortunate William was a drunken mail-van driver who ran his vehicle off the road, over-turning it in the pond and drowning himself in the process. A casual inspection of the site confirms the improbability of this story as the pond is set well back from the lane up a steep bank. Recent research suggests that the name 'Headless William' was in use as early as 1372 and refers to a roadside stone, that still exists, rather than to the pond.

Cross the barrier behind the pond to follow the footpath along the Roman road. This is an overgrown but well preserved raised section of the road which ran from Dorchester (*Durnovaria*) to Salisbury and ultimately onto London; it cut across *Egdon* in a straight line to the hill fort at Badbury Rings, west of Wimborne, where it turned sharply northward. 'The Roman Road runs straight and bare / As the pale parting-line in hair / Across the heath' (CP 218). Somewhat ironically, the Roman road is no longer a public right of way but a permissive route across the privately owned Duddle Heath. Here, also, the heath has been extensively cleared of trees and rhododendrons, allowing the Bronze Age Rainbarrows to re-emerge from the deep coniferous cover which had obscured them for fifty years. The downside of this clearance is that the next stretch of path, which used to be a well defined route under the trees, is now hard to follow in the summer months.

After about 400 yards (360 metres) of Roman road there is a path on the right beside a holly bush which cuts down through some pines to the open heath. On reaching the heath turn left and follow the narrow path along the edge of the heath curving to your right; this should bring you past Rainbarrows one and two and on to Rainbarrow number three, which stands on the crest of the ridge, surmounted by a holly tree. This is Eustacia Vye's *Blackbarrow* (First Edition), subsequently amended by Hardy to Rainbarrow (plate 1.3). There is no evidence that this barrow was ever known locally as Blackbarrow but a tumulus of that name still exists on the heath, just north-east of Lulworth, confined within the military zone. At quieter times of day/seasons of the year, you can expect to meet deer on or near this

1.3 Rainbarrow

path. In the summer and early autumn, watch out for the occasional adder sunning itself on the path – descendants of the viper which bit Mrs Yeobright, contributing to her untimely death.

If the path to the right off the Roman road is not readily visible, follow the 'road' straight on to a stile and turn left along a track. After about 400 yards (360 metres) a small stile will appear in the fence on your left – cross this and follow the path ahead to Rainbarrow.

Diggory Venn stops to rest his tired ponies in the shadow of Rainbarrow:

> The scene before the reddleman's eyes was a gradual series of ascents from the level of the road backward into the heart of the heath. It embraced hillocks, pits, ridges, acclivities, one behind the other, till all was finished by a high hill cutting against the still light sky. The traveller's eye hovered about these things for a time, and finally settled upon one noteworthy object up there. It was a barrow. This bossy projection of earth above its natural level occupied the loftiest ground of the loneliest height the heath contained.

On the summit of the barrow, Diggory notices a motionless form, Eustacia, scanning the horizon. Ahead of her, in the distance, the chalk downs obscure

Osmington Bay, where 'hill hid tides throb throe on throe' (CP 563); to the left, on a clear day, there are extensive views to Purbeck Hills and right to the Hardy Monument on Blackdown. Closer to and further to the right Kingston Maurward House dominates the middle-distance. Beyond it lie the chimneys and spires of *Casterbridge* (Dorchester), the prison being clearly visible from here, at times magically illuminated by the early morning sun. Beyond *Casterbridge* lies the unsightly sprawl of Poundbury new town.

Sit down on the far (south) side of the barrow. Spread before you is the *Valley of the Great Dairies*; you can see the cattle grazing in the water meadows and hear their intermittent disgruntled bellows. At 'half-past four o'clock' listen out for the 'Waow! Waow! Waow!' of the cows being driven to milking, for this is the enchanted land where Tess fell in love with Angel. The distinctive cream-coloured buildings ahead are the cottages of Norris Mill Farm, the model for *Talbothays* Dairy. Below here and slightly to the left is Duck Dairy Farm, the site of Wildeve's home, the *Quiet Woman Inn*. The original building – referred to elsewhere by Hardy as 'The Travellers' Rest' (CP 563) and marked as such on the first Ordnance Survey map – has been demolished, but it is easy to see how Eustacia standing alone on the barrow would have been visible both from the road below and to Wildeve at the door of his inn. The extensive woods to the left, beyond the *Quiet Woman*, cover the former Islington Heath, at the edge of which lies *Shadwater Weir*, where Eustacia and Wildeve drown on that stormy 6 November night.

Head westward from Rainbarrow along a narrow path just behind the tumulus to a cross stile in a stock fence. Turn left along the track, heading back into the heath. Continue straight on beside the fence for about 500 yards (460 metres), passing the end of the Roman road path, then take the next track on your right. When it forks, after less than 100 yards (ninety metres), turn left and follow this path gently downhill through woodland. Cross the track at the bottom and continue on gently uphill until you meet a broad gravelled trackway. Turn left and follow this curving track uphill. As you approach the top of the hill, the likely site of *Mistover Knap* is on your left.

Hardy describes *Mistover Knap* as a 'small hamlet' consisting of two cottages and 'the only remaining house – that of Captain Vye and Eustacia, which stood quite away from the small cottages, and was the loneliest of lonely houses on these thinly populated slopes'. Lea informs us that '*Mistover* was the fictitious name given to a few houses which were scattered upon the heath in this locality; but being built only of mud, they have completely disappeared. As long as the roof is kept in good repair these mud-walled houses will last a long time, but directly that becomes defective the walls literally melt away. This method of building is practically a lost art.' (4)

There is no evidence of there ever having been permanent dwellings on this part of the heath. However, this area would have been known intimately by Hardy, lying as it does on the ridge behind his home. On damp winter mornings one can quite often see the mist clinging to the ridge at this point, strongly suggestive of *Mistover Knap*. The *Knap* stood beside a pond, the only immediate candidate for which is Green Hill Pond. **This can be reached by going straight ahead on the semi-metalled track across the junction at the top of the hill. Follow it until it descends round a corner and the pond lies on your right.** This pond is indeed nowhere near a hilltop, so it does not match Hardy's description.

Retrace your steps back to the fiveways junction. Here take the grassy track straight ahead through the birch trees (this represents a sharp first left from the original track from Rainbarrow). Beside this track is a low earthen wall – the common boundary markers on the heath – and a small permanent pond surrounded by a crescent of water reeds, suggesting that this was once a larger pond. The low wall behind the house, separating it from the pond, is clearly described in *The Return of the Native*, so this seems as reasonable a place as any to imagine *Mistover Knap*. There is a significant swallet hole here also, which could well be a pond. The slope to the south of the path is covered in young pine trees; seven years ago, when it was clear of vegetation, it formed an excellent viewpoint straight down the valley and giving clear views of Rainbarrow to the right. This is how it would have appeared in Hardy's lifetime when the whole area was open heathland. This is as close as one can get to the description Hardy gives of *Mistover Knap*, as Eustacia waits for Wildeve to respond to her 5 November signal:

> Before going on her walk again the young girl stood still on the bank for a few instants and listened. It was to the full as lonely a place as Blackbarrow, though at rather a lower level; and it was more sheltered from wind and weather on account of the few firs to the North. The bank enclosed the whole homestead, and well protected it from the lawless state of the world without; it was formed of thick square clods, dug from the ditch on the outside, and built up with a slight batter or incline, which forms no slight defence where hedges will not grow because of the wind and wilderness, and where wall materials are unattainable. Otherwise the situation was quite open, commanding the whole length of the valley which reached to the river behind Wildeve's house. High above this to the right, and much nearer than the Quiet Woman Inn, the blurred contour of Blackbarrow obscured the sky.

When, in due course, the Forestry Commission fell their timber, we may once more be able to experience Hardy's *Mistover Knap*.

As you emerge from the trees at the next junction (also a fiveways), take the second left and go straight on. This path goes slightly uphill, is often a bit muddy and follows the boundary wall. At the next junction take the main path slightly right and follow on downhill ignoring all turnings. You emerge onto open heathland with the rear of the Hardys' Cottage a white blob behind the trees in the distance (plate 1.4). This is the situation, if not the exact orientation, of the Yeobrights' home, *Blooms-End*, as first encountered by Eustacia Vye on a reconnaissance mission; descending the hill from *Mistover Knap* she observes, 'a row of white palings which marked the verge of the heath in this latitude ... beyond the white palings was a little garden; behind the garden an old, irregular, thatched house, facing the heath, and commanding a full view of the valley'.

Lea, guided by Hardy, states unequivocally, that 'Blooms-End was drawn from a farmhouse called Bhompston, which stands in a grass field just off the margin of the heath.' (5) Bhompston Farm, in reality, is situated just above the banks of the Frome in the *Valley of the Great Dairies*. Even on the earliest of maps (Ordnance Survey 1811), it stands over half a mile (800 metres) from the nearest outpost of heath. So why was Hardy in 1913, thirty-five years after the publication of *The Return of the Native*, trying to deliberately mislead his

1.4 *Blooms-End*

readers about its topography? Hardy started from exactly the opposite position, for the first map of any kind to accompany his works was the map, 'copied from the one I used in writing the story', which Hardy requested Smith Elder to display in a prominent position in the first three-volume edition of 1878. This map is displayed here alongside a reprint of a mid-twentieth-century Ordnance Survey map (maps 1.1 and 1.2). Hardy's map is aligned east–west rather than the more conventional north–south, but the relationship between the four main locations – in particular the triangle between *Mistover*, *Blackbarrow* and *Blooms-End* – is very clearly reproduced in the Ordnance Survey map.

At the time of writing *The Return of the Native* Hardy was himself a returning native, a son of the heath who had gone to the great metropolis to make good. He had left in the solid profession of architect, but returned in the much less secure and dubious position of author of serial fiction for magazines.

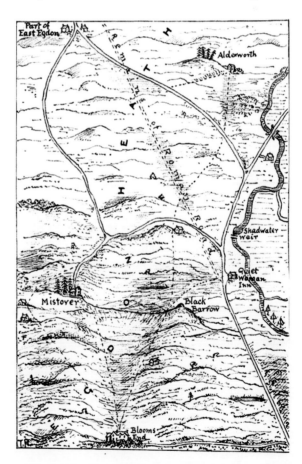

Map 1.1 Hardy's map of *Egdon* Heath

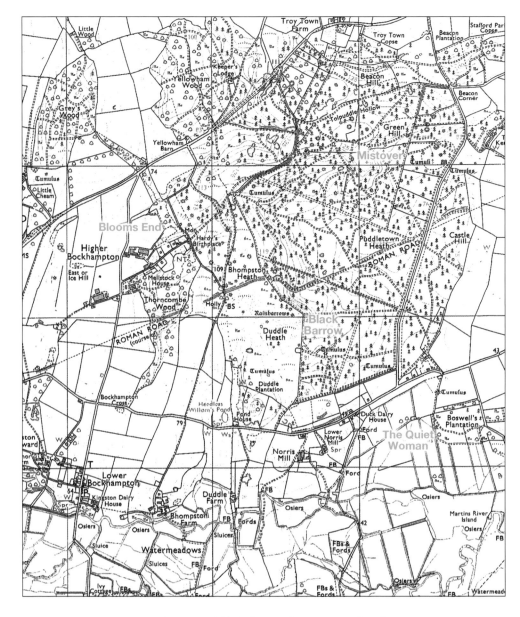

Map 1.2 Old Ordnance Survey map of *Egdon*

The landscape of the novel as Hardy wrote *The Return of the Native* was very much the landscape of his own mind and many of the events in the lives of the characters are reflections of his personal experience. *Egdon* Heath was his

28

own backyard, the intimately familiar playground of his childhood and adolescence. As Michael Millgate observes:

> ... while the map had been deliberately disorientated ... it still clearly showed – to anyone familiar with the countryside around Dorchester – that the place whose unity Hardy sought so earnestly to preserve – was the tract of heathland immediately adjacent to Higher Bockhampton with the position of the fictional Bloom's-End approximating to the house in which he himself was born and his parents still lived. (6)

Tony Slade picked up this issue in the current Penguin Classics volume:

> The map, therefore, would surely have precisely and directly conveyed a clear message to two very specific readers in the first instance: the 'young woman' of his past (Tryphena Sparks or whoever) and Hardy's mother. To yet another reader (his wife, Emma) there would have been still another signal which she would have picked up in the ms after only a few moments of transcribing and contemplation: namely, not only the suggestion of a strong autobiographical element in the novel, but also disturbing reverberations (to her mind) of 'lower-class' life, of its author's better-hidden 'low' origins, and his awareness of the heath as a scene of intense passion and tragedy. What, she must have wondered, was driving him now to publish such a map which surely – all too clearly – would make his self-revelations even more obvious and public? (7)

Hardy's initial motivation was undoubtedly his wish to demonstrate the unity of place preserved by his novel, as in Greek tragedy. Somewhat ironically, in his letter to Smith Elder, he argued that, 'nothing could give such reality to a tale as a map of this sort'. Hardy, naively, had not foreseen the kind of reality that readers and critics would extract from an apparently autobiographical novel containing as its frontispiece a map at the bottom centre of which was the cottage of his birth. By the second edition the map had been relegated to the rear of the book and was expunged from the Wessex edition of 1895, never to resurface. In his co-ordinated Wessex edition, *Blooms-End* was a farmhouse beside the Frome, more than a mile distant from its true location in the thatched homestead at the top end of Bockhampton Lane, that gateway to *Egdon*.

Imbibe the atmosphere of his cottage, if you are lucky enough to find it open, and then take the clearly signposted path behind the cottage up through Thorncombe Wood and back down to the car park. Alternatively follow 'Cherry Lane' straight ahead from the cottage.

Mrs Yeobright's Last Walk

Extended *Egdon*

By foot (nine miles/fourteen kilometres)

This a more ambitious walk, retracing Mrs Yeobright's steps – as far as is possible with current land usage – from her home at *Blooms-End* to Clym's Cottage at *Alderworth* and then back onto the heath. The walk is linear, starting once more from Thorncombe Wood Car Park and finishing at Cull-peppers Dish Car Park near Affpuddle.

Hardy informs us of the exact date of Mrs Yeobright's last walk – Thursday 31 August – and the year was 1843, for the action of *The Return of the Native*, which lasts one year and one day, starts 5 November 1842. Mrs Yeobright is a strong character, a powerful, controlling woman, who has run out of people to control. Her husband has died, her niece, Thomasin, has married away from home, and, against her wishes, her son has now done the same. She has just had a blazing row with her daughter-in-law, Eustacia, to whom she cuttingly describes herself as, 'only a poor woman who has lost her son'. Thus utterly defeated and depressed, she sets off across the heath seeking reconciliation with Clym and Eustacia, bearing china as a gift. Hardy's description of Mrs Yeobright's 'Journey across the Heath' is a magnificent melding of landscape and emotion, in which *Egdon* becomes the external expression of the dying woman's innermost torment.

Thursday 31 August was one of a series of days of stifling heat when 'stinging insects haunted the air, the earth and every drop of water that was to be found', plants were flagging and 'even stiff cabbages were limp'. The sun 'had branded the whole heath with his mark' 'the air was like that of a kiln' and the paths incinerated … this 'torrid attack made the journey a heavy undertaking for a woman past middle-age'. She continued, however, 'the air around her pulsating silently, and oppressing the earth with lassitude'. In the twenty-first century, you are more likely to encounter driving rain on 31 August but it is still sensible to be adequately prepared for there are no facilities at all on the heath.

From the Hardys' cottage head straight onto the heath, with the American Monument on your left – the track is signposted Puddletown. Follow it back, past Mistover Knap, to Greenhill, passing the pond on your right and ignoring all side-turnings, to emerge onto the narrow lane, currently termed 'Rhododendron Mile'. After 200 yards (180 metres), bear right onto a track and, after a similar distance, left through the wood, past the old kennels. At this point, Mrs Yeobright would almost certainly

have carried straight on into Islington Wood, probably picking up the old Roman road towards Tincleton Heath, but the felling of most of the wood for agricultural purposes, the lack of public rights of way and the fact that this land, although originally heath, does not qualify as 'Access Land' under the Countryside Act 2000, means the modern walker has no choice other than to take a northerly diversion via Puddletown.

Emerging from the wood, follow the path beside the electricity poles, passing to the west of the now deserted Coombe Farm, to the lane; here turn right through the trees and down the Coombe (seats for the weary on your left) and straight along the picturesque New Street to turn right along the edge of the main Athelhampton Road. After 100 yards (ninety metres), take Millom Lane (third on your right). Follow this until you see a footpath sign in the hedge on your left; take this path up across the meadow, crossing the barely visible remains of the Roman road, through a farmyard to a drive. Turn right and then left onto a signposted path past a cottage and into Cowpound Wood. This waymarked path will lead you two-and-a-half miles (four kilometres) due east across the largely afforested remains of Tincleton, Southover, Pallington and Affpuddle Heaths, eventually emerging on Waddock Drove, directly opposite the Affpuddle Car Park.

Pause in the field just beyond Cowpound Wood beside the solitary memorial to a rifleman killed in Calais in 1940 and look behind you. There are fine views over Islington Wood to Rainbarrow and the adjoining heath; otherwise views are generally restricted by the forest. The track passes close to Pallington Clump – the *Clyffe-hill Clump* of 'Yellham-Wood's Story' (CP 244) and 'The Paphian Ball' (CP 769) – but it is no longer distinguishable from the surrounding pine trees into which it has become absorbed. If you wander south from the path in this area, there are still extensive views to be gained over the Frome Valley. In various puddles on the route, and especially in a carefully fenced-off pond just beyond Pallington Clump, view 'amid the vaporous mud, the maggoty shapes ... heaving and wallowing with enjoyment' as witnessed by Mrs Yeobright. To her over-heated mind these 'ephemerons' resembled Clym and Eustacia, delighting in the transient pleasures of the flesh, whilst she struggled on alone, rejected, and unpleasured.

The most direct route from the Affpuddle Car Park to *Alderworth* is to continue straight ahead along the grassy track which runs parallel to the lane until you reach Cull-peppers Dish Car Park. Bear diagonally across this, taking the path downhill at the far right corner, turn left along a track at the bottom, through a gate, to emerge behind Clym's cottage. Here the thoughtful owner has provided a bench for the weary walker to rest and enjoy the tranquillity of *Egdon*, for you have once more emerged

on open heath after so much woodland (plate 1.5). Walk past the cottage, whose rendering conceals cob upon a brick foundation, to the lane. Here bear left uphill, left again at the top, and then left down the track back onto the heath. You have circled the Devil's Bellows, now, unfortunately, fenced off as an extension of the cottage gardens. This is the black knoll where Mrs Yeobright, having followed her son, in the guise of a furze cutter, towards his cottage and feeling 'distressingly agitated, weary and unwell', sits down beneath trees which were 'singularly battered rude and wild … not a bough but was splintered, lopped and distorted by the fierce weather' and where 'on the present heated afternoon, when no perceptible wind was blowing, the trees kept up a perpetual moan'. Mrs Yeobright has become the landscape; or rather it has become an exaggerated expression of her innermost agonies.

Continue on the path downhill from the Devil's Bellows and follow it straight ahead, ignoring other tracks. After a short while Rimsmoor Pond will appear below in the open heathland to your left. Excluded by the closed door, Mrs Yeobright walks determinedly away from the cottage, her eyes fixed on the ground until she encounters Johnny Nunsuch gathering whortleberries. This child, like the young Hardy, is well versed in local geography. Mrs Yeobright sits down, exhausted and desperate for water:

1.5 *Alderworth*

Mrs Y: Now can you tell me if Rimsmoor Pond is dry this summer?

JN: Rimsmoor Pond is but Oker's Pool isn't, because he is deep and is never dry …

Mrs Y: Is the water clear?

JN: Middling – except where the heath-croppers walk into it …

In this era of climate change, Rimsmoor Pond does not seem to ever dry up. Although Okers Pool lies only a few hundred yards away, it is not easy to find, as witnessed by several, otherwise reputable, guides to Hardy's Wessex which claim that it was a figment of his imagination.

To find Okers Pool, retrace your steps from Rimsmoor back towards *Alderworth*. Take the first turning on your left and after about 250 yards (230 metres) on this track – just before trees appear on your left – cut across the open uneven heathland to the left of these pine trees; there is a deer track for much of the way. After about 200 yards (180 metres) you should find yourself on the top of a bank with the deep irregular pond in front of you (plate 1.6). Kay-Robinson describes its surface as 'spectacularly green', but I have never witnessed this. Late winter, when the bracken has died down, is the best season to find it; on one occasion I encountered a herd of Sika deer beside the pond.

1.6 Okers Pool

From Okers Pool, retrace your steps to the main trackway, turn left and left again back to the car park. Cross the road to inspect Cull-peppers Dish, hidden in the trees opposite. This is the largest of the many hundreds of swallet holes on *Egdon*.

Dying on *Egdon*

Mrs Yeobright throws away the water from Okers Pool because it is warm and nauseating. Johnny, bored by her immobility, heads for home, casting off the broken-hearted woman in the same way that she imagines Clym has done. Although her exertions have 'well-nigh prostrated her' she continues 'to creep along in short stages with long breaks between' eventually reaching 'a slope about two-thirds of the whole distance from *Alderworth* to her home'. Whilst this 'knoll covered with shepherd's-thyme' cannot be identified with certainty, it is likely to lie on the western edge of Tincleton Heath and thus is most probably the knoll in the field with the memorial stone and the views towards Rainbarrow, where little pockets of heath still survive amongst the pasture.

The western sun beats down upon her pallid and dyspnoeic body 'like some merciless incendiary, brand in hand, waiting to consume her'. She is excluded from the garden – and it is a spurious Eden. The ancient heath is subject to Darwinian laws. Firstly, the survival of the fittest; Mrs Yeobright knows that she is not fit and that she cannot survive. Secondly, the adaptation of species; Mrs Yeobright senses that she belongs to a species that is poorly adapted. All around her is abundant evidence of the Insecta, the most successful and adaptable order of animals on the planet. She looks down upon 'an ant thoroughfare, which had been in progress for years at the same spot'; she hears 'the intermittent husky notes of the male grasshoppers' which show 'that the insect world was busy in all the fullness of life'. In the sky above, a solitary heron flies away from her towards the sun. Like Lear or Henchard on the heath, she is broken down by filial ingratitude, which finds expression in the oppressive elements: for Lear the raging tempest, for Mrs Yeobright the raging heat.

Hardy's text is a masterful tapestry of interwoven themes as rich as the life of the heath itself; for now her estranged son sets off through a cloud of 'white miller-moths' to visit his mother. He pauses to inhale 'a soft perfume' which 'wafted across his path' and discovers a collapsed female form comatose and moaning. He attempts to carry his moribund mother home across the darkened heath but eventually 'lays her down in a clod-built hut', about a mile from *Blooms-End* and 'runs with all his might for help'. Just as *Mistover Knap* and the surrounding cob-built cottages have disappeared beneath the mists – and more specifically the rains – of time, so there is no chance of now identifying Mrs Yeobright's death-place on the eastern side of Piddletown Heath, as yet still heavily afforested.

In *The Mayor of Casterbridge* Henchard, believing himself to be rejected by a daughter rather than a son, follows suit and wanders off onto the heath to die. One month after her stepfather's disappearance, Farfrae and Elizabeth-Jane set out in their gig to find him. They know that he has taken the *Melchester* Road as far as *Weatherbury* and then forked off eastward along the 'forking highway which skirted the north edge of Egdon'. This is the old A35 through Tolpuddle to Bere Regis, beyond which this road still traverses the ancient heath, though mostly buried at present by the conifer plantations of Wareham Forest. No longer can the traveller along this road be said to be:

> Bowling across that ancient country whose surface had never been stirred to a finger's depth, save by the scratching of rabbits, since brushed by the feet of the earliest tribes. The tumuli these had left behind, dun and shagged with heather, jutted roundly into the sky from the uplands, as though they were the full breasts of Diana Multimammia supinely extended there.

These shagged tumuli, resembling exposed breasts – a somewhat surprising image for the closing chapter of a book in which eroticism is tightly suppressed – have been carefully tidied from vision by the intense efforts of the Forestry Commission. Past Morden Park, the forest disappears, the heath being wholly subsumed into farmland. By afternoon, Farfrae and Elizabeth-Jane had reached 'the neighbourhood of some extension of the heath to the north of *Anglebury*, a prominent feature of which in the form of a blasted clump of trees on the summit of a hill'. Despite extensive urbanization, this hill can still be readily identified as Beacon Hill, Lychett, now occupied by a touring caravan site just north of the most westerly roundabout on the A35 dual carriageway; in fact the best view of this blasted clump is obtained from the slip road off the A35 heading north onto the A350. A safer spot is the Harbour-View burial ground just off Blandford Road North, which also affords a vista over Poole Harbour towards Purbeck.

Farfrae is correct in his estimate 'that they were now a score of miles at least from home' – it is exactly twenty miles (thirty-two kilometres) from *Casterbridge* (Dorchester) to Beacon Hill. That humblest of humble dwellings in the ravine below the clump has perished along with Mrs Yeobright's 'clod-built hut'. The trees remain, but the constant roar of hurtling motor traffic and industrial, human and air-borne pollution totally detract from the potential solemnity of the site. You will not find Henchard's ghost here. This destruction can perhaps be seen as consistent with Henchard's last testament: 'that no man remember me'.

So, where, if anywhere, can one find unpolluted, unimproved heathland?

Native Heath

About three miles (five kilometres) west of Lychett Beacon, on the route taken by Henchard on his final journey, lies the village of Slepe, formerly 'Sleeping Green', under which guise it appears in *A Laodicean*. South-east of Slepe lies Morden Bog National Nature Reserve and, within it, the remains of Decoy Heath. At the beginning of *The Hand of Ethelberta*, the heroine walks from the Red Lion across the railway onto the open heath; her saunter becomes a 'rapid run' as she chases after a duck-hawk (marsh harrier) pursuing a wild duck. 'Her feet suddenly became as quick as fingers' as she raced along over the uneven ground, her patent heels crippling the heather twigs and sucking 'the swampy places with a sound of quick kisses'. The duck dives below the surface of the decoy pond, leaving the frustrated buzzard to fly away in satanic moodiness. Ethelberta realizes that she has run a long distance and is afraid that she will become lost on the heath. Old decoy pond lies nearly three miles (five kilometres) from the Red Lion. Somewhat ironically, the decoy ponds were originally used for trapping and shooting wild birds and it is because of this so-called 'sport' that this area of heathland has survived. As an example of 'unspoilt heath' it is a disappointment: stock-fenced, heavily trampled by cattle, criss-crossed by electricity pylons, the views in all directions spoilt by surrounding forest plots.

More rewarding places to visit, which give a feel of the ancient unspoilt *Egdon*, are the adjoining remains of Winfrith and Tadnoll Heaths. **Take the lane to the north opposite the Red Lion at Winfrith Newburgh. Just beyond the hamlet of Blacknoll, Blacknoll Hill appears on the right, projecting into the grounds of the Winfrith Heath Technology Centre; shortly afterwards on the left is a path onto Winfrith Heath (plate 1.7). Follow the waymarked paths into Whitcombe Vale and onto Tadnoll.** Here is virgin heath (and plentiful bog), divided by pale sandy tracks – 'long, laborious, dry, empty and white' – exactly matching Hardy's description of the road from *Anglebury* as traversed by Captain Vye at the beginning of *The Return of the Native*. If you avoid looking behind at the Atomic Energy Research Centre (soon to be decommissioned) or towards the forests on the northern horizon, you can safely imagine yourself back in that 'obscure, obsolete, superseded country' so beloved by Hardy.

1.7 Unspoilt (Winfrith) Heath

The *Quiet Woman*

Beside that empty road which bisected the vast dark surface of the heath 'like the parting-line on a head of raven hair' is situated, as the traveller nears Bockhampton, the inn 'known in the neighbourhood as the *Quiet Woman*, the sign of which represented the figure of a matron carrying her head under her arm' (plate 1.8). The front of the house faces towards *Blackbarrow*, towering 200 feet (sixty metres) above it. Sadly the original building has been completely demolished and the house (Duck Dairy Farm) and outbuildings – now craft workshops – show no sign of their original function. It was at 'the Quiet Woman, a lone roadside hostel on the lower verge of Egdon Heath', that Car'line Aspent suffered her final disastrous encounter with the acoustic magnetism of Mop Ollamoor and his fiddle in 'The Fiddler of the Reels'. Leaving Car'line unconscious on the floor, Mop snatched his daughter and disappeared across the highway into the mass of not easily accessible dark heathland, 'where jutted into the sky, at the distance of a couple of miles, the fir-woods of Mistover backed by Yalbury coppices – a place of Dantesque gloom at this hour'.

In *The Return of the Native* it is on this road, at a spot just below the inn,

that Wildeve waits, 'slightly sheltered from the driving rain by a high bank' (still identifiable), for Eustacia to join him in her bid to escape the darkness of life on the heath. As he waits, he can hear 'the roaring of a ten-hatch weir a few yards further on'. As always, Wessex is 'a partly real partly dream coun-try', for at its nearest point the Frome is over a third-of-a mile (500 metres) from the road. So whilst one can identify the point at which Wildeve shel-tered his horses from the worst of the tempest, even on the stillest night no one would be able to hear the sound of a body falling into the stream adjoining *Shadwater* Weir.

Shadwater Weir lies on the Frome nearly a mile (one-and-a-half kilometres) south-east of the *Quiet Woman*, officially known as Nine-Hatches, Islington (plate 1.9). In this age of obsessive health and safety, it is protected by locked gates and barbed-wire fencing, emblazoned with notices proclaiming 'Danger/No Entry/Keep Clear/Strong Currents', so that a latter day Eustacia would have great difficulty finding a way through in the dark. Exactly as described by Hardy, 'it is a large circular pool, fifty feet in diameter', out of which 'the water flowed through ten [actually nine] huge hatches, raised and lowered by a winch and cogs in the ordinary manner. The sides of the pool

1.9 *Shadwater Weir*

were of masonry....' The appearance of the weir itself has changed little over the intervening 130 years. It is on private land but readily reached by the (often muddy) track which crosses the remains of Islington Heath (now farmland), passing through Boswell's plantation to the weir on the Frome.

Magical Mysteries: The Heathen Heath

To Hardy, haggard *Egdon* was in essence an ancient pagan landscape where the soil had remained unturned since Bronze Age men built their hilltop barrows and where primitive beliefs, superstitions and magic still held sway. As night closes in at the start of *The Return of the Native*, the archetypal Romantic figure is displaced from *Blackbarrow* by faggot-bearing heathmen, who rekindle the Neolithic funeral pile and then tread a 'demoniac measure' in the embers of the conflagration as a 'lineal descendant of jumbled Druidical rites'. Beside the fire and afraid to dance, stands that 'slack-twisted slim-looking maphrotight fool', Christian Cantle, a caricature of Christian man, terrified of the dark wilderness in which the robust (and pagan) heathmen feel perfectly at ease. The very word 'heathen' is itself a contraction of 'heath-men' – Church attendance on *Egdon* being more honoured in the breach than

39

the observance, for as Humphrey observes: "'tis so terrible far to get there; and when you do get there 'tis such a mortal poor chance that you'll be chose for up above'. The heath folk see Eustacia Vye as a witch, who 'overlooks' Susan Nunsuch's children, deals in crooked sixpences, summons up Damon (Daemon?) Wildeve with an enchantress's bonfire, but eventually succumbs to the burning of her effigy, accompanied by the backward incantation of the Lord's Prayer. An intermediary between the isolated heath folk and devil's advocate appears (and disappears): that startling 'Mephistophelean visitant', Venn the reddleman, like a goblin in a fairy tale.

The heath was naturally, therefore, the appropriate home for Conjuror Trendle, the 'white wizard' to whom Gertrude Lodge turns for help in 'The Withered Arm'. His home is an isolated cottage 'in the heart of Egdon', reached by a protracted climb 'into the interior of this solemn country', where 'the wind howled dismally over the slopes of the heath – not improbably the same heath which witnessed the agony of the Wessex King Ina, presented to after ages as Lear'. There is dispute as to the site of Gertrude Lodge's home – it is one of those instances where Lea appears to be deliberately confusing. It would, however, be impossible to better Kay-Robinson's painstaking research on this subject, particularly on the route of Gertrude's secret journey to *Casterbridge*. Farmer Lodge's house was at Hethfelton, the only heathland farm mentioned in Domesday, and Rhoda's Brook's cottage lay between Stokeford and Stokeford Farm. From the text of the story, Conjuror Trendle's secluded valley was upon Holme Heath, now buried within the MOD firing range, north of Tyneham.

In Hardy's childhood, a maypole was annually installed on the grass outside the cottage at Higher Bockhampton. In 'Aftercourses', Hardy's postscript to *The Return of the Native*, following the several deaths of the witch and the bewitched and the 'translation' of the reddleman, the heath is likewise transformed into a benign place where Thomasin can safely gather flowers and where a maypole is erected beside the cottage at *Blooms-End*. Here, as the sun sets on a fine May evening, illuminating the 'new leaves, delicate as butterflies' wings and diaphanous as amber', the local women are engaged in wreathing the pole 'from top to downward with wild flowers'.

Hardy notes that:

> … the instincts of merry England lingered on here with exceptional vitality and the symbolic customs which tradition has attached to each season of the year were yet a reality on Egdon. Indeed the impulses of all such outlandish hamlets are pagan still: in these spots homage to nature, self-adoration, frantic gaieties, fragments of Teutonic rites to divinities whose names are forgotten, have in some way or other survived medieval doctrine.

Inspection of Hardy's manuscript reveals that he initially wrote 'medieval Christianity', subsequently amended as above.

Hardy the Naturalist

In 1898, as Hardy prepared to publish his first volume of poetry, he defended the change from fiction by declaring:

> It was not as if he had been a writer of novels proper, and as more specifically understood, that is, stories of modern artificial life and manners showing a certain smartness of treatment. He had mostly aimed, and mostly succeeded, to keep his narratives close to natural life, and as near to poetry in their subject as the conditions would allow, and had often regretted that these conditions would not let him keep them nearer still. (8)

Hardy 'had mostly aimed to keep his narratives close to natural life', and nowhere did he come closer to natural life than on *Egdon* Heath and in the text of *The Return of the Native*. The text is imbued with descriptions of the changing face of the heath as it moves through its five acts; from autumn, to winter, to spring with its joys (the fascination), to summer with fulfilment (the closed door), leading inexorably to the second autumn of death and destruction. Co-existent with human activities is the parallel world of the true natives of the heath: the insects, spiders, glow-worms, lizards, heath-croppers and birds. Their lives also change with the seasons and are woven intricately into the text. Indeed the abundant, independent natural world has the effect of reducing human life to a humble Darwinian context. Hardy extended this sense of 'no superiority to a single living thing under the sun' into an active concern for the protection and conservation of the heath and its wildlife. As Venn ascends the hill towards *Mistover Knap* on a wintry morning, the narrator observes that:

> Feathered species sojourned here in hiding which would have created wonder if found elsewhere. A bustard haunted the spot; and not many years before, five-and-twenty might have been seen in Egdon at one time. Marsh Harriers looked up from the valley by Wildeve's. A cream-coloured courser had used to visit this hill – a bird so rare that not more than a dozen had ever been seen in England; but a barbarian rested neither night nor day till he had shot the African truant so cream-coloured coursers thought fit to enter Egdon no more.

The great bustard, a turkey-like bird, became extinct in Britain nearly 200 years ago, to be followed later in the nineteenth century by the marsh harrier or duck hawk. The cream-coloured courser had never been more than an occasional migrant from North Africa. Hardy's indignation at the execution of the courser was well ahead of his time, for in the nineteenth century shooting a bird was regarded as the proper means of identifying it. His interpretation of Darwin's theories made Hardy a conservationist before conservationism had been invented. Hardy's acceptance of Darwinism was the natural development of his own astute observations of life on *Egdon*; from the deer at the cottage window, to the heathcroppers watching the game of dice, to the lizards, the vipers and the ancient ant thoroughfares, and from the death's head moths to the microscopic ephemera gyrating upon the surfaces of the stagnant summer pools. Hardy observed and understood; human life paled into insignificance against the immense complex ecology of the natural world. Yet from the spurious Eden of *Egdon*, man alone had emerged with the capacity not only to destroy but also to preserve this treasure house, which he was only just beginning to understand (see 'An August Midnight' CP 113).

Egdon in the Twenty-First Century

Beside the American memorial at the corner of the Hardys' cottage stands a cross-ways; from here footpaths lead in four different directions. But whichever route you follow onto the heath at whatever season of the year and whatever hour of day or night, you will never find the unbroken stillness experienced by Clym and described by Hardy, not unless you are totally deaf or wearing silencing earphones (plate 1.10). Wherever you choose to wander on modern *Egdon*, you cannot escape the roar of the internal-combustion engine. It is ubiquitous. The dual carriageway which has sliced like a manic meat cleaver through Puddletown Heath is just one of a series of road 'improvements' which have divided and decimated *Egdon*, especially on its southern and eastern boundaries; here birdsong is drowned out day and night by deep, disgusting decibels, the stars are obscured by an orange halo of streetlighting and the darkness of the night destroyed by the repetitive flashing of car headlamps. Hardy notes that every night *Egdon's* 'Titanic form seemed to await something; but it had waited thus, unmoved, during so many centuries ... that it could only be imagined to await one last crisis – the final Overthrow'. Whether that final Overthrow turns out to be the Second Coming or an environmental apocalypse remains to be seen. But on a more sanguine note, the exhaustion of carbon-fuel resources may put a stop to motor transport as we currently know it (and the pressurized lifestyle which goes with it) and allow a return to calmer days and a more tranquil *Egdon*.

There is also hope that the Forestry Commission's blanket coverage of heathland with conifer plots may be on the wane; this is not for sound

1.10 The American Memorial
and some Hardy fans

environmental reasons but because with a turning economic tide the Ilchesters, who own most of western *Egdon*, are likely to opt for grazed heathland rather than renew the Commission's lease. A return to heath-cropping would be wonderful, tightly fenced medium-density cattle grazing – as has happened on Sussex heathland – less desirable.

But Hardy was a poet with a poet's insight and a poet's vision. At times his sensitivity extends so far beyond the common as to be beyond common sense. At twilight, *Egdon* embrowns itself moment by moment so that it wears:

> ... the appearance of an instalment of night which had taken up its place before its astronomical hour was come ... the face of the heath by its mere complexion added half-an-hour to eve; it could in like manner retard the dawn, sadden noon, anticipate the frowning of storms scarcely generated, and intensify the opacity of a moonless midnight to a cause of shaking and dread ...

Reality is much more prosaic; if you stand on *Egdon* at dusk the heath, being elevated and treeless, is brighter and lighter than the surrounding woodland and the meadows below in the Frome Valley. At daybreak also, the heath lightens first. So in Dorset rather than Wessex, *Egdon* retards nightfall and accelerates dawn. This opening passage from *The Return of the Native* parallels the opening passage of *Under the Greenwood Tree*:

To dwellers in a wood almost every species of tree has its voice as well as its feature. At the passing of the breeze the fir-trees sob and moan no less distinctly than they rock; the holly whistles as it battles with itself; the ash hisses amid its quiverings; the beech rustles while its flat boughs rise and fall. And winter, which modifies the note of such trees as shed their leaves, does not destroy their individuality.

Thus the trees whisper distinctively to Dick Dewy as he heads up Bockhampton Lane on a starry December night and, being a local lad, he can tell his position in the wood by the sound of the trees. Go down to the woods at night and try this one out – as Mike Irwin has done – and find to your disappointment that all you can hear is the wind. Branches may knock against each other – a deciduous wood is obviously different from a conifer plantation – but what you can hear is the wind itself. The countryman's responses are undoubtedly coloured by his foreknowledge; he has been there during the daytime and throughout the seasons, he knows which trees grow where.

Review: Hardy was a child of the heath who, as a middle-aged refugee from the metropolis, made *Egdon* the centre of his creative universe. Not only was *The Return of the Native* to become the core text of his fiction but *Egdon* became the central locus of an expanding Wessex to which he was to return time and again in his writings. Hardy's early enthusiastic reading of Darwin led him to reject the Wordsworthian ideal of a beneficent nature and thus the heath becomes a metaphor for nature's indifference to human suffering and despair; a place he considered to be, 'absolutely in keeping with the more thinking among mankind'. *Egdon* Heath has altered almost beyond recognition since Hardy's childhood, decimated by a combination of urbanization, afforestation, militarization and agricultural enclosure. 'Civilization was its enemy,' but the heath is an artefact created by our Mesolithic and Bronze Age forefathers, and paradoxically now principally preserved by the army. 'Haggard Egdon' is best explored at twilight in an atmosphere which evokes the opening pages of *The Return of the Native*. *Rainbarrow*, *Mistover Knap* and *Blooms-End* are readily accessible on foot and a longer walk retraces Mrs Yeobright's journey to *Alderworth*, and thence via Rimsmoor Pond and Okers Pool to her resting place upon a 'knoll covered with shepherd's-thyme'; the landscape becoming the external expression of the dying woman's innermost torment. In his Darwinian descriptions of this essentially pagan landscape Hardy became a conservationist before conservationism had been invented. Sadly, the pen has not proved mightier than the bulldozer, for only a few patches of (partially) unspoilt heath survive in the twenty-first century.

CHAPTER TWO

Beyond *Egdon*

From the beginning of his career, Hardy is a poet inhabiting a poet's complex, personally symbolised world, and signifying the imprint upon his heart of everything, even the associations of local geography. Many minor details of Hardy's broad terrain of Wessex are actually found near Bockhampton, so Hardy's Wessex may have evolved less as an organising device than as a necessary enlargement to mask the archetype's tellingly localised origins. (1)

MICHAEL RABIGER IS here making an astute observation, fundamental to a proper understanding of Hardy's Wessex. The cottage at Higher Bockhampton and the surrounding heathland formed the centre of Hardy's poetic universe. Although the Wessex delineated on the map which accompanied all later editions of his novels covered half of southern England, from Tintagel and the Isles of Scilly in the south-west to Oxford in the north, the essence of Hardy's Wessex lay within a few square miles surrounding his 'Domicilium' (map 2.1). His fictive Wessex is the outward extension of a very narrow landscape; an attempt to resist that constant centripetal poetic force which drew all locations back towards their heart on *Egdon*. This process was demonstrated in chapter one, where *Blooms-End* was shown to belong at Higher Bockhampton rather than Bhompston Farm and where *Shadwater Weir* was similarly transported nearly a mile (one-and-a-half kilometres) closer to the heath. As Hardy's fiction extended beyond the margins of *Egdon* into the surrounding agricultural communities, so the telescopic reduction of distances, that drawing-in process, continued in *Far From the Madding Crowd*, *Tess of the D'Urbervilles* and *Two on a Tower*. This process inevitably calls into question some of the recognized and accepted identifications of Hardy's Wessex locations; at times he was deliberately trying to obscure places that were too personal, at others merely to expand outwards into appropriate alternative areas of Dorset.

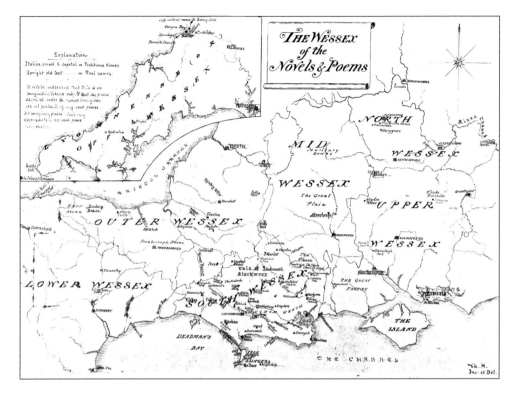

Map 2.1 Hardy's Wessex

Talbothays Dairy

'On a thyme-scented, bird-singing morning in May,' Tess sets out from *Marlott*
for the *Valley of the Great Dairies*. Taking the carriers van from *Stourcastle* to
Weatherbury, she continues 'her pilgrimage' on foot towards Farmer Crick's
dairy. The walk across the 'intervening uplands and lowlands of Egdon' was
more troublesome than she had anticipated, but after two hours 'she found
herself on a summit commanding the long-sought-for vale ... the valley in
which milk and butter grew to rankness – the verdant plain so well watered
by the Var or Froom'. Having crossed the heath in a south-westerly direction
from Puddletown, this summit can only be Rainbarrow. From her lofty viewpoint, Tess compares the landscape below with her native Blackmoor (also
known as Blackmore) and notes that 'the world was drawn on a larger pattern
here. The enclosures numbered fifty acres rather than ten ... the myriads of
cows stretching from far east to far west outnumbered any she had ever seen

at one glance before'. Like Hardy's *Egdon* Heath, which stretches from Bockhampton to Bournemouth, his *Valley of the Great Dairies* is a titanic creation, extending beyond the known horizon. Tess's bird's-eye perspective arouses a religious enthusiasm for this valley where the waters 'were clear as the pure River of Life shown to the Evangelist', so that she spontaneously chants the Benedicite Omnia Opera. What a contrast to *The Return of the Native*, where the same viewpoint is haunted by the solitary witch Eustacia and used by local heathens for enacting wild nocturnal druidical rites!

Tess descends from the heath, stands for a moment 'upon the hemmed expanse of verdant flatness, like a fly on a billiard table of indefinite length', disturbs a solitary heron and then follows 'the red and white herd nearest at hand' into 'the barton by the open gate'. She has arrived at *Talbothays*. But where is *Talbothays*? The modern reader can readily retrace the final part of Tess's journey.

From your perch on Rainbarrow (p.22) take the same narrow path westward but, after crossing the stile in the barbed-wire fence, turn right downhill. The track descends steeply through wooded heathland to enter a meadow. At the lower end of this, cross the lane and follow the track straight ahead into the farmyard of Norris Mill Farm.

Current consensus, following Kay-Robinson's groundbreaking *Hardy's Wessex Re-appraised*, is that Hardy's *Talbothays* was based on Lower Lewell Farm, which lies in West Knighton parish. This is the standard identification to be found in walk booklets, tourist information sheets and on guided tours, television programmes, Wessex DVDs etc. As always, Kay-Robinson's research is meticulous and clearly argued, but his conclusions do not fit the facts. Hardy's detailed description of Tess's arrival in the *Valley of the Great Dairies* cannot be interpreted as including the one-and-a-half mile (two-and-a-half kilometres) trek across the valley; passing through the entire territory of two other dairy farms to emerge on the other side of the vale onto a road, which she then follows to reach Lower Lewell. **The modern walker can easily follow this route by continuing on the byway straight through Lower Norris Farm, crossing a sequence of footbridges over the Frome and its tributary streams, to reach the road at Lewell Mill Farm. Follow the road straight ahead, then bear left at three consecutive T-junctions to arrive at Lower Lewell Farm.**

Evidence from Hardy himself is conflicting. He confirmed to Clive Holland that Windle (1901) was correct in his statement that 'Norris Mill Farm, by situation and general characters, has the best right to be considered as the original for *Talbothays*'. Lea states 'that the dairy-house is drawn from no particular building, but is typical of many of the dairies which occupy the Froom Valley'. Significantly, no photograph is offered. Windle lamented the sad alterations which had taken place at Norris Mill by the turn of the century. Neither here nor in the buildings at Lower Lewell is it possible to match the farm where the milkmaids slept in a dormitory with Angel ensconced in the loft above. Norris Mill was the dairy farm most familiar to Hardy, situated just one mile (one-and-a-half kilometres) away – straight down the track which ran behind his home. In the November of Tess's stay at *Talbothays*, batches of animals were sent away daily 'to the farmhouse on the slopes above the vale', to the 'lying-in hospital' 'in the straw-barton to which they were relegated'. This fits well with 'the lonely barton by yonder coomb / Our childhood used to know' (CP 468), then known as Higher Bockhampton Farm, a short distance from Hardy's cottage (p.77).

The other topographical arguments given in support of Lower Lewell Farm can be fairly easily dismissed. When Angel returns from visiting his parents, he also pauses on an elevated point to survey the valley. I agree with Kay-Robinson that this 'detached knoll' is Frome Hill tumulus, to the east of Max Gate on the West Stafford Road. It is well worth visiting on a clear day for the extensive views, which rival those from Rainbarrow. As Angel observed, to the north-east the Var Valley, 'that green trough of sappiness and humidity', extends before you with Norris Mill and the Traveller's Rest prominent and Rainbarrow and *Egdon* beyond. Due north stands Kingston Maurward House, enshrouded in green parkland, whilst to the south-west Maiden Castle is dominant with the Hardy Monument on Blackdown behind it. Straight ahead the chalk downs obscure Osmington Bay. This tumulus is an eastern extension of Conquer Barrow, one of a series of aligned ancient earthworks including Hell Stone, Maiden Castle, Conquer Barrow and Rainbarrow.

Hardy describes the knoll as being 'a mile or two west of Talbothays' – it is indeed just under two miles (three kilometres) from both the farms in question – and Hardy offers no description of Angel's journey from the knoll to the dairy. Hardy's description of Tess wandering along 'creeping paths which followed the brinks of trickling tributary brooks' and of her taking refuge in the 'thicket of pollard willows at the lower side of the barton' can be attributed to both farms, although there are more wandering brooks in the immediate vicinity of Norris Mill. *Talbothays* possessed a watermill, as did Norris Mill but not Lower Lewell. The description of Tess and Angel's journey to deliver the milk churns to the railway station is consistent with a drive from either farm to Moreton Station, but the sentence 'as they drove the fragment of an old manor house of Caroline date rose against the sky' has caused much confusion. Could Hardy have meant Woodsford Castle visible on both routes? But it is fourteenth rather than seventeenth century, and Angel's reference to the D'Urbervilles strongly suggests the Caroline *Wellbridge* Manor. It is then argued by many that the trip was to Wool Station, but

Wellbridge Manor is *at* Wool, it is not 'passed and left behind' on a journey to the station. This view is backed by Rebekah Owen's assertion that Hardy told her that the station intended was Moreton and demonstrated the holly under which Tess took shelter. Here, I think, one has to accept that Hardy was sacrificing topographical veracity to plot necessity.

The same may be said of the thorny issue of Angel carrying the milkmaids over the flooded length of lane as they head for Sunday service at *Mellstock* Church. The most obvious site for this is the low-lying stretch of road between the two bridges over the Frome at Lower Bockhampton. This is used as a strong argument to support the case for Lower Lewell as *Talbothays*. However, the girls were obviously not regular churchgoers for Tess 'had now been two months at Talbothays, and this was her first excursion'. Why then trek all the way to Stinsford when they had to pass the door of West Stafford Church only one mile (one-and-a-half kilometres) into their two-and-a-half-mile (four-kilometre) journey? Plot necessity? Coming from Norris Mill to Stinsford, the girls would have encountered the same flooding at the start of the Fromeside path, having just crossed Lower Bockhampton Bridge.

It is generally presumed that Tess and Angel were married in West Stafford Church because this was the nearest church to Lower Lewell and because Hardy described it as having a 'louvred belfry'. The text states, however, that 'they were obliged to drive' because 'the church was a long way off'. Elsewhere in the text, both Angel and Tess reveal themselves to be strong and experienced walkers; this church was not a long way off, so why were they obliged to drive? In any case, the parish church for Lower Lewell is at West Knighton not West Stafford. I would contend that the reason they were obliged to drive was because Hardy envisaged the farm being at Norris Mill, which is in Puddletown Parish – the church being over three miles (five kilometres) distant and also having a 'louvred belfry'.

Wellbridge: An Unconsummated Digression

The multiple rivulets, streams and tributaries which moisten and nourish the great dairies of the valley above have converged into the mighty Frome by the time their waters reach Wool. Hence the most popular illustration to guides to Hardy's landscape of *Wellbridge* Manor and 'the great Elizabethan bridge' viewed from across the river (plate 2.1). Although Wool itself is reaching the status of a small town, the ancestral home of the Turbervilles remains isolated in the riverside flats. When the unfortunate newly-weds stayed there the building was no more than 'the mouldy old habitation' which Hardy describes. Now sympathetically restored, it seems at peace with

2.1 *Wellbridge* Manor

itself, the hag-like profiles faded into brown obscurity and the motor traffic diverted away to the east. Hardy's contracting kaleidoscope was at work here, also, for the mill which Angel went to study and the semi-submerged tomb in the ruins of Bindon Abbey where he somnambulistically laid his 'angel' to rest are more than a mile (one-and-a-half kilometres) by foot from the mansion. On their first morning as a married couple, Angel mechanically sets off over 'the great stone bridge' and across 'the railway beyond', heading for Bindon Lane. Neither the mill nor the abbey are open to the public, but discretionary access may be obtained and an excellent view of the mill can be seen from the train. The abbey at Bindon stood just outside the heath on fertile ground; *Egdon* itself was always pagan. When the abbey was demolished in 1539, much of the stone was transported to Weymouth for the building of Sandsfoot Castle. On *Egdon* Heath, one mile (one-and-a-half kilometres) due north of the mill, stands Hethfelton – the *Holmstoke* of Farmer Lodge – its grand isolation now compromised by its raucous new neighbour, Monkey World.

A few miles downstream from Bindon, Frome and Piddle converge on the ancient Saxon walled-town of *Anglebury* (Wareham), the town where Thomasin and Wildeve failed to marry at the start of *The Return of the Native*.

It is here that we are first introduced to Ethelberta, staying at the Red Lion, which continues 'an old and well-appointed inn', little changed in the 130-year interim. I will not judge whether it is fair to say that the inn still remains 'the fashion among tourists because of the absence from its precincts of all that was fashionable and new'!

From *Lew-Everard* (West Stafford) to *Warborne* (Wimborne)

Beyond the Boundaries of *Egdon*

By bicycle (seventeen miles/twenty-seven kilometres)

Having decried the positive identification of Lower Lewell as Tess's *Talbothays*, I would still recommend a visit to the farm, where the thatched barn (dating from 1704) has recently been sumptuously restored, the farmhouse is graceful and the yard enchanting. To one side of the yard can be seen the somewhat dilapidated remains of a shepherd's hut on wheels – of the kind in which Gabriel Oak nearly suffocated on *Norcombe Hill*. This area is probably best explored by bicycle as there is rather too much tarmac for the pedestrian, but is equally accessible to the motorist.

From Lower Lewell head back towards West Stafford. You will pass Talbothays cottages on the right and, immediately afterwards, Talbothays Lodge on the left. These were all built by Henry Hardy to the design of his brother, Thomas, on farmland owned by their father. Here Hardy's three siblings spent their later years together. **Continue straight ahead through the picturesque centre of West Stafford past the thatched 'Wise Man' inn and seventeenth-century church. A quarter-mile (400 metres) further, beyond a bend in the lane, you encounter the magnificent 'mullioned and transomed' Elizabethan Stafford House.** This is *Froom-Everard House*, the home of Squire Everard and his daughter Christine in 'The Waiting Supper'. Christine meets her tenant-farmer lover at 'the Sallows', a (still-surviving) willow plantation beside a weir and waterfall on the Frome to the north of the house, the same point at which her husband Bellston subsequently drowns, his body lying undiscovered for seventeen years until a new owner clears the waterway. Christine's lover, Nicholas, farmed at *Elsenford*, which is Duddle Farm – immediately south of Heedless William's Pond and adjoining Norris Mill Farm. Nicholas, who wears long water-boots above his knees, is an expert at wading through the Frome (unlike the violent and hapless Bellston); even in the darkness he 'transverses the alluvial valley' in a direct line to his farmstead, bypassing deep pools, morasses and gullies – his sure local knowledge matches that of Eustacia upon the heath.

In the story, Nicholas travels from Dorchester to *Elsenford* via *Froom Hill* barrow; this is exactly the same route taken by the returning Angel to Norris Mill and relevant to the *Talbothays* debate because it is assumed that this route from Dorchester would only be taken to West Stafford (and hence Lower Lewell), rather than to Bockhampton and Norris Mill. Nicholas and Christine are thwarted in their initial marriage plans by that recurring Hardyan theme of, 'The Poor Man and the Lady', and subsequently by the belief that Christine is still married to the absent (in fact long-dead) Bellston. After many years of separation, Nicholas and Christine re-encounter each other on the heath beside Rushy Pond (see p.21).

Having admired Stafford House (east façade 1633: west 1850), turn left at the next junction onto the flooded lane where Angel carried the three milkmaids. Keeper's Cottage, on your right, is the house which Nicholas built 'large enough for his wants' 'on the nearest spot to her home ... on the opposite bank of the Froom'. Pause at Bockhampton Bridge to admire the cattle in the water meads and the swans on the Frome, and then continue straight up Bockhampton Lane and over the Cross to Cuckoo Lane and the main road. Bear left across the bridge – obtaining very clear views of the destruction wrought upon Puddletown Heath/Forest by the road builders – and as the flyover curves round, turn left onto the old main road. This is *Yell'ham Bottom* (CP 261), also known as *Yalbury Plain*, the spot where Henchard tried unsuccessfully to persuade Farfrae to return to his dying wife in the aftermath of the skimmity ride in *The Mayor of Casterbridge*. Ahead lies Yellowham (*Yalbury*) Hill and Yellowham Wood, ancient beech woodland, so unlike the spurious pine plots of Puddletown Forest. In Hardy's day, *Yalbury* Wood was home to the Wild Man o' Yall'm, who was held responsible for fathering many of the 'love-children' born in the neighbouring villages – the mythological equivalent of Ralph Blossom (CP 238).

Pass Yellowham Barn (Vaughan Agri) and take the bridleway on the left into the wood. After a short distance this brings you to Keeper Day's Cottage, which stands precisely as Hardy describes it in *Under the Greenwood Tree*, with the grass in front and the great trees behind. One of these trees, though no one can now tell which, may be the Greenwood Tree under which Dick and Fancy's wedding was celebrated with feasting and country dances. The cottage, which still sports the thickly leaded diamond glazing described by Hardy, was the home of Keeper Browne, whose daughter was the inspiration for 'To Lizbie Browne' (CP 130). This cottage, at least, remains reassuringly nineteenth-century in aspect and usage, with sheep and hens grazing the lawns and pigs and game-birds in pens (plate 2.2).

2.2 Keeper's Cottage

If on foot (or mountain bike) continue along the track to the right of the cottage and through the woods to emerge on the Ridgeway. Here turn left, then take the first right, to descend to Waterston Manor (see p.58). Otherwise, retrace your steps to the old main road and ascend Yellowham Hill, now reverting to the lovely tranquil highway of Hardy's time, the mossy edges gradually encroaching upon the tarmac. It was here – the setting of the poem 'Ice on the Highway' (CP 704) – that the quarrelling Bathsheba and Troy encountered Fanny Robin on her last journey to the Union in *Far From the Madding Crowd*. And it was in *Yalbury* Wood that the hapless Joseph Poorgrass, fortified by Keeper Day's metheglin, becomes lost on a dark night and 'much afeared, and not able to find his way out of the trees nohow, 'a cried out, "Man-a-lost! Man-a-lost!" An owl in a tree happened to be crying "Whoo-whoo-whoo!" and Joseph, all in a tremble, said, "Joseph Poorgrass, of Weatherbury, sir!"' (also CP 704).

As you descend the hill and the wood opens into pasture, a fine nineteenth-century farmhouse with a handsome brick-built barn, sadly disfigured by a corrugated-iron roof, appears on your left. This is Troy Town (*Roy Town*), 'a roadside hamlet on the old western turnpike road'. Set back in the field opposite the farm stood the once-important coaching-inn, the Buck's Head; all that remains of it now is part of an outhouse, converted into a shelter for livestock. Here the returning Nicholas Long stopped, expecting 'a lively old tavern', but finding instead a house 'cavernous and chilly, the stable-roofs hollow-backed, the landlord asthmatic, and the traffic gone' in 'The Waiting Supper'. Here the melancholy Poorgrass, becalmed in the autumn fog with his pallid burden, again indulges in 'very pretty drinking' until distressingly afflicted by 'a multiplying eye' in *Far From the Madding Crowd*. Also in this novel, here Gabriel Oak crept into the back of a wagon to sleep on his first journey to *Weatherbury*; due to the darkness, he noticed neither the Buck's Head nor the celebrated signpost which 'hung from the horizontal bough of an elm on the opposite side of the way'. Alas, not only has the hostelry vanished, but all elms from the vicinity also. The railways came, the coaches went and so did the inn, the road was quiet; the motor car came, the road was noisy, busy and polluted as never before; the bypass came, the road was quiet: *Roy Town* slumbers once more. 'So do flux and reflux – the rhythm of change – alternate and persist in everything under the sky.'

Beyond Troy Town, you reach the feeder road for the dual carriageway; bear left onto this then straight ahead to double metal gates, signposted 'Public Route to Public Path'. Here are 180 yards (160 metres) of old highway rapidly reverting back to nature; the former A-road reduced to three yards (two-and-a-half metres) in width, edged by a delightful hazel coppice, beyond which lies the interminable roar of high-speed motor traffic – once more a lovely place, if you are hard of hearing! Towards the end of this stretch, on the right-hand side, is supposed to be the fourth milestone out of *Casterbridge*; it is clearly marked on the newest Ordnance Survey map but currently buried or removed. These were the markers on Fanny Robin's Via Dolorosa in *Far From the Madding Crowd*. The third milestone was located beside Yell'ham Wood but was buried during the war and never retrieved, and those who could locate it are now buried likewise; this is 'The Milestone by the Rabbit-Burrow' (CP 674). The second milestone, against which Fanny rests following her encounter with Troy and Bathsheba, has recently been restored and is clearly visible opposite the Stinsford lay-by and public toilets. You put your life at serious risk crossing the road to inspect it but, if you manage to do so, you are rewarded by a fine vista across open farm-land down to Kingston Maurward House. The first and, for Fanny, final milestone stands proud of the undergrowth just below the roundabout as you descend Stinsford Hill.

At the end of this obscure cul-de-sac, you can turn left up a leafy bridle path which joins the Ridgeway with onward connections to Waterston Manor or Puddletown. Otherwise retrace your steps, cross under the dual

carriageway and follow the old road into Puddletown. This is Hardy's
Weatherbury; the name comes from the original spelling of what is now known
as Weatherby Castle, the Iron Age hill fort at nearby Milborne-St-Andrew.
Puddletown, correctly Piddletown, was a thriving small market town in the
nineteenth century and the one closest and best known to Hardy during his
childhood – it being a mere two-and-a-half miles (four kilometres) across
Egdon on broad tracks whilst Dorchester was a minimum of three-and-a-
quarter miles (five-and-a-quarter kilometres) away by footpath and road. The
Hardys' cottage was the most easterly dwelling in Stinsford Parish; all that was
beyond them was Piddletown. Hardy had ten cousins in Piddletown – the
children of his mother's sisters Maria Sparks and Mary Antell – and his great-
aunt Elizabeth Hardy lived there also. **As you approach the traffic lights
entering Puddletown on the old main road, pause and look left.** Hidden
behind a high brick wall and enshrouded by trees stands an anonymous large
grey house. This is the location of Bathsheba's *Weatherbury Farm* as described
in *Far from the Madding Crowd*, but not the actual building; Hardy admitted
that this had 'taken a witch's ride of a mile or more from its actual position'.

**Turn down Mill Street and then right into the square. The centre of the
town has changed very little in the last 150 years, apart from the ubiquitous
motor car. Take the lane to the left of the thatched house with the projecting
window supported on Tuscan columns – this is Back Street.** *Warren's
Malthouse*, from *Far From the Madding Crowd*, was situated just north of here in
the area now absorbed by the Walpole Court development. The irregular
single-storey building called the Bakehouse may well incorporate part of 'the
old wall inwrapped with ivy' – all that remains of Smallbury's premises.

Hardy accurately describes the church tower as being 'a square erection of
fourteenth-century date', the rest of the building being a century or so older.
The netted entrance porch on the north side contains a pair of narrow
benches, both sufficiently antique to be the original on which Troy spent an
uncomfortable night as the rain spouting from the 'gurgoyle' on the north-
west corner of the tower washed the plants away from Fanny's grave. The
'gurgoyle' remains *in situ* but with its output carefully piped away. The
gargoyles at Puddletown are functional rather than fiendish; for the grotesque
gargoyles described in the text you need to look elsewhere, at Stinsford or
Sydling St Nicholas. Ancient yews still populate the corner where Fanny was
buried and in the south-western corner of the graveyard lie the remains of
Hardy's aunt and uncle, Maria and James Sparks (parents of Tryphena) –
although their headstone has recently been moved to make way for the new
church hall.

Despite this twentieth-century blemish, Piddletown Church thankfully
escaped the heavy hand of the Victorian restorers, for inside it retains its oak

box pews, pulpit and reading desk, west end gallery, font cover and open chancel screen, largely unaltered from the refurbishment of 1634–7. It is a joy to behold. In the box pew immediately to the left of the gallery stairs is carved the name 'HENERY' – the local variant spelling insisted upon by Henery Fray. This church is the setting of that wonderful poem 'The Christening' (CP 214), a satire on both marriage and Christianity. In an arched alcove off the south of the nave lie a number of knightly tombs, each topped by a reclining representation of the occupant. At the entrance to this chapel is the battered seven-foot alabaster figure of Sir William Martyn of Athelhampton commemorated in 'The Children and Sir Nameless' (CP 584) – his effigy now restored to its proper place on his tomb (plate 2.3). Hardy's description of the D'Urberville tombs in *Kingsbere* Church – upon one of which Alec reclined pretending to be an effigy – owes much to these figures at Puddletown.

A one-mile (one-and-a-half kilometre) diversion from Piddletown Square along the old High Road brings you to Athelhampton, one of the finest houses in Wessex; its great hall has a magnificent timbered roof, musician's gallery and vast oriel window and there are superb gardens. *Athelhall*, which is open to the public throughout the summer, was built by the afore-mentioned Sir William Martyn, Lord Mayor of London in 1493 and extended by his descendants (plate 2.4). Hardy was familiar with this great house; his father had worked on it as a stonemason and the architect John Hicks restored the church whilst Hardy was working for him. Hardy records in *The Life* that he

2.3 'Sir Nameless'

2.4 Athelhall

was lunching at Athelhampton at the moment when war was declared with Germany. The description of *Endelstow House* in *A Pair of Blue Eyes* is principally based upon *Athelhall* rather than its local model, Lanhydrock. In 'The Waiting Supper', Christine and Nicholas dance together on the lawn at *Athelhall* whilst attending a christening party. See 'The Dame of Athelhall' (CP 124).

Beyond Athelhampton lies Tolpuddle. This is *Tolchurch* in *Desperate Remedies* where Owen superintends the restoration of the church. The description of the church itself may more closely resemble the one at Turnworth, which Hardy himself restored, but the situation is correct. The 'one half of an old farmhouse' where Cytherea and Owen lodge is easily recognizable in the Manor House, just below the church on the Affpuddle road.

In creating *Weatherbury*, Hardy performed a telescopic contraction of the countryside around Piddletown. Thus Waterston Manor, the model for Bathsheba's farmhouse, is to be found two miles (three kilometres) distant from its situation in the text, and Boldwood's *Little Weatherbury Farm* stands, on the ground, over a mile (one-and-a-half kilometres) north of the village square. One of the results of the construction of the dual carriageway is the effective detachment of the agricultural world from the village, which has the feel of a dormitory and retirement town.

Remount your bicycle or return to your car and head out of Piddletown on the Blandford Road. As you do so you will pass the Blue Vinney; this has replaced the Cat, an old thatched inn which sadly burnt down, but survives in a local motto which reinforces Hardy's account of the town's reputation for heavy drinking:

> Into Church
> Out of Church
> Into Cat
> Out of Cat
> Into Piddle

Go straight across the first roundabout, and turn left at the second. The realigned Druce Lane now runs beside the bypass, then heads north-west on its old route. Where the road turns sharply left, the long, low, grey structure of Druce Farm is on your right. The track past the house is a bridleway so make full use of your rights to inspect *Little Weatherbury Farm*. Then resume your original route and, after nearly a mile (one-and-a-half kilometres) traversing the Piddle water meads, Waterston Manor comes into view on your right, screened initially by a beech hedge, then by a wall with a red post-box. Pause here and admire the house through the trees – the garden is occasionally open to the public in the summer. Hardy describes this 'stone building of the Jacobean stage of Classical Renaissance' in chapter IX of *Far From the Madding Crowd*; Pevsner considers Waterston to be the most charming of seventeenth-century Dorset manor houses (plate 2.5).

The swamp where Bathsheba spent the night after the opening of Fanny's coffin cannot readily be identified, nor can 'the hollow amid the ferns', although a number of authorities have made unsubstantiated assertions. The hollow was most probably a swallet hole and therefore back upon *Egdon* – ferns do not grow in the lush water meadows of the Piddle Valley. A whole cluster of swallet holes riddle the heath between Troy Town and Green Hill, so it was most likely here that Troy gave his erotic display.

Turn around at Waterston and head back towards Puddletown. The first group of cottages form the hamlet of Lower Waterston. On your right as the road then bends left downhill stood a thatched cottage, now demolished, which is thought to have been Gabriel's residence (between the corner and the elegant nineteenth-century Chine Hill Cottages). The sheep-washing pool lay in the water meadows to your left; still in working order until the 1990s, it has since vanished almost without trace. **At Druce's Farm take the narrow Birch Lane straight ahead.**

2.5 Bathsheba's Farm

On this hill stood *Nest Cottage* (now replaced by a house called 'Holm Bush') 'to which Gabriel had retired before taking his final departure from the locality' after being dismissed by Bathsheba for voicing his opinion of her conduct. **We are now heading for Milborne-St-Andrew and the territory of *Two on a Tower*. If on bicycle or foot, keep straight ahead at the top of Birch Lane until you reach the bridleway which brings you to Basan Hill on the A354 where you turn left. By car, it is a right turn back to the roundabout by the dual carriageway from where you turn left for Basan Hill.**

Two on a Tower is a tale of two localities deliberately entwined by Hardy into a single text. Like *The Return of the Native*, it is dominated by an elevated viewpoint, but here the observers have their eyes fixed on celestial happenings, rather than upon the earth below. As in *The Return of the Native*, the action is geographically very compact, being principally confined to a small stage, a single, thinly populated parish. Anyone travelling east from Dorchester on the highway towards Wimborne and the New Forest cannot fail to notice two miles (three kilometres) beyond Bere Regis, near the crossroads known as Red Post, a stone tower projecting starkly from the top of the wooded hill straight ahead. This is the phallus of Charborough Park, which Hardy must have known from a young age – it is in many ways more startling and graphic than the reclining giant of Cerne Abbas. When he chose to write a further novel on the theme of 'The Poor Man and the Lady' with an astronomical twist – astronomy being all the rage in the 1880s – his mind inevitably turned to the well known but secret tower.

The Drax family, owners then and now of the Charborough Estate, allow no public access to their land, and in 1841 successfully rerouted the main road to greatly enlarge the park and keep the lowly populace yet further away – an event which Mr Sawbridge Erle Drax celebrated by erecting the triumphant Lion Lodge and Stag Gate. Even Hardy, the grand old man of English and Dorset letters, did not manage to breach this barrier until the very end of his life – being invited to the great house for lunch in September 1927.

Hardy was considerably more familiar with the village of Milborne-St-Andrew, its decaying Manor House beside the church, the monument on Weatherby Castle, and the adjoining bivallate Iron Age hill fort. In the novel he amalgamated these features with the unfamiliar Charborough House, church and hilltop tower. That he did this can pass without question because Hardy commissioned the artist Macbeth Raeburn to draw the house and tower at Charborough as a frontispiece for the novel, embodying the actual location of *Welland* House; whilst in the text of the novel he refers several times to the column as Rings-Hill Speer, the local name for Weatherby Castle – as Swithin explains to Lady Constantine on their first encounter. In his 1895 preface, Hardy confirms that 'the scene of the action was suggested by two real spots in the part of the country specified, each of which has a column standing upon it'.

In Milborne-St-Andrew, make for the southern end of Chapel Street. Note the church (above you to the right), the features and fabric of which resemble the fictional *Welland* Church. **Beyond Church Hill, when Chapel Street bears sharp left, continue on the track straight ahead. You will soon pass through a pair of decayed stone gate pillars, isolated in the field, then the remains of the manor house (mostly demolished in 1802) will appear on your left. Follow this path straight ahead along the edge of two meadows, then turn left onto a track, then right over a stile onto a path along the edge of a further field. At the end of this take the stile on your left and head uphill. You will soon see before you a partially wooded hill fortification with no sign of a column. Follow the irregular path into the wood, where beech, ash and thorn have replaced Hardy's conifers; in a minimal clearing stands a sixty-foot brick-built obelisk, surmounted by a dull copper ball, erected in 1761. Continue through to its southern extremity and emerge into a sloping field of twenty-five acres (ten hectares).** In chapter one of *Two on a Tower*, Lady Constantine, who has become somewhat fascinated by this obscure obelisk, listlessly asks Nobbs, her coachman, whether he can drive her to the edge of the plantation:

The coachman regarded the field. 'Well, my lady,' he observed, 'in dry weather we might drive in there by inching and pinching, and so get across by Five-and-Twenty Acres, all being well. But the ground is so heavy after these rains that perhaps it would hardly be safe to try it now.'

Looking north from the Old *Melchester* (Roman) Road:

The central feature of the middle distance, as they beheld it, was a circular isolated hill, of no great elevation, which placed itself in strong chromatic contrast with a wide acreage of surrounding arable by being covered with fir-trees. This pine-clad protuberance was yet further marked out from the general landscape by having on its summit a tower in the form of a classical column, which, though partly immersed in the plantation, rose above the tree-tops to a considerable height.

Unless you are fortunate to have hit upon an exceptionally dry spell for your walk, you will have already encountered the heavy (muddy) ground, aggravated by the grazing cattle; and thus completely understood why Hardy christened this wet and miry parish *Millpond St Jude's*. The first citation is pure Milborne, the second an amalgam. Neither column is Tuscan, but the architecture of Charborough Tower, which still projects well above the tree-line, closely resembles Hardy's fictional portrait, and, more essentially, it also has a door, interior staircase and a flat roof with a parapet, ideal for positioning an equatorial. The tower, which is approached by a now somewhat neglected triumphal causeway from the house, was erected in 1790 but rebuilt higher in 1840 after being struck by lightning. One hundred feet (thirty metres) tall, it is constructed of five octagonal Gothic storeys; from the top, as well as celestial catastrophes, you can spy over four counties and the Isle of Wight.

The park is generally open to the public once or twice in the spring when the rhododendrons are at their best; on these occasions you can inspect the tower in a colourful setting and admire, from a distance, the 'long, low front of the Great House' with its church adjoining. As implied earlier, there are no public rights of way anywhere near this landscaped park which Pevsner describes as 'the most splendid in Dorset'.

Circle back round the grassy fortification with views over (afforested) *Egdon*, then retrace your steps over the two stiles. On reaching the lane after the second stile, keep going straight ahead down the often muddy broadway, bearing left beyond the farmyard for Chapel Street. Now reunited with your wheels, turn left at the southern end of Chapel Street, then right into the somewhat quaintly named Little England. Follow this to

the hilltop crossroads and here turn right. This narrow lane gives you an alternative view of Ring's-Hill Speer. As you descend the hill, the entrance to the public footpath, forming the most direct access to the obelisk, has unfortunately become completely overgrown and the path fallen into disuse. At the bottom of the hill, as the lane turns sharp right to cross the Milborne, a bridle path continues ahead to Ashley Bottom, a close match for Hardy's description of *Welland Bottom*.

Here, at the opposite end of the parish from the church, Swithin walks 'along a narrow lane flanked by a hedge' to reach a 'little dell', which occurred 'quite unexpectedly on the other side of the field fence' and descends 'to a venerable thatched house' – the abode of his grandmother, Mrs Martin. This is the location but not the appearance of the present Roger's Hill Farmhouse. Swithin has here just parted from Lady Constantine, who walks in exactly the opposite direction to reach her home – topographically correct for Manor Farm at Milborne.

Hardy had no first-hand knowledge of Charborough other than his distant visioning of the tower; he therefore borrowed from a third source for his text. Thus, whilst the status of *Welland* Church as the sole survivor of a demolished village is taken from Charborough, the juxtaposition of the church tower to the house, terraced walk and yard – as described in chapter 27, where Swithin, concealed in the belfry, watches Lady Constantine and her brother Louis play bowls with the Bishop of *Melchester* – owes much to Stinsford. Stinsford House adjoins the west side of the churchyard and is very close to the church tower, and the terraced walk along the south front of the house abuts the churchyard wall, exactly as described in the novel where Louis, lurking in an arbour, listens over the wall to Swithin and the bishop engage in a private conversation.

Not far beyond the track to *Welland* Bottom, our lane encounters the dual carriageway. We are heading for *Kingsbere-sub-Greenhill*, so the simple option is to take the main road for just under two miles (three kilometres), slipping off for Bere Regis at the first opportunity. A far more pleasant route is to go under the bypass and take the first left for Briantspuddle. This is a delightful, sleepy, mossy-thatched village, originally known as 'Pidel Turberville' but renamed in the fifteenth century to preserve the name of Brianus-de-Thorbeville who was lord of the manor 200 years earlier.

Turn left at the crossroads and, as you leave the village, the footpath on your right beside the dairy is the one mentioned in *The Return of the Native* as a short cut to *Alderworth*. A few hundred yards further on, the road turns sharp right in a hollow – this is Throop Corner where Eustacia and Wildeve, returning together from the Gipsying, are observed by Venn.

If on foot or bicycle, turn left here up the path to Turner's Puddle, then right and subsequently left into Yearlings' Drove for Bere Regis. By car, follow the road to the right; this brings you to Throop Clump – sadly isolated by army exclusion zones on both sides – turn right again here for Yearlings' Drove and Bere Regis. The word 'drove' indicates the proximity of Woodbury Hill – the site of *Greenhill Fair*.

Kingsbere, 'a little one-eyed blinking sort of place', 'the half-dead townlet' where the D'Urbervilles had resided 'for full five-hundred-years', is another former market town reduced to village status. The town, where the Durbeyfields failed to secure lodgings, has indeed little to recommend it apart from the church. On your right as you approach the church door (on the southern side) is the spot where Joan and her children set up camp in the old four-post bedstead, adjacent 'to the D'Urberville aisle beneath which the huge vaults lay. Over the tester of the bedstead was a beautiful traceried window, of many lights, its date being fifteenth century.' Viewed from the inside, on a sunny day, the window is indeed beautiful (plate 2.6). On the

2.6 The D'Urberville Window

floor you can just distinguish the words '*ostium sepulchri antiquae familiae Turberville 24 Junii 1710*'. The pair of tombs, 'their brasses torn from the matrices, the rivet-holes remaining like marten-holes in a sand-cliff', disappoint in comparison to the tombs in the south chapel at Piddletown. By way of compensation, admire the fifteenth-century nave roof, painted and gilded, adorned with multiple carved heads and full-length figures of the twelve apostles portrayed as fifteenth-century Dorset men.

Beyond the east window of the church, across Southbrook, lies a rough paddock which is the site of the D'Urberville mansion. This was demolished in 1832, apart, probably, from a small area of masonry incorporated into the structure of the cottages on the further side of the field. Behind the remains of the mansion, Woodbury Hill rises to a height of 360 feet (110 metres). It is a univallate hill fort, enclosing twelve acres (five hectares) and from 1267 until 1914 was the site of the annual Woodbury Hill Fair:

> Greenhill was the Nijni Novgorod of South Wessex; and the busiest, merriest, noisiest day of the whole statute number was the day of the sheep fair. This yearly gathering was upon the summit of a hill which retained in good preservation the remains of an ancient earthwork, consisting of a huge rampart and entrenchment of an oval form encircling the top of the hill, though somewhat broken down here and there. To each of the two chief openings on opposite sides a winding road ascended, and the level green space of ten or fifteen acres enclosed by the bank was the site of the fair. A few permanent erections dotted the spot, but the majority of visitors patronized canvas alone for resting and feeding under during the time of their sojourn here.

This is the first occasion on which Hardy used the word 'Wessex' in his published writings. In September 1873, whilst writing *Far from the Madding Crowd*, Hardy walked the thirteen miles (twenty-one kilometres) over *Egdon* Heath from Higher Bockhampton to see the sheep fair; it was a day he would never forget, for that evening his friend and mentor, Horace Moule, committed suicide in his rooms at Cambridge.

To walk to *Greenhill* from *Kingsbere*, leave the churchyard by the northeast gate, turn right, then left, into North Street and immediately right into Blind Street. Follow this to the main road. Take the bridleway opposite and follow the signposted route uphill, across a lane and through a small wood. Then bear left to a gate, then diagonally across a field, passing to the right of some cottages to reach a stile onto a lane. By bike or car, turn left at the roundabout (A35) and then take the first right into Cow Drove. At the top of hill turn left up the steep uneven track to the summit of Woodbury Hill; this is the southern of the two winding roads described by Hardy, its

northern partner, known as Sturt Lane, continues as far as Winterborne
Kingston. The 'few permanent erections' remain beside the cottages already
mentioned. On a clear day this is a magnificent viewpoint, to the south and
west, over *Egdon* and the Frome Valley to the Purbeck Hills beyond. On a dull
day, it is hard to imagine this bleak, unattractive farmland as being the focal
point to which the crowds flocked to see 'The Royal Hippodrome Performance
of Turpin's Ride to York' and other associated marvels. In its heyday it was the
largest fair in Dorset, lasting a full five days. Monday was Wholesale Day,
Tuesday was Gentlefolk's Day (Oysters and Pork), Wednesday was Allfolk's
Day, on Thursday the Sheep Fair was held, and Friday was Pack-and-Penny
Day, when the remaining goods were sold off cheap.

**Make your way back to the main road, then turn right and right again
for Wimborne, passing Red Post with its view of the Tower then the three-
mile (five-kilometre) long brick wall which marks the northern boundary
of the extended Charborough Park.** Hardy and Emma lived in Wimborne for
two years from June 1881 at Llanherne, 16 Avenue Road. It is a pleasant tree-
lined street of well maintained suburban detached houses, remembered in a
poem about the lime trees, long-since replaced by flowering cherries (CP
943). On his first night in this house, Hardy watched Tebbutt's Comet from
the garden, and whilst living there he wrote *Two on a Tower*. Swithin attended
Queen Elizabeth's Grammar School, a not unattractive mid nineteenth-
century pastiche of a Tudor Mansion, well preserved and now converted into
apartments. This was the school where, according to Amos Fry, 'they draw up
young gam'sters' brains like rhubarb under a ninepenny pan'. Wimborne
Station, which features several times in the novel, has followed the majority
of Dorset railways into oblivion. Whilst the town has a certain archaic charm,
the Minster itself is large and grim, and impressive only perhaps because of its
bulk and its dedication to St Cuthburga, sister of King Ina of Wessex. This is
the setting of 'Copying Architecture in an Old Minster' (CP 369).

An *Under the Greenwood Tree* and *Far From the Madding Crowd* Walk

An Alternative Approach to *Weatherbury*

By foot (eight miles/thirteen kilometres)

**Start, once more, from the Thorncombe Wood Car Park and take the
waymarked path through the wood to the Hardys' cottage. Pass directly**

behind the cottage, noting the small window used for paying the workmen their weekly wages, and head straight uphill through the beech trees. This is Snail Creep, the path along which Dick went nutting without Fancy in *Under the Greenwood Tree*. Descend onto the main track towards the bypass. Cross it by the Cuckoo Lane Bridge and then follow the directions on p.52 to Keeper Day's Cottage.

Snail Creep continues on the other side of the Old Road up into Grey's Wood; it was here that Dick 'entered a hazel copse by a hole like a rabbit's burrow' and 'nutted as never man had nutted before'. Sadly this route is not a public right of way. But this sadness is nothing compared to the Hardyan environmental disaster caused by the construction of the dual carriageway.

For reasons, which no one now in authority can explain, all the paths heading from Puddletown Heath northwards across the old High Road were simply stopped at the edge of the new dual carriageway when it was built in the early 1990s. Thus all the northward paths from Higher Bockhampton, known to Hardy and featuring frequently in his fiction and poetry, have been blocked off. The routes can no longer be followed. There is no alternative on but to clamber down a brambly bank onto the dual carriageway, risk life and limb crossing four lanes of traffic, and then descend a highly overgrown and potholed embankment on the other side. Snail Creep escaped lightly because it passes only a short distance from the new Cuckoo Lane Bridge. The next path north, which used to go to Yellham Barn, stops at the edge of the bypass; the one beyond it, which is the direct route from the Hardys' cottage to Keeper Day's Cottage – used several times in *Under the Greenwood Tree* – stops dead. The next two paths, which are bridleways – the first a track which joined the old High Road in *Yalbury* Wood, the next the direct route from the heath to Troy Town and the Buck's Head – have been diverted over half-a-mile (800 metres) each to the Troy Town underpass, then it is a further half-mile (800 metres) back on the other side.

From Keeper Day's Cottage, continue on the same track uphill through the wood (plate 2.7) and between sheep pastures until you reach the hilltop crossroads. Here turn left along the Ridgeway and, after nearly half a mile (800 metres), take the waymarked bridleway to your right down towards Waterston. On reaching the road, turn right and you will see Waterston Manor ahead to your left. These downland pastures are usually well stocked with sheep, a tradition which dates from long before Gabriel Oak for the Exeter Domesday Book records there being 1,600 sheep at Piddletown (plate 2.8).

From *Weatherbury Upper Farm* (p.58) it is half-a-mile (800 metres) along the road and past the sheep-wash water meadows to *Little Weatherbury Farm* (Druce Farm). From here retrace your steps to the right-angled bend and here turn left up the first bridleway. Follow the dog-leg to cross

2.7 Yell'ham Wood

2.8 Piddletown sheep

the bypass and then the track beside the playing field to the High Road at Puddletown. Inspect *Weatherbury* as already described (see p.55–6).

Take the footpath which starts directly opposite the high brick wall which conceals the site of Bathsheba's house and follow it up behind the school and down to White Hill Lane. Cross over and take the bridleway here, as waymarked, through the field beside the telegraph poles rather than along the main track which stays to your left. This is Coombe Farm, well known to Hardy as a favourite area for 'Gipsying', as recorded in 'In a Eweleaze near Weatherbury' (CP 47).

The path passes through a pleasant little wood and then bears sharply right to the lane (Rhododendron Mile). Here turn left and then first right. Follow this broad track up onto the (afforested) heath. Keep going straight on, ignoring turnings – you will soon pass Green Hill Pond and reach *Mistover Knap*. Follow the route back to *Mellstock*, as described in chapter one (pp.25–6).

A Walk to Fiddler's Green

'The Three Strangers'

By foot (two miles/three kilometres)

'The Three Strangers', subsequently dramatized by Hardy as 'The Three Wayfarers', was the first *Wessex Tale* and has always been one of his most popular short stories. All major Hardy topographers, including Lea and Kay-Robinson, have placed *Higher Crowstairs* – Shepherd Fennel's cottage – on Hog Hill, near Grimstone, off Long Ash Lane to the north-west of Dorchester. However, as Fred Pitfield sagely pointed out in 1992, the third stranger was travelling from *Shottsford* (Blandford) to visit his condemned brother in *Casterbridge* Gaol – in other words from a north-easterly direction – so it is inconceivable that his route could have passed over Hog Hill. Moreover, the Fennels' house stands 'on the long, grassy and furzy downs … not three miles, by actual measurement, from the county town' and 'the only reason for its precise situation seemed to be the crossing of two footpaths at right angles hard by, which may have crossed there and thus for a good five hundred years'. The only such crossing-point on Hog Hill is a place called Jackson's Cross, which is a good four-and-a-half miles (seven kilometres) from Dorchester by the shortest route.

To find *Higher Crowstairs*, one needs to look closer to home, in this case within the boundaries of Stinsford Parish and less than two miles (three kilometres) from the Hardys' cottage, for a much more probable site, which fits both the criteria of lying between *Shottsford* and *Casterbridge*, and being within three miles (five kilometres) of the latter, can be found on the lonely, exposed and beautiful Waterston Ridge.

This, the continuation of the same Ridgeway track used on the *Far From the Madding Crowd* Walk, can be reached simply by not turning down to Bathsheba's Farm but keeping straight on along the down. Alternatively, take Slyer's Lane (B3143) out of Dorchester and pick up the Ridgeway at Waterston Ridge. Heading west, with fine views towards Dorchester nestling in its cluster of hills – the Poundbury development is that carbuncle to the right – you soon come to a wooded tumulus which stands 420 feet (130 metres) above sea level but still in Stinsford parish.

From here the track sweeps down towards a green corrugated-iron barn, shaped like an aircraft hanger; this stands beside the crossing of two ancient trackways and is the spot suggested by Pitfield as being *Higher Crowstairs*, certainly a far more probable location than the 'magnificent thatched barn' at Grimstone photographed by Kay-Robinson. Walk on along the Ridgeway, a true Wessex Height, where 'one's next neighbour is the sky' (CP 261) (plate 2.9). Less than half a mile (800 metres) beyond the barn you come to a T-junction below a wood. Here turn left and within

2.9 Near Fiddler's Green

2.10 The cottage at *Higher Crowstairs*

a short distance a track joins you from the right – thus making a staggered crossroad. This wild and isolated spot on Wolfeton Down – frequented by deer – would also seem a likely site for *Higher Crowstairs*. Continue down this track with the hedge first on your left, then on your right until you reach the cross-ways at Seager's Barn – diminished to no more than a water tank, surrounded by mud. Here take the grassy track on your left towards Three Cornered Coppice. Beside the coppice bear right and follow the track round to the left towards a tumulus and ivy-enshrouded ruin.

Stop and admire the ruined cottage, constructed from a mixture of brick, stone, chalk and flint and displaying in places the remains of a slate roof. This old house beside the tumulus is known as Fiddler's Green (plate 2.10). Fiddler's Green in folk mythology is 'the happy land imagined by sailors where there is perpetual mirth, a fiddle that never stops playing for dancers, who never tire, plenty of grog and unlimited tobacco'. (2) This description has uncanny resonances with 'The Three Strangers'. At *Higher Crowstairs*, the first stranger (an escaped convict rather than a sailor) obtains tobacco and a pipe; the second stranger (the gentleman in cinder-grey) drains the 'huge family mead mug' until it is empty and then obtains a complete refill, against Mrs Fennel's better judgement. But these are minor coincidences compared with events in the cottage, prior to the arrival of the strangers:

The fiddler was a boy of those parts, about twelve years of age, who had a wonderful dexterity in jigs and reels, though his fingers were so small and short as to necessitate a constant shifting for the high notes, from which he scrambled back to the first position with sounds not of unmixed purity of tone. At seven the shrill tweedle-dee of this youngster had begun, accompanied by a booming ground-bass from Elijah New, the parish-clerk, who had thoughtfully brought with him his favourite musical instrument, the serpent. Dancing was instantaneous, Mrs. Fennel privately enjoining the players on no account to let the dance exceed the length of a quarter of an hour. But Elijah and the boy, in the excitement of their position, quite forgot the injunction. Moreover, Oliver Giles, a man of seventeen, one of the dancers, who was enamoured of his partner, a fair girl of thirty-three rolling years, had recklessly handed a new crown-piece to the musicians, as a bribe to keep going as long as they had muscle and wind. Mrs. Fennel, seeing the steam begin to generate on the countenances of her guests, crossed over and touched the fiddler's elbow and put her hand on the serpent's mouth. But they took no notice, and fearing she might lose her character of genial hostess if she were to interfere too markedly, she retired and sat down help-less. And so the dance whizzed on with cumulative fury, the performers moving in their planet-like courses, direct and retrograde, from apogee to perigee, till the hand of the well-kicked clock at the bottom of the room had travelled over the circumference of an hour.

There could hardly be a clearer description of 'a fiddle that never stops playing for dancers'! This episode has a strong autobiographical element, for a remark-ably similar passage in *The Life* describes how little Thomas Hardy 'loved adventures with the fiddle' and how on one occasion:

> … at a homestead … he was stopped by his hostess clutching his bow-arm at the end of three-quarter-hour's unbroken footing to his notes by twelve tire-less couples in their favourite country-dance 'The New-Rigged Ship'. The matron had done it lest he should 'burst a bloodvessel', fearing the sustained exertion to be too much for a boy of thirteen or fourteen.

The next paragraph describes 'queer occurrences accompanying these merry minstrellings'. It would seem likely, therefore, that *Higher Crowstairs* was sited on the downs within Stinsford Parish and that Hardy had played fiddle at such a 'randy'. As was so often the case, Hardy transported Fiddler's Green a few hundred yards away from its actual position to a nearby cross-ways to suit his narrative purposes. It indeed stands less than a quarter of a mile (400 metres) from the barn identified by Pitfield.

Follow the track on from Fiddler's Green back towards the farmhouse on Waterston Ridge, taking the permissive route up their boundary to rejoin the Ridgeway rather than crossing through fences and livestock. Bear right back to Slyer's Lane.

A left turn 'Up the lane I knew so well, the grey, gaunt, lonely Lane of Slyre' ('The Revisitation' CP 152) takes you across the Pydel at Higher Waterston and soon into Hardy's *Longpuddle*: first Piddlehinton (*Lower Longpuddle*) and then Piddletrenthide (*Upper Longpuddle*). Kay-Robinson's detailed exposition of the routes taken by Burthen's carriers van and Tony Kyte's wagon in 'A Few Crusted Characters' remains the definitive text on this subject, so I will not repeat it here. *Upper Longpuddle* Church, which has long-since lost its gallery, is the setting of 'Absentmindedness in a Parish Choir' and of 'Andrey Satchel and the Parson and Clerk', whilst at the eighteenth-century Manor House, just down the street, the older Andrey was unmasked in his attempts to pass himself off as a musician. *Longpuddle Spring*, where Philip Hookhorn drew water in 'The Superstitious Man's Story', can be found at Morning Well beside the wood, just north-east of *Longpuddle* Church.

Review: This chapter expands on the theme set out in chapter one, that the essence of Hardy's Wessex lay within a very few square miles surrounding his birthplace at Higher Bockhampton. His fictional territory is thus the outward extension of a very narrow landscape, an attempt to resist that constant centripetal poetic force which draws all locations back towards their heart on *Egdon*. Beyond *Egdon* lies the fertile landscape of *Tess, Far From the Madding Crowd, Under the Greenwood Tree* and *Two on a Tower* as well as the short stories 'The Waiting Supper', 'The Three Strangers' and 'A Few Crusted Characters'. Careful examination of the effects of Hardy's contracting kaleidoscope calls into question some of the previously accepted identifications of Hardy's Wessex locations. In particular, I contend that *Talbothays* can be most closely identified with Norris Mill Farm, that Tess and Angel were married at Puddletown and that *Higher Crowstairs* can be found upon Waterston Ridge within Stinsford Parish. Outer *Egdon* is best explored on a seventeen-mile (twenty-seven-kilometre) bicycle ride which takes in *Talbothays*, Stafford House, Yellowham Hill, Troy Town, Puddletown, Athelhampton, Milborne-St-Andrew, Briantspuddle, Throop Corner, Bere Regis and Woodbury Hill before ending at Wimborne. An eight-mile (thirteen-kilometre) walk from Thorncombe Wood includes Snail Creep and Keeper's Cottage before exploring the heart of *Weatherbury* and returning across the heath via Coombe Farm, a favourite local spot for 'Gipsying'.

CHAPTER THREE

Mellstock (Stinsford Parish)

Mellstock was a parish of considerable acreage, the hamlets composing it lying at a much greater distance from each other than is ordinarily the case. Hence several hours were consumed in playing and singing within hearing of every family, even if but a single air were bestowed on each. There was Lower Mellstock, the main village; half a mile from this were the church and vicarage, and a few other houses, the spot being rather lonely now, though in past centuries it had been the most thickly-populated quarter of the parish. A mile north-east lay the hamlet of Upper Mellstock, where the tranter lived; and at other points knots of cottages, besides solitary farm-steads and dairies.

IN HARDY'S 'partly real, partly dream country' the fictional *Mellstock* Parish equates very closely to the actual parish of Stinsford, and still does so 170 years after the setting of *Under the Greenwood Tree*. The parish remains large, scattered and thinly populated, reaching from the heights of Waterston Ridge in the north (425 feet (130 metres) above sea level) to the lowly Frome water meadows in the south. In the west the parish abuts the Fordington end of Dorchester and in the east merges into Puddletown Heath. Grey's Bridge and Ten Hatches Weir span the boundary between county town and rural parish – we can be truly thankful that throughout the twentieth century this boundary remained sacrosanct. The population of Stinsford Parish in the 2001 census was only 346, twenty-seven people less than in 1851, and remains scattered between three small hamlets and the Kingston (Maurward) Estate; although the number of houses in the parish has more than doubled in the last 150 years, Stinsford no longer boasts a single shop or public house.

A *Mellstock* (Poems) Walk

The Heart of Hardy's Wessex

By foot (four miles/six kilometres)

The best way to explore Hardy's *Mellstock* is to follow this gentle four-mile (six-kilometre) walk, which starts from Kingston Maurward, visits Higher and Lower Bockhampton, and finishes at Stinsford Church. Alternatively, all the main points on the route can be reached quite easily by car.

A good starting point is the Garden Centre which is clearly signposted, and where there is car parking. Follow the path from here straight ahead to the imposing front of Kingston House, bearing in mind that until you reach the Old Manor House you are on private paths, forming part of the Kingston Maurward College Farm and Estate, rather than designated public rights of way. You are approaching *Knapwater House* in the opposite direction to Cytherea Graye in *Desperate Remedies* but Hardy's detailed architect's description still holds true:

> The house was regularly and substantially built of clean grey freestone throughout, in that plainer fashion of Greek classicism which prevailed at the latter end of the last century ... the main block approximated to a square on the ground plan, having a projection in the centre of each side, surmounted by a pediment. From each angle of the inferior side ran a line of ... subsidiary buildings being half buried beneath close-set trees and shrubs. The natural features ... were of the ordinary, and upon the whole, most satisfactory kind, namely, a broad, graceful slope running from the terrace beneath the walls to the margin of a placid lake lying below, upon the surface of which a dozen swans and a green punt floated at leisure. An irregular wooded island stood in the midst of the lake ...

Although the garden is only occasionally open for public viewing, you will catch indirect glimpses of the lake and irregular wooded island during the course of this walk; swans still frequent both the lake and the adjoining Frome-side path. The new house at Kingston Maurward, built of brick in 1720 by George Pitt – who had married Lora Grey, the last survivor of the family from the old Manor House – was resurfaced in Portland stone in 1794 after George III had derisively exclaimed 'Brick, brick, brick!' In 1845 the Pitt family sold the house to Francis Martin, whose childless wife, Julia Augusta Martin, was particularly attentive to the frail but precocious young Thomas Hardy who, in return, nourished a romantic attachment to her throughout his adolescence.

Martin was the Squire of Stinsford and, as Hardy records in *The Life*, the withdrawal of Julia's favourite pupil from the school, which she had started at Lower Bockhampton, so angered the Squire's wife that her husband reciprocated by removing 'the estate-building work ... out of the hands of Tommy's father' – a significant, though temporary, blow to the family business. 'In Her Precincts' (CP 411) is an expression of young Tom's grief at 'the loss of his friend the landowner's wife' whilst 'Amabel' (CP 3) is based upon their painful re-encounter in London in 1862 when Hardy was shocked by 'her ruined hues', for time had transfigured 'the lady of his earliest passion' (now aged 52) into 'an old woman'. A later, happier, poem associated with this house is 'To C.F.H. On Her Christening-Day' (CP 793), written for his goddaughter Caroline Hanbury, whose parents owned Kingston Mauward in the 1920s, and was presented to her in a silver casket.

Follow the path from the left corner of the front of the house down some steps, past some new buildings and across a stretch of lawn to pick up the drive heading towards the Old Manor (plate 3.1). This beautiful stone house, built by Christopher Grey in 1591, is described by Pevsner as 'the late Elizabethan E-plan manor house refined to a point of perfection'. Approaching the house, you can hear the gentle murmur of the weir as the lake empties itself into the Frome – an inoffensive cascade in comparison to the waterfall which you can hear 'in every room of the house, night or day ...

3.1 *Old Knapwater House*

enough to drive anybody mad', a necessary exaggeration from the author of that 'sensation novel', *Desperate Remedies*.

In Hardy's day the Old Manor, that 'glad old house of lichened stonework' (CP 634), was in a very poor state of repair and subdivided into cottages, thus accurately forming the basis for *Old Knapwater House*:

> In front, detached from everything else, rose the most ancient portion of the structure – an old arched gateway, flanked by the bases of two small towers, and nearly covered with creepers ... behind this ... came the only portion of the main building that still existed – an Elizabethan fragment ... the mullioned and transomed windows, containing five or six lights, were mostly bricked up to the extent of two or three, and the remaining portion fitted with cottage window-frames carelessly inserted, to suit the purpose to which the old place was now applied, it being partitioned out into small rooms downstairs to form cottages for two labourers and their families; the upper portion was arranged as a storehouse for divers kinds of roots and fruit.

When Cytherea is forced to find shelter during a thunderstorm, the Old House becomes the Gothic backdrop for Manston's masterful and seductive organ recital, which leaves the mesmerized girl wondering 'O, how is it that man has so fascinated me?' As often in Hardy, his fiction was to transmute into reality, for in the 1880s a dairyman called Thomas Way moved from Toller Porcorum into the Old Manor, then a farmhouse, bringing with him his four daughters. Hardy spotted the youngest daughter, Augusta Way, as she milked the cows in the adjoining byre and was fascinated by the beautiful teenager; she became the model for Tess of the D'Urbervilles, and her daughter, Gertrude Bugler, later played Tess on stage both in Dorchester and in the West End. Hardy's original fascination with this place dates, however, from his attraction to Julia Martin; whilst in pursuit of her he attended a harvest-home celebration held in a barn adjoining the Old Manor House, commemorated in 'The Harvest-Supper (*c.* 1850)', a poem which reverberates into *Far From the Madding Crowd*.

From the Manor House, now a superb bed and breakfast establishment, turn left onto the waymarked bridleway through the farmyard. The Dog Grooming Salon and Animal Care Centre form the adapted remains of the byre where Hardy spied 'Tess' milking the cows and the long brick walled enclosure attached at right-angles to the end of this building is all that remains of the barn where the 'Harvest Supper' was held. Follow this bridleway on to the track which curves between fenced fields to the lane at Hollow Hill. Cross the lane, and again following the waymarked route, bear right to a stile at the top corner of a field beside

a copse. **Look back for fine views of Kingston Maurward from this path.** On reaching the stile you have joined Hardy's route – trudged daily as a young man – from Higher Bockhampton to school and then work in Dorchester. Hardy's path westward from here followed a higher trajectory than the one which you have just climbed. The old route, prior to a modern footpath diversion, ran straight ahead along the ridge past the clump of beech trees (Grey's Copse) to the far corner of the field where it joined the lane in front of Birkin House; from here Hardy would continue in a straight line along the road to Grey's Bridge and Dorchester. Just across the main road to the right of this path is Kingston Mauward Eweleaze, the setting of 'An Anniversary' (CP 407). Looking to the left, still with your back to the stile, read 'When Oats Were Reaped' (CP 738).

Cross the stile and follow the path straight on to Bockhampton Lane. Pause on the far side of the lane at the gravelled entrance; note a stone gatepost straight ahead and then find its partner, transposed to a redundant position behind the magnificent wrought-iron gateway on your right. These are the gateposts of 'At Middle-Field Gate in February' (CP 421). The buildings in front of you form the Greenwood Grange holiday complex, at the heart of which is a brick-built quadrangle of barns, constructed by Hardy's father for Francis Pitney Brounker Martin in 1849.

To adhere to public rights of way, head north up Bockhampton Lane, turning right at the signpost for Hardy's cottage. Alternatively, and quietly – respecting the privacy of those on holiday – go through the open gateway straight ahead, then bear left past a long low byre (now a gym), fork right down a path and through a door in a fence. On your left is an indoor pool, but to your right on the gable at the end of the farm building you will see the brick inscription '1849 FPBM', commemorating Hardy's Squire. This was known as Higher Bockhampton Farm, 'the lonely barton by yonder coomb / Our childhood used to know', the setting of Hardy's magical Christmas Eve poem 'The Oxen' (CP 403), written in the dark days of 1915.

Follow the path towards the main entrance to Greenwood Grange and turn left for the lane to Hardy's cottage, but first take a brief diversion to your right to peer under the archway entrance to this enchanted farmyard.

The Oxen

Christmas Eve, and twelve of the clock.
 'Now they are all on their knees,'
An elder said as we sat in a flock
 By the embers in hearthside ease.

We pictured the meek mild creatures where
  They dwelt in their strawy pen,
Nor did it occur to one of us there
  To doubt they were kneeling then.

So fair a fancy few would weave
  In these years! Yet, I feel,
If someone said on Christmas Eve,
  'Come; see the oxen kneel

'In the lonely barton by yonder coomb
  Our childhood used to know,'
I should go with him in the gloom,
  Hoping it might be so.

Turn left out of Greenwood Grange, then right at the junction and follow the sandy track towards the Hardys' cottage. On page one of *The Life*, Hardy describes the 'quaint, brass-knockered, green-shuttered domiciles' scattered along the length of 'Veterans' Valley' or 'Cherry Alley' as the lane was dubbed in his childhood. He then laments how 'the quaint residences have been replaced every one by labourers' brick cottages and other new farm buildings, a convenient pump occupying the site of the mossy well and bucket'. The Hardys' cottage, built in 1800 by Hardy's great-grandfather, John Hardy, was the first dwelling in New Bockhampton and the only one to survive into the twenty-first century.

As you walk up the lane, the third house on your right is called Greenwood. This building was originally a pair of brick cottages, constructed by the Hardy family. They are similar in style to the pair of cottages set back diagonally opposite and built somewhat later by Henry Hardy. In Hardy's childhood, abutting the lane in what is now the garden of Greenwood, there stood a thatched cottage. This was the home of William Keats, tranter, and Mary his wife – the models for Tranter Reuben and Ann Dewy in *Under the Greenwood Tree*. The Keats's romance is alluded to by Hardy in *The Life*. In the other half of this cottage lived Hardy's uncle, James, a stonemason, and family. James's daughter, Teresa, four years Hardy's junior, never married and spent her entire life in Bockhampton, playing the organ at Stinsford Church for many years. Teresa, interviewed by *The Daily Mail* shortly after Hardy's death, is reported to have said, 'Poor Tom he was a clever boy, but I never thought he would take to writing and I did not like it when he did. Writing, I think, is not a respectable way of earning a living.' The remains of the village well – the sole source of water for the Hardy household – can still be identified in the ivy-covered mound beside the lane to the right of the entrance to Greenwood. This was the well in which 'The Rash Bride' drowned herself (CP 212).

The appearance of Hardy's cottage (the house has never had any other name) closely fits Hardy's description of the Tranters': 'It was a long low cottage with a hipped roof of thatch, having dormer windows breaking up into the eaves, a chimney standing in the middle of the ridge and another at each end.' Hardy's cottage was also built as two separate dwellings; marked by the higher roofline is the house dating from 1800, carefully constructed, with two rooms above and one below – the original core extended from the central chimney stack to the lane. The extension south-wards is of inferior construction and appears to have been built hastily, probably to provide accommodation for Hardy's grandmother, Mary, on the marriage of his parents in 1839. At a later date, possibly following her death in 1857, the two halves were joined together and the present off-centre front door with porch added. The second window from the left marks the site of the original entrance door, described in the poem 'The Self-Unseeing' (CP 135):

> Here is the ancient floor,
> Footworn and hollowed and thin,
> Here was the former door
> Where the dead feet walked in.

This original front door opened straight from the garden into the large parlour. This layout appears in scenes in both *Under the Greenwood Tree* and *The Return of the Native*; in the latter Eustacia and the mummers are trapped in the frosty garden because 'the door opens right upon the front sitting-room' in 'this quaint old habitation' and to open the door would stop the dance (plate 3.2). Hardy was born in the central of the three upstairs chambers. The room with a window seat (right-hand window), where Hardy is thought to have written his early fiction, was originally in the separate 'granny annex'. In his early years, Hardy slept in the left-hand bedroom, which he shared with his sister Mary. The outhouses to the right of the main building were the scene of home cider-making as described in 'Shortening Days at the Homestead' (CP 791), *Desperate Remedies* and *Under the Greenwood Tree* where Reuben taps his cask 'a drop o' the right sort … a real drop o' cordial from the best picked apples – Sansoms, Stubbards, Five-corners, and such … and there's a sprinkling of they that grow down by the orchard-rails – streaked ones – rail apples we'd call 'em, as 'tis by the rails they grow, and not knowing the right name'.

3.2 The Hardys' cottage

Hardy's birthplace is the property of the National Trust who open it for public viewing in the summer months, except on Fridays and Saturdays. In the winter it is a rather different story; the cottage appears forgotten, looking damp, dark, cold and neglected with green mould rapidly rising up the exterior walls. A heathland dwelling build of cob, tree branches and wheat straw (albeit faced with brick) needs to be warmed in winter to ensure its survival; that central brick inglenook should be put to its original purpose on a daily basis. Hardy prophetically foresaw this problem in the poem 'Starlings on the Roof' (CP 320), written after his siblings had moved to Talbothays Lodge in September 1912: 'No smoke spreads out of this chimney-pot, / The people who lived here have left the spot.'

Here read again 'Domicilium' (CP 1), Hardy's earliest surviving Wordsworthian poem. As Mary Hardy tells her grandson in the poem 'change has' indeed 'marked the face of all things', but the surrounding heath (since the recent clearances), the cottage and the garden have altered very little in appearance since Hardy's childhood. The 'high beeches' which 'bending, hang a veil of boughs, and sweep against the roof' are a major contributor to the dampness of the cottage. Maybe the time has come to return the house to the state described in the final stanza of the poem when 'those tall firs and beeches were not planted'? On a winter's evening 'The Fallow Deer at the Lonely House' (CP 551) is a beautiful poem to read here, as are three of Hardy's poems about memory and regret: 'Logs on the Hearth', his simple but poignant elegy for his sister Mary (CP 433); 'Night in the Old Home' (CP 222) written 9 October 1924, when Hardy was eighty-four years old; and 'Concerning His Old Home' (CP 839), published posthumously in 1928.

On a happier note, and to put a spring in your step as you leave the birthplace, read 'When I Set Out for Lyonnesse' (CP 254), Hardy's recollection of his first magical trip to Cornwall, which started so inauspiciously at 4 a.m. and included a starlit walk down Veteran's Alley to catch the train for Cornwall from Dorchester West station:

> When I set out for Lyonnesse,
> A hundred miles away,
> The rime was on the spray,
> And Starlight lit my lonesomeness
> When I set out for Lyonnesse
> A hundred miles away.

Monday 7 March 1870

From the cottage, pause by the American monument and then follow the path signposted 'Rushy Pond' behind the cottage into Thorncombe wood. As you ascend the slope watch out for the small wooden sign directing you to the left onto the path which runs through the trees to Rushy Pond. In 'At Rushy Pond' (CP 680), the 'half-grown moon' illuminating 'the frigid face of the heath-hemmed pond' reminds the poet of the break-up of his relationship with a woman whom he had 'once, in a secret year' called 'from across this water, ardently – and practised to keep her near'. The similarity of this late poem (published 1925) to his greatest early poem 'Neutral Tones' (CP 9, dated 1867) has led some authorities to place 'Neutral Tones' here also, rather than at Tolmare Pond in West Sussex (p.186). Quite apart from Millgate's compelling evidence in favour of Tolmare, this latter pond, which is illuminated by 'the god-curst sun' rather than 'the troubled orb' of a moon, is shaded by an ash tree. There are no ash trees growing within at least a quarter of a mile (400 metres) of Rushy Pond whilst an ash sapling flourishes beside the desiccated remnant of Tolmare. Here also read 'Moonrise and Onwards' (CP 517), another *Egdon* elegy directed to Diana 'the Wan Woman of the waste up there'.

Follow the path on the open (west side) of Rushy Pond over exposed heathland and down to a ferny crossway with a picnic bench; on a sunny spring day, this makes a luxuriant green resting place. This is an ideal spot to read 'Childhood Among the Ferns' (CP 846), another late poem based on an early experience. Hardy describes in *The Life* how as a young child he lay on his back in the sun, 'thinking how useless he was', and 'came to the conclusion that he did not wish to grow up'; his mother 'was very much hurt' by these early conclusions on the futility of existence. These themes meld into his bleak, self-critical, nihilistic trilogy 'In Tenebris', dating from the dark, despairing days of 1896, particularly 'In Tenebris III', which contains in the fourth stanza a celebration of his early dependence upon Jemima:

> Or on that loneliest of eves when afar and benighted we stood,
> She who upheld me and I, in the midmost of Egdon together,
> Confident I in her watching and ward through the blackening
>   heather,
> Deeming her matchless in might and with measureless scope
>   endued. (CP 138)

Cross the stile beyond the picnic bench and follow the path straight on between fenced cow pastures to Pine Lodge Farm. Glance back from this path for fine views of Rainbarrow (half-right). Pine Lodge is an excellent stop for refreshments. Heedless William's Pond (p.22) is enshrouded in the clump of trees below, to the left of the farm drive.

Cross the lane and continue on the track towards Bhompston Farm. On reaching the farm, follow the signposted track to your right (a deviation onto the path to your left will take you across the water meadows to Norris Mill, the model for *Talbothays* and thus *Tess* territory, see p.47–9). Bear left over a stile and follow the waymarked path diagonally across (down) this meadow to a gate in the corner by an osier coppice. Continue straight ahead across the next field towards Kingston Dairy beyond. This path affords a fine perspective of the Frome as it meanders through the water meadows from Bockhampton Bridge; if cattle are not grazing these meadows, deer may often be spied, taking advantage of their absence.

Follow the path through the dairy to emerge on the lane in Lower Bockhampton. This southern end of the village, with its mellow thatched cottages, has changed little in appearance over the last hundred years, but has changed significantly since the time of *Under the Greenwood Tree* (1830). **Turn up Bockhampton Lane.** The thatched house on your left (Bridge Cottage) originally doubled as both a blacksmith's and the village beer shop. Opposite this ran a lane, now completely vanished, populated by 'several old Elizabethan houses, with mullioned windows, and doors, of ham hill stone'; the first of these is thought to have been Farmer Shiner's 'queer lump of a house' where the quire were subject to unexpected abuse.

Climb Bockhampton Lane. The thatched cottage on your right, opposite the lane now known as Knapwater, was until recently the village post office. 'Geographical Knowledge (A Memory of Christiana C———)' (CP 237) commemorates the postmistress with scant understanding of local geography but a global sense of direction, gleaned from her sailor son, Frederick Coward. This is also the setting of 'The Thing Unplanned' (CP 763). Opposite the post office stands the school, endowed by Julia Martin and opened in 1848. This is where Hardy recalls in 'He Revisits His First School' (CP 462) that he was 'the first pupil to enter the new school-building, arriving on the day of opening, and awaiting tremulously and alone, the formal entry of the other scholars from the temporary premises near'.

The schoolhouse formed the second halt for the *Mellstock* Quire in 'Going the Rounds'; directed towards the upstairs window, there 'passed forth into the quiet night an ancient and time-worn hymn, embodying a quaint Christianity in words orally transmitted from father to son through several generations down to the present characters, who sang them out right earnestly:

> Remember Adam's fall,
> O thou Man:
> Remember Adam's fall
> From Heaven to Hell.

It takes two further carols to draw out the sleeping schoolmistress but the result is worth the wait for, in a typical Hardyan scene, the blind slips upward to reveal 'a young girl, framed as a picture by the window architrave, and unconsciously illuminating her countenance to a vivid brightness by a candle she held in her left hand ... She was wrapped in a white robe of some kind, whilst down her shoulders fell a twining profusion of marvellously rich hair, in a wild disorder'; from that moment of fascination the captivated Dick Dewy is a lost man.

The school survived until 1961 when it was sold by auction and sympa-thetically converted into a house, as it now stands. Beyond Yalbury Cottage modern dwellings have replaced the ancient cottages. The last house on the left, now Martins, marks the site of Robert Penny's workshop in *Under the Greenwood Tree*:

Mr Penny's was the last house in that part of the parish, and stood in a hollow by the roadside so that cart-wheels and horses' legs were about level with the sill of his shop-window. This was low and wide, and was open from morning till evening, Mr Penny himself being invariably seen working inside ... facing the road, with a boot on his knees and the awl in his hand ... rows of lasts, small and large, stout and slender, covered the wall which formed the background ...

This workshop, which belonged to Robert Reason, did not survive Hardy's lifetime, being replaced by the Mellstock Hut, a reading room and club opened by Hardy in December 1919 as a memorial to the seventy-five men of Stinsford Parish who fought in the First World War. The hut in turn was demolished after being declared unsafe in 1957 and Stinsford was once more without a village hall. Appearing lonely and somewhat dilapidated on the hill above Martins is the original Peakhill Cottage (*Carriford*), home of Adelaide Hinton, long affianced to her cousin Edward Springrove, whom she suddenly jilts in favour of Farmer Bollens (in *Desperate Remedies*).

The lane runs due north from here to Bockhampton Cross and Higher Bockhampton. This is the setting of 'To Louisa in the Lane' (CP 822): 'Meet me again as at that time / In the hollow of the lane.' This poem, published posthumously in *Winter Words* (1928), is an expression of Hardy's long-lasting devotion to Louisa Harding, whose father farmed at Stinsford Farm (just north of the church and now absorbed within the college). A year younger than Hardy, but socially his superior, they never exchanged a word, but as late as 1859 he travelled to Weymouth, where Louisa was at boarding school, in the hope of catching a glimpse of her in church. Louisa never married and spent her whole life in Stinsford, where she is buried in an unmarked grave, which Hardy often visited in old age. The poem 'The Passer-By (L.H. recalls her Romance)' (CP 627) is written from Louisa's perspective, implying that her failure to marry was the result of having fallen in love with her silent admirer, who then passed by no more! A subsequent poem, 'Louie' (CP 739), links her death with Emma's: 'Long two strangers they and far apart; such neighbours now!'

Bockhampton Cross is also the setting of 'By Mellstock Cross at the Year's End' (CP 588), published in December 1919, but, possibly in view of the implications of its personal content, relocated to Henstridge in Somerset (with an explanatory headnote) when the poem was collected. This is a typical example of Hardy's habit of moving geographical settings away from Bockhampton both to disguise their autobiographical nature and to fill the outlines of his expanded Wessex.

Retrace your steps through the village. Remember as you go the other local Hardy characters such as Jude, who started life here, and Mop Ollamoor, from 'The Fiddler of the Reels', the 'musician, dandy and company-man' who 'lodged awhile in Mellstock village', most probably at Bridge Cottage. Pause on Bockhampton Bridge, looking downstream to imbibe the atmosphere of the *Valley of the Great Dairies*, and note the threat of transportation from T. Fooks on the central span and the injunction to 'persons in charge of ponderous carriages' on the corner brickwork from E. Archdall Ffooks. **Take the signposted footpath beside the stream (plate 3.3).**

3.3 *Froomside* path

Here you will often find a pair of swans nesting alongside coots and moorhens. You are retracing the midnight steps of the quire that 'crossed Mellstock Bridge, and went along an embowered path beside the Froom towards the church and vicarage, meeting Voss with the hot mead and bread-and-cheese as they were approaching the churchyard'. Somewhat bleak in winter, this path is at its most luxuriant in early summer, teeming then with nature; the water is crystal clear, reminiscent of the Valency River, that 'purl of a runlet that never ceases / In stir of kingdoms, in wars, in peaces' (CP 276). On wintry days, this is an appropriate place to read 'She Hears the Storm' (CP 228), and, as you near the turning up to Stinsford, look at 'The Third Kissing-Gate' (CP 895), set on the continuation of this path back to Dorchester. The original kissing gates have decayed and disappeared; the third kissing gate was in the field-boundary just beyond the thatched dwelling, now enlarged into Three Bears Cottage. This path, often frequented by the young Hardy on his daily walk to and from Dorchester, lost much of its charm with the construction of the A35 viaduct. Despite this violent and noisy intrusion, kestrels can still be seen hovering over-head or on the lookout from electricity poles and, if you are lucky, you will catch the gold-and-blue flash of a kingfisher darting past.

At the junction of paths by the brick bridge, turn right towards the church. The left-hand path beside the stream, signposted 'St George's Road', will take you across the water meadows to Max Gate, and was the route used by Hardy when walking from his home to Stinsford Church. As you follow in Hardy's footsteps, read the opening lines of 'The Dead Quire' (CP 213):

> Beside the Mead of Memories,
> Where Church-way mounts to Moaning Hill,
> The sad man sighed his phantasies:
> He seems to sigh them still ...

The poem starts on the Church-way where you are now walking; the dormered inn is the beer-house at Bridge Cottage; and 'the Quick pursue the Dead / By crystal Froom' along the path which you have just taken to the graves ahead 'by gaunt yew tree' and 'ivied wall'. **Enter the lower graveyard by the gate on your left, immediately beyond the cottage drive, and follow the grassy path beside the hedge into the main churchyard.**

The first grave which you encounter on your right is that of Fanny Hurden, the lettering of which was restored through the generosity of the late Dr James Gibson (plate 3.4). She is the first of Hardy's 'Voices from Things Growing in a Churchyard' (CP 580): 'These flowers are I, poor Fanny Hurd, / A little girl here sepultured. / Once I flit-flitted like a bird / Above the grass, as now I wave / In daisy shapes above my grave.' Hardy was attracted to Fanny, a fellow

3.4 *Mellstock*

pupil at Lower Bockhampton. One winter's day he accidentally pushed her against the schoolroom stove, burning her hands – an action for which he never forgave himself, particularly following Fanny's premature death in 1861 at the age of twenty.

There is a memorial to 'Bachelor Bowring, "Gent"' within the church on the south wall of the gallery. Squire Audeley Grey (stanza 6) is commemorated twice in the church, most strikingly in the monument on the north wall with its skull and two weeping cherubs in pale Purbeck marble. This Gothic display left a deep impression on the young Hardy; he is reputed to have learnt the inscription by heart on those long 'afternoons of drowsy calm' as he 'stood in the panelled pew' watching the swaying branches of the 'gaunt old yew tree' under which he and so many of his family were subsequently to lie. This memorial, which is taken to be the source of the name 'Angel' Clare, also refers to George Trevelyan, the family name of Eve Greensleeves (stanza 5), as explained in Hardy's own footnote to the poem. The grave of Voss, the character who takes care of the refreshments for the *Mellstock* Quire, can still be identified near to the Hardys'; his name was also adopted by Patrick White, the Australian Nobel-prize winner, for the eponymous hero and title of his greatest novel. The proud Lady Gertrude (stanza 4) alone remains unidentified.

From Fanny's grave, inspect the gargoyles on the southern aisle; the most grotesque is the one on the south-east corner, the exact position on Weatherbury Tower of the 'gurgoyle' which caused such damage to Fanny Robin's grave in *Far From the Madding Crowd* (see. p.55). It is surely no coincidence that we are dealing here with two Fannys who were both beautiful and died young; the fictional Robin in childbirth, the real Hurden probably from the same cause in those days of high maternal mortality? **Continue up past the east end of the church to the Hardy graves.** En route you pass the grey slate memorial to C. Day-Lewis, poet laureate and former Professor of Poetry at Oxford, now at rest beside his much-admired fellow poet. See Day-Lewis's 'Birthday Poem for Thomas Hardy':

> Great brow, frail frame – gone. Yet you abide
> In the shadow and sheen,
> All the mellowing traits of a countryside
> That nursed your tragi-comical scene;
> And in us, warm-hearted and brisker-eyed
> Since you have been.

Here nestling in the shade of an ancient yew Hardy's heart lies buried between the remains of Emma and Florence, flanked on the right by the grave of his parents and to the left by the shared grave of his siblings: Mary, Henry and

Kate (plates 3.5 and 3.6). The line extends with the graves of his paternal grandparents, his uncle James, then that of his Aunt Jane and her daughter, Teresa – the organist, who survived her more famous cousin by exactly eight weeks – all undergoing such wonderful natural 'Transformations' (CP 410): 'Portion of this yew / Is a man my grandsire knew ...' Whilst you are here also take a look at 'Friends Beyond' (CP 36), a poem which includes a number of characters from *Under the Greenwood Tree*, and remember 'The Choirmaster's Burial' (CP 489), that story of the burial of Thomas Hardy I, Hardy's grandfather. The events in this poem appear to foreshadow the difficulties the *Mellstock* Quire experienced with the young, new reforming vicar, although Edward Murray, the incumbent at the time of the choirmaster's death, was himself a violinist and a firm supporter of the church musicians who frequently practised at his home, Stinsford House.

In *The Life* Hardy offers an alternative explanation, that 'there could be no such quiring over his grave as he had performed over the graves of so many, owing to the remaining players being chief mourners'. Throughout his life, Hardy was a regular visitor to his 'Friend's Beyond', as reflected in the poem 'Paying Calls' (CP 454). This was particularly so after Emma's death, as explained in 'Rain on a Grave' (CP 280), 'I Found Her Out There' (CP 281), 'If You Had Known' (CP 593), written fifty years after their first meeting, and as viewed from the dog's perspective in 'Why She Moved House' (CP 806).

The Hardy graves afford a fine view of the pair of stone urns that top the brick gate pillars at the main entrance to the churchyard. These were drawn by Hardy for the illustration opposite the frontispiece in *Wessex Poems*, with a view of the church beyond. Behind the yew tree which overshadows the graves stands the solitary memorial to Mary and William Keats, the models for Tranter Reuben and his wife. Over the wall beyond this grave is the Old Vicarage, in outward appearance little changed since Parson Maybold's time in *Under the Greenwood Tree*. It was here, in the study, that the young Hardy

3.5 Hardy's heart

3.6 Hardy graves

took confirmation classes, and where the *Mellstock* Quire confronted the
Vicar about their threatened redundancy as a result of his scheme for
replacing them with a barrel organ. It is a charming extended Georgian
building and, like many old Dorset vicarages, of greater square footage than
the church its occupant served.

As you head for the door in the church tower, the stone on your right, just
past the Higginson memorial, marks the grave of Robert Reason, boot and
shoemaker. Beyond this, the graveyard is bounded by the wall of Stinsford
House, now carefully restored and divided into ten separate dwellings; as you
turn to enter the church, the main façade of this building stretches away over
the wall behind you. This house, originally a manor mentioned in Domesday,
was long the property of the Strangways family, Earls of Ilchester, whose principal seat is at Melbury House near Evershot (p.192–3). In 1764, Lady Susan
O'Brien, daughter of the then Earl, scandalized society by eloping with
William O'Brien, an actor and protégé of Garrick. Eventually, partially reconciled to the family, they settled at Stinsford House, where Lady Susan was
generally remembered for her kind-heartedness. Hardy's grandfather built a
special vault under Stinsford Church just large enough for the two lovers, and
Hardy's father sung for Lady Susan in her old age. After her death the house
was occupied by Edward Murray, an Ilchester relative and incumbent of the

3.7 Stinsford House and Church

parish. Hardy's mother Jemima came to Stinsford House in 1836 as Murray's cook. Here she encountered Thomas Hardy II doing building work on the house. Family tradition has it that Hardy's father promptly seduced her in the bushes by the neighbouring Frome (cf. 'The Third Kissing Gate' CP 895). The couple did not marry until three years later, Jemima safely pregnant with Thomas Hardy III. When Stinsford House burnt down in September 1892, two months after the death of Hardy's father, Hardy helped carry books and furniture from the conflagration and experienced an understandable 'bruising of tender memories' (plate 3.7). (For the connection between Stinsford House and *Two on a Tower* see p.62.)

Stinsford Church, described by Hardy as being 'of various styles from Transition-Norman to late Perpendicular', is mainly thirteenth-century in structure. Internally, it has undergone many changes since Hardy's birth, most particularly at the hands of the High Church reformer Arthur Shirley, who succeeded Edward Murray in 1837. The contrast between Shirley's innovative zeal and Murray's *laissez-faire* are reflected in the contrast between Parson Maybold and old Mr Grinham in *Under the Greenwood Tree*. Mr Penny complains 'that the first thing he done when he came here was to be hot and strong about church business'. Shirley, on his arrival, greatly increased the number of church services, instituted a Sunday school and, with Julia Martin, was instrumental in founding the new National School – all of which had a great influence on Hardy, leading, most especially, to his deep familiarity with both the Bible and the Book of Common Prayer.

Maybold's second offence was 'to think about altering the church, until he found 'twould be a matter o' cost and what not, and then not to think no more about it'. No such financial restraints limited Shirley who carried out sweeping internal changes including the removal of the chancel pews and the installation of a barrel organ. Maybold's third crime 'was to tell the young chaps that they were not on no account to put their hats in the christening font during service', and his fourth to abolish the stringed choir – a target which Shirley attained within a year of Hardy's birth. Shirley removed the remaining box pews from the nave in 1868 and in a final set of internal revisions took away the gallery itself in 1880. Hardy, temperamentally conservative and yearning for a Stinsford he had never really known, took his revenge on Shirley by attributing Maybold's sweeping reforms not to religious conviction but rather to a socially humiliating infatuation with the local schoolmistress: 'The music is second to the woman … and God A'mighty is nowhere at all.' Incidentally, Hardy's Uncle James faithfully played the barrel organ at Stinsford Church for forty years until his sudden death at the organ on Sunday 19 March 1880.

Hardy's romantic vision of his parents' first encounter is described in the sonnet 'A Church Romance (Mellstock: *c*. 1835)' (CP 211) in which his mother Jemima Hand, newly arrived at Stinsford, 'turned in the high pew, until her sight / Swept the west gallery, and caught its row / Of music-men' one of whom responded with 'a message from his string to her below, / Which said: "I claim thee as my own forthright!"' After approximately 115 years without a west gallery, a splendid new structure was erected in 1996, complete with a modern organ, which occupies the space needed for the choir. Whilst it is wonderful to see a west gallery in Stinsford Church once more, it seems quite bizarre that it was constructed in such a way that it can never fulfil its original purpose.

Displayed on the west wall below the new gallery stairs is Hardy's plan of the West Gallery from *c*. 1835, 'Shewing Positions of Choir', including the four musicians: Thomas Hardy I and his two sons, accompanied by James Dart on violin. Nearby is the brass tablet put up by Hardy with its Latin inscription commemorating '*Thomae Hardy patris Jacobi et Thomae filiorum*' (1903). At the back of the nave is the restored Norman font. This was found broken up and buried in the churchyard, but was repaired in 1920, with a new base designed by Hardy. The restoration was instigated by Mrs Cowley, the vicar's wife, as a memorial to her two brothers, one of whom, Captain Cecil Prowse, is also commemorated in Hardy's poem 'The Sea Fight' (CP 782). On the north wall, admire the Grey monument with its morbidly realistic skull, mentioned by Hardy in both *Desperate Remedies* and *An Indiscretion*. Nearby is a memorial to John and Marcia Pitt of Encombe – suggesting the source for Marcia Bencomb

3.8 The memorial window

in *The Well-Beloved*. On the south wall of the chancel is the memorial tablet, with its 'two joined hearts enchased there' (CP 239 'The Noble Lady's Tale'), to William O'Brien and Lady Susan, whose mortal remains are buried below in their special vault for two. In *A Pair of Blue Eyes*, Hardy transferred this tomb to Cornwall, where it became the model for the Luxellian family vault.

As you pause by the chancel, read that sadly prophetic poem 'Channel Firing' (CP 247), published just three months before the onset of the First World War, for here at Stinsford 'The mouse let fall the altar crumb'. The south aisle is dominated by the Hardy memorial window, showing Elijah on Mount Horeb (plate 3.8). The glass illustrates the earthquake, wind and fire from 1 Kings 19, Hardy's favourite biblical passage. This passage is reflected in several poems, notably 'Quid Hic Agis' (CP 371). To the right of the memorial window is a tablet to William Harding Gent, the grandfather of Louisa, whose unmarked grave Hardy tended in later years.

As a child Hardy regularly attended Stinsford Church, where his father had until recently played the fiddle in the quire (see *Under the Greenwood Tree*), and until his mid-twenties Hardy's cherished ambition was to be ordained into the Anglican Church. However, as a young man in London in the 1860s, his religious convictions appear to have slowly subsided and Hardy began to doubt his religious faith — see 'The Impercipient' (CP 44). His readings of Darwin sharing a close affinity with his innate pessimistic outlook upon the world.

However, he remained, in his own words, 'churchy; not in an intellectual sense, but so far as instincts and emotions ruled'. Throughout his life he remained a regular church-goer, continuing to annotate significant personal events against passages in his bible and prayer book. Particularly fond of the language, traditions, seasonal ritual and music of the church, he had a strong sense of the social value of religious observance in a rural community. Hardy cared deeply about the human condition and believed that the way ahead lay through 'loving-kindness', his personal variant on Christian charity. (For more information see Michael Millgate's book *Thomas Hardy: A Biography* and Timothy Hands's *Thomas Hardy: Distracted Preacher?*) The poem 'Afternoon Service at Mellstock (c. 1850)' (CP 356) suggests that Stinsford offered Hardy the possibility of sentimental reminiscence over childhood religious security:

> On afternoons of drowsy calm
> We stood in the panelled pew,
> Singing one-voiced a Tate-and-Brady psalm
> To the tune of 'Cambridge New'.
>
> We watched the elms, we watched the rooks,
> The clouds upon the breeze,
> Between the whiles of glancing at our books,
> And swaying like the trees.

So mindless were those outpourings! –
Though I am not aware
That I have gained by subtle thought on things
Since we stood psalming there.

In his later years, after the end of Shirley's long incumbency (1837–91), and particularly after the death of Emma in 1912, Hardy turned back to Stinsford Church as a source of tranquillity, continuity and tradition in a rapidly changing world – as a central focus, it is second only to the cottage on *Egdon* in his fiction, poetry and imagination. It was also increasingly the place where so many of his family, friends, neighbours and girls, whom he might have wished to marry, were laid to rest. In the poem 'Looking Across' (CP 446), written shortly after the death of his sister Mary in 1915, Hardy, bereft of sleep in the small hours, looks across the Frome Valley from Max Gate towards Stinsford. There beneath the yew tree lie the first four: his father, mother, Emma and Mary; number five is the poet himself. Hardy chose to be buried at Stinsford, for this was the resting place of so much (and so many) that was close to his heart. Perhaps appropriately, though contrary to his wishes, only his heart was allowed to remain in the yew-enshrouded spot.

To complete the walk, head up the road from the churchyard gates and bear right back to the nursery either through the farmyard, currently the Casterbridge Training Centre, or else along the drive beyond. Alternatively continue down the road towards the roundabout and you will be at the start of the *Casterbridge* walk in chapter four.

Review: Hardy's *Mellstock* (Stinsford Parish) has changed very little in the 170 years since he was born; the human population has dwindled although the number of dwellings has more than doubled. *Mellstock* is best explored on foot starting in the territory of his first novel, *Desperate Remedies*, where *Knapwater House* and the Old Manor still match Hardy's descriptions. From here the walk follows his childhood route from Dorchester to the farmyard of 'The Oxen' – built by Hardy's father – and up Veteran's Alley, through the landscape of *Under the Greenwood Tree*, to Hardy's cottage (which features as Tranter Dewy's home). The walk then crosses the heath to Rushy Pond and *Lower Mellstock*, following the footsteps of the quire to reach *Mellstock* church and graveyard in an explosive medley of characters and scenes from Hardy's early fiction, poetry and life; for here his heart lies buried between the bodies of his two wives, beside his siblings and generations of his ancestors and close by the earthly remains of many of the 'original characters' from this 'partly real partly dream country'.

CHAPTER FOUR

———

Casterbridge (Dorchester)

T HE THIRD landscape to profoundly influence the young Hardy, after *Egdon*
and Stinsford, was the urban territory of Dorchester, a three-mile (five-kilometre) walk from the isolated family cottage at Bockhampton. From September
1850 until the summer of 1861, Hardy daily made this return journey; for the first
six years to Isaac Last's non-conformist school in Greyhound Yard and then as
architectural apprentice to John Hicks at 39 South Street. In 1850 Dorchester
was – and remains now – a small country town, with a population, at that time,
of less than 6,000 people. In 1850, as described in *The Mayor of Casterbridge*, it
had hardly begun to overflow its Roman boundaries. However, because it was the
county town and as such the administrative and judicial centre for Dorset, it was
in many senses intensely urban. It was also a garrison town with a long, violent
and, at times, frightening history; home to the County Assizes and the County
Gaol, where public executions could still be regularly witnessed. The sensitive
young boy from the lonely heath absorbed this stimulating atmosphere through
every pore of his body. As he records in *The Life*:

> Owing to the accident of his being an architect's pupil in a county-town of
> assizes and aldermen, which had advanced to railways and telegraphs and
> daily London papers; yet not living there but walking in every day from a
> world of shepherds and ploughmen in a hamlet three miles off, where
> modern improvements were still regarded as wonders, he saw rustic and
> borough doings in a juxtaposition peculiarly close.

This 'accident' was to play a decisive part in his understanding of the nineteenth-century world around him and its place in the continuum of human
history, particularly in a town where evidence of human occupation extended
over five millennia; Maumbury Rings, on a hill to the south of the town, and
Mount Pleasant, currently buried beneath Waitrose, are Neolithic henges

dating back to 2,000 BC Maiden Castle, one of the largest and most spectacular Iron Age hill forts in Europe, carved out of the Downs to the south-west of Dorchester, originates from a late Stone-Age 'causewayed enclosure' dated 3,000 BC. Hardy grew up playing on Rainbarrows, just one of the several hundred Bronze Age sites in the immediate vicinity. His perception of all these things, coupled with an intense nostalgic drive to conserve the past, was a major influence on his creative output.

In AD 44, the Roman army under Vespasian defeated the Durotrigian tribe, routing both Maiden Castle and the newer fort of Poundbury, on the banks of the Frome. The Romans established a garrison nearby to keep the tribes subdued; the local population gravitated towards this, thus forming the town of Durnovaria. The fortified boundaries of Dunrovia regulated the outline and layout of Dorchester right up until the late nineteenth century. The Roman walls on the south and west sides of the town survived until the eighteenth century when they were demolished to make way for the 'Walks', the tree-lined avenues which feature prominently in *The Mayor of Casterbridge*.

Two seventeenth-century events significantly influenced the atmosphere of the town in which Hardy was educated. Firstly, the fire on 6 August 1613, which destroyed most of the timber-framed medieval heart of Dorchester; for it was harvest time and – just as described by Hardy over 200 years later – the urban population were out in the fields and not available to fight the flames. John White, the radical young Calvinist minister, declared that it was 'Fire from Heaven' – God's punishment for the evil ways of his parishioners – and succeeded in imposing an extreme, puritanical regime upon the town, whereby, amongst numerous other stringencies, fines were imposed for non-attendance at church. In search of religious freedom many Dorchester men became 'Pilgrim Fathers', migrating across the Atlantic. Aspects of this radicalism pervaded through to Hardy's time, though human nature had generally reasserted itself for, as Christopher Coney states: 'we be bruckle folk here – the best o' us hardly honest sometimes, what with hard winters, and so many mouths to fill'.

Secondly, in 1685, the vicious slaughter of Monmouth's rebels following his defeat on Sad Sedgemoor, as Buzzford relates in *The Mayor of Casterbridge*: ''Tis recorded in history that we rebelled against the King one or two hundred years ago, in the time of the Romans, and that lots of us was hanged on Gallows Hill, and quartered, and our different jints sent about the country like butcher's meat.' 'Such was Casterbridge in the days when Henchard and Farfrae were Mayor.'

The Mayor of Casterbridge is unique in Hardy's canon because the narrative is contained, almost exclusively, within the boundaries of an ostensibly fictional town, which equates very closely with Dorchester as it was around the time of Hardy's birth. As so often in his fiction, he is writing about a place just before he actually knew it; his focus being upon 'the immediately recoverable past'. When Susan and Elizabeth-Jane first arrive in *Casterbridge*, the reader is given a detailed description of the buildings: 'There were houses of brick-nogging, which derived their chief support from those adjoining. There were slate roofs patched with tiles, and tile roofs patched with slate, with occasionally a roof of thatch …' to which the author adds the footnote '*most of these houses have now been pulled down (1912)'. We are being told that this Wessex is more real than imagined.

A Twenty-First Century Walk through *Casterbridge* (Dorchester)

The Mayor of Casterbridge

By foot (three-and-a-half miles/five-and-a-half kilometres) (map 4.1)

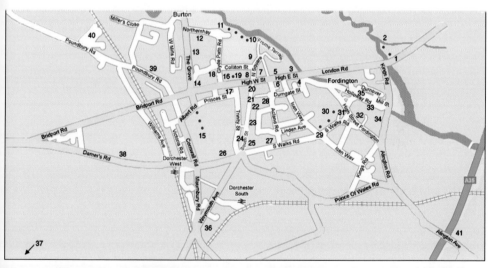

Map 4.1 – Key to *Casterbridge* Map

1. Grey's Bridge	12. Roman Town House	23. Napper's Mite	33. Durnover Barton (site of)
2. Ten Hatches Weir	13. Chalk (Colliton) Walk	24. The Gorge Café	34. Fordington Cemetery
3. The White Hart	14. Hardy Statue	25. United Church	35. Mixen Lane
4. Dorford Chapel	15. West Walks	26. Bowling Alley Walk	36. Maumbury Rings
5. Three Mariners Inn	16. Shire Hall	27. South Walks	37. (To) Maiden Castle
6. Phoenix Inn	17. Ship Inn	28. Henchard's corn store	38. Casterbridge Union
7. The King's Arms	18. Colliton House	29. Gallows Hill	39. The Barracks
8. The Bow	19. Seed & Grain Shop	30. Salisbury Fields	40. Poundbury
9. Casterbridge Gaol	20. Town Pump	31. Fordington Vicarage	41. Max Gate
10. Jopp's Cottage (site of)	21. Antelope Hotel	(site of)	
11. Hangman's Cottage	22. Henchard's house	32. St George's Church	••••• footpath

It was on a Friday evening, near the middle of September and just before dusk, that they reached the summit of a hill within a mile of the place they sought. There were high banked hedges to the coach-road here, and they mounted upon the green turf within, and sat down. The spot commanded a full view of the town and its environs.

The ideal approach to *Casterbridge* is along the route taken by Susan and Elizabeth-Jane; the same route down Stinsford Hill which Hardy followed daily on his way thither from Bockhampton. The new roundabout and bypass do not facilitate this: on the Dorchester side of the roundabout, the old road (not on the traffic sign) continues straight ahead to the left. This short stretch of old highway is indeed enclosed within high banks; but to mount these and sit on the green turf above is almost impossible now, even in winter, so you have to settle for a less than perfect view down Stinsford Hill (B3150). 'The level eye of humanity' now detects a less compact town: the churches and the prison still dominate the foreground but the skyline behind is occupied to the right by the fairytale paraphernalia of Prince Charles's Poundbury and to the left by that building 'higher than the handsomest hotel', the Dorset County Hospital. **Follow the footpath beside the road.** On the bank to the left you will see the recently restored one-mile milestone, upon which the retreating Henchard, 'an outcast and a vagabond', rested his basket, giving way 'to a convulsive twitch, which was worse than a sob' in *The Mayor of Casterbridge* (plate 4.1). In contrast, this same stone gave comfort to Fanny Robin on her desperate last journey to the workhouse in *Far From the Madding Crowd* – from here on she advanced by dragging herself along the fence rails. Further along this fence, a signposted brand-new kissing gate indicates the path back to Stinsford (CP 895).

On Stinsford Hill, Elizabeth-Jane commented to her mother on the apparent squareness of the antiquated borough laid out before them. The narrator confirms that 'it was compact as a box of dominoes. It had no suburbs – in the ordinary sense. Country and town met at a mathematical line.' From the east and the north, this arrangement still holds to the present day. Grey's Bridge and the Frome do indeed mark the abrupt boundary between *Mellstock* and *Casterbridge*; the river being the only buffer between isolated parish and bustling town.

Before crossing the Frome (strictly, here the Cerne) turn right onto the path along the riverbank. You are rewarded with a fine prospect of the town across the water meadows, dominated by the prison to the right and the spire of All Saints and the tower of St Peter's to the left (plate 4.2). You soon reach the rusting remains of Ten Hatches Weir, with five hatches missing and no longer controlling the main flow of water. This means that Ten Hatches Hole, immediately beyond, the pool which Henchard 'was intending to make his death-bed' until shocked out of it by the appearance

4.1 The first milestone

4.2 Town from near Ten Hatches Weir

of his skimmity doppelganger, appears less deep and less daunting. The path beyond still leads 'to a deep reach of the stream called Blackwater', now almost obscured by overhanging willows. On the evening of Thursday 25 September 1873, Hardy sat beside Ten Hatches Hole looking towards Fordington Church, where an open grave awaited the body of Horace Moule, who had committed suicide in his rooms at Cambridge on the previous Sunday – see 'Before My Friend Arrived' (CP 804).

Return to Grey's Bridge ('Sitting on the Bridge' CP 385). Here Parson Maybold, on receiving the news that Fanny was already Dick's chosen-one, 'leant over the parapet of the bridge and saw without heeding' the water gliding beneath the arches and how 'the dace, trout, and minnows sported at ease among the long green locks of weed' in *Under the Greenwood Tree*. Here Henchard gravitated in his time of sorrow; to this remoter bridge, habituated by 'the miserables ... of a politer stamp' who watched the water intensely as if observing some strange fish 'though every finned thing had been poached out of the river years before' in *The Mayor of Casterbridge*. Since the two novels are set at the same time, this fishy discrepancy is surely a reflection of their very different tone and as such a typical example of Hardy's use of landscape to reflect mood. Not infrequently, these men 'allowed their poor carcases to follow that gaze' so they were found in the water here or at Blackwater. Hardy records that 'it had been no uncommon thing for desperate men to wrench the coping off and throw it down the river, in reckless defiance of the magistrates': hence the further warning from T. Fooks.

Head straight towards town up the London Road. This is no longer lined by an avenue of sycamores; it is now a noisy, polluted, ugly highway. Firstly, the water meadows have been sacrificed to a ribbon development of utilitarian red brick houses and bungalows; this was duchy land sold off by Edward Prince of Wales to finance his relationship with Wallace Simpson. Beyond the houses is an extended shrine to the motor car – vehicles for sale packed deep on both sides of the road and then the glorious Shell petrol station. No longer does the main approach to the town reveal 'an indistinct mass behind a dense stockade of limes and chestnuts, set in the midst of miles of rotund down and concave field'; rather it presents a jumble of sorry housing and cheap industrialization. But maybe this tells us as much about the town now as the 'the class of objects displayed in the shop windows' did then.

Pause between the garages for a view straight up to Top-o'-Town. This is little changed from that in the earliest photographs (1840s), if you ignore the motor vehicles and the tarmac. The view is dominated by the two churches aforementioned, plus the spire of the Corn Exchange, with the grey façade of Top-o'-Town House and the tower of the Military Museum forming

4.3 West from Swan Bridge

the backdrop. Ahead on your left a signpost directs traffic to the Casterbridge Industrial Estate (plate 4.3).

Cross Swan Bridge. This is not the brick bridge on whose parapet Troy sat waiting in vain for Fanny – that collapsed in 1954. You are now entering the Roman heart of the town.

On your right a tethered White Hart confirms that this is the ruin of the (rebuilt) inn of that name. This proud beast, somewhat worn at the edges, also adorned the entrance porch of the original tavern, at which Hardy was known to pause for a drink and which he described in 'A Changed Man' as marking the dividing line between the poor quarter of *Mixen Lane* 'and the fashionable quarter of Mr Maumbry's former triumphs'. It was here that Troy was discovered 'smoking and drinking a steaming mixture from a glass' before his assault on Boldwood's Christmas party in *Far From the Madding Crowd*. Here also Gertrude Lodge stabled her horse, whilst a crowd of boys at the harness-maker's next door watched the manufacturer of the hangman's rope in 'The Withered Arm'. The quadrangular forecourt of the White Hart, now fenced off, was the starting point for Burthen's van on its journey to *Longpuddle*, during which the travellers told their tales of 'A Few Crusted Characters'. C.G. Harper describes how in 1904 the courtyard of the White Hart was still packed on market days with 'such a concourse of carriers' carts as rarely witnessed nowadays'. (1)

To the left of the bridge, as the Roman boundary heads up High Street Fordington, is the original Dorford Baptist Chapel where Maumbry preached, now converted into a combined Terracotta Warriors and Teddy Bear Museum! The Dorford Chapel, so called because it stood on the boundary between Dorchester and Fordington, is the setting of the poem 'The Chapel Organist' (CP 593), a soliloquy on the night of her suicide. In 1890 the Baptists moved to their new larger premises at Top-o'-Town.

Head up High East Street towards the projecting portico of the King's Arms. On your right, beyond the Casterbridge Hotel, you come to another abandoned inn, this one stone-built with a green-tiled lower fascia and an archway adjoining inscribed 'Pale Ale Brewery'. This is the former Three Mariners Inn, the replacement of that 'ancient house of accommodation for man and beast, now, unfortunately, pulled down' with 'bay window projecting into the street, whose interior was so popular among the frequenters of the inn'. Just above it, on the left-hand side of the road, note the building currently trading as the Glaze and Graze Craft Café and the 'Hardcore Ink Tattoo Shop'; this is the dilapidated remains of the Phoenix Inn, the setting of 'The Dance at the Phoenix' (CP 28) where Jenny enjoyed her final fling with the 'King's Own Cavalry'. Although there were many taverns much closer to the barracks, this inn was indeed much favoured by the military.

Beyond the Phoenix stands the redundant All Saints Church, setting of 'The Casterbridge Captains' (CP 29). The garden of All Saints is now a nature reserve and, as such, a welcome sanctuary from the bustle of the town. Next door, the West Dorset District Council Housing Advice Centre has taken the place of the wagon office, described in both *The Mayor of Casterbridge* and 'The Waiting Supper'. Opposite, the Kings Arms (plate 4.4) may still be called 'the chief hotel in Casterbridge' and its nineteenth-century frontage (disguising a much older timbered interior) has hardly changed since Hardy's childhood with 'spacious bow-window projected into the street over the main portico' and arched entrance to the stables beyond. In the eight-eenth and nineteenth century it was the principal coaching inn and Royal Mail staging post – it does not seem to have found its role since that time.

Beyond the Kings Arms is the Corn Exchange and Town Hall; the present building, which dates from 1847, appears to be the one described by Hardy as the scene of Bathsheba's first public appearance as a farmer in her own right in *Far From the Madding Crowd*. Troy subsequently teases her with the epithet 'Queen of the Corn-market'. It was here that she fainted on the news of Troy's supposed drowning and Boldwood, for once rising to the occasion, sweeps her

4.4 The Kings Arms

up and carries her unconscious form along the pavement to the nearby hotel. Lea, writing in 1913, described how the scene had little changed in the interim – the hall still packed with farmers 'with their sample bags of corn, pouring out the contents into their hands', only the 'town-bred fowls' had disappeared.

Lucetta's house in *The Mayor of Casterbridge* – High Place Hall – was located by Hardy on the corner directly across the road from the Corn Exchange in the position now occupied by Hardy's Jewellers. However, the building he describes matches Colliton House, a quarter of a mile (400 metres) away, but translocated to a more central position. Kay-Robinson observed that Hardy varied the position of High Place Hall 'not merely within each new edition, but within any single edition': *The Mayor of Casterbridge* contains a number of such inconsistencies. High Place Hall was positioned so as to give Lucetta a 'raking view of the market-place ... the carrefour being like the regulation Open Place in spectacular dramas, where the incidents that occur always happen to bear on the lives of the adjoining residents'. Here Lucetta is subtly commenting on her creator's operatic style: Hardy's use of the landscape to dramatize feelings, as music does in opera. The few market stalls at the top of Cornhill are the vestigial remnants of the great weekly markets, biannual livestock fairs, occasional hang fairs and 'the yearly statute or hiring fair' which used to occupy the carrefour formed by the junction of High East and West Streets with Cornhill and *Bull-Stake Square*. Here the impoverished

Gabriel Oak stood amongst 'two to three hundred blithe and hearty labourers waiting upon Chance' at the annual Candlemas Fair in *Far From the Madding Crowd*.

At this 'Crossways', the church wall used to project in a 'Bow' into the thoroughfare; after the town council straightened this out to improve the flow of traffic, Hardy paid for the erection of 'The Bow' sign so that another piece of Dorchester history might not be completely lost. It is 'up here by the Bow' that the neglected wife stood shivering whilst waiting for her unfaithful husband who was 'treading a tune' 'at the dance in the Club-room below', presumably at The Phoenix, in one (CP 199) of the seven-poem sequence 'At Casterbridge Fair' (CP 194–200). The weekly markets and periodical fairs survived at the carrefour until the mid-1930s when pressure from motor traffic through the town forced its removal to a site between Charles Street and the South Walks.

Turn right into North Square. This narrow entrance between the Bow and the Town Hall was originally enclosed within an archway. It was here in *The Mayor of Casterbridge* that Henchard's wagon capsized after becoming entangled with Farfrae's, 'the bright heap of new hay' spread across High Street, illuminated by the moon's rays. *Bull-Stake Square* has, however, always known harsh times, for the town stocks stood here as did 'a stone post ... to which oxen had formerly been tied for baiting with dogs to make them tender before they were killed in the adjoining shambles', and beyond the square stands the entrance to the prison – a late Victorian replacement for Hardy's *Casterbridge* Gaol. All that remains of the original prison is the great stone 'classic archway of ashlar' on the flat roof above which public hangings were conducted. Today the arch is partially obscured by trees but it can still be seen from the water meadows below. This is where the hang crowds used to gather including, on the morning of 9 August 1856, the impressionable young Thomas Hardy at the execution of Martha Browne: 'I remember what a fine figure she showed against the sky as she hung in the misty rain, and how the tight black silk gown set off her features as she wheeled half-round and back.' Today's prison has capacity for around 250 inmates, serving courts covering a wide area of Dorset and Somerset, the population being divided approximately equally between remands and convicted prisoners. The prison stands on the site of a Norman Castle dating from 1070.

Head down Friary Hill. As you do so, note the blue plaque on the wall to your left, which links the building to a letters patent of Edward I, March 1305.

Cross the Frome by the footbridge at the bottom of the hill. The attractive white cottage on your left marks the site of the Old Priory and is as close as one can get to 'Jopp's Cottage', that 'sad purlieu to which Henchard had wandered' on the night of his discovery that Elizabeth-Jane was not his daughter.

Turn left beside the river. Hardy described it as 'slow, noiseless, and dark – the 'Schwarzwasser of Casterbridge' running 'beneath a low cliff, the two together … rendering walls and artificial earthworks unnecessary'. Here 'the back hatch of the original mill yet formed a cascade' 'which roared like the voice of desolation'. On a winter's day the river in full flood still surges round the bend of the old millpond and the spot remains frosty, dark and gloomy, never penetrated by the low solstical sun.

Follow the path through this 'seed-field of all the aches, rheumatisms, and torturing cramps' and turn left at the T-junction over the bridge. The innocuous seeming pool on your right is that 'wherein nameless infants had been used to disappear' in *The Mayor of Casterbridge* – one of the undoubted conveniences of High Place Hall, the original of which can be rapidly reached by 'the steep back lane into town' straight ahead (along Glyde Path).

Bear left past the extensive thatched building. This is known as 'Hangman's Cottage', originally a group of cottages, one of which housed the resident executioner, that 'Waterside Hermit' interrupted by Gertrude Lodge in 'The Withered Arm' as he retired to bed by way of an exterior staircase, long-since demolished. Harper states that Dorchester paid its hangman a regular salary for performing 'between his more important business' (2) other punishments such as 'whipping, scourging, putting in the stocks and pillorying'. Other authorities doubt whether Dorchester ever had a resident hangman, suggesting that the cottage gained its name from a traditional belief that a public executioner lodged there temporarily during the Bloody Assizes.

Cross the road and follow the path opposite signposted 'Top-of-Town and Roman Town House'. The latter soon becomes apparent through a gate in the wall on your left, occupying the north-west corner of Colliton Park, behind County Hall. Excavated in the 1930s the house comprises two separate ranges forming an L-shape around a small courtyard; especial features include a well and a beautifully preserved mosaic. This confirms Hardy's observation that 'Casterbridge announced old Rome in every street, alley, and precinct. It looked Roman, bespoke the art of Rome, concealed dead men of Rome.'

Follow the North Walk to the corner where it turns left into Chalk (Colliton) Walk. There are fine views behind to the north and west, emphasizing the fact that you are standing on a great Roman earthwork, once topped by the walls which enclosed Dorchester on all sides, except the northern Schwarzwasser. It was here that Henchard persuaded Farfrae not to continue on his journey to America but to turn around and settle as his manager in *Casterbridge*. The North Walks are entirely planted with lime trees, Colliton walk is lime infiltrated with some whitebeam and other sorbus. As you ascend the walk, a small turning way below you to the right (School Lane) marks the site of Henry Moule's chapel-of-ease, referred to in 'A Changed Man'.

As you **approach Top-o'-Town,** you encounter Eric Kennington's effigy of Hardy, seated with heathland vegetation around his feet. This is a somewhat awkward statue, its position rendered increasingly more awkward by the rise and rise of the ubiquitous motor car. It is not an easy place to remember the quiet, thoughtful man from the heath; it is hard to notice the 'man who used to notice such things' when to do so involves a continuous battle with the traffic.

Continue straight ahead over the Belisha crossing into the West Walks proper. Note on your left the surviving fragment of uncovered original Roman wall. Somewhere halfway down these walks was the cottage which Henchard rented for Susan 'Newson' – only one or two large town houses remain, which do not begin to fit Hardy's description. At the time of *The Mayor of Casterbridge* the town ended abruptly at the South Walks – beyond this was open farmland with views towards 'the tumuli and earth-forts of the distant uplands'. It was in the West Walks that Farfrae ingeniously constructed a gigantic tent without poles or ropes by suspending rick-cloths to make a barrel roof at the 'densest point of the avenue of sycamores', the resulting enclosure being 'like the nave of a cathedral with one gable removed' – ideal as a dance venue. Today the lower end of the West Walks remains almost exclusively sycamore – and could still serve this purpose – whilst the upper reaches are mainly lime with some horse chestnut.

Retrace your steps back to the northern side of High West Street. The long view down the High Street from here is that described in the first paragraph of 'A Changed Man'; the house on the further side of the crossing, No. 41 (currently the property of Mustoe Shorter Solicitors), is the dwelling of Laura Maumbry in this story. Hardy identified No. 51 (currently Jackson-Stops Estate Agents) as the house 'having an oriel window on the first floor', from which the invalid Burgher spent 'a great many hours in the day' observing the comings and goings of his neighbours. The oriel window was still in place in 1975 but sadly disappeared in a subsequent refurbishment. Two doors further up (No. 49) was the Hardys' doctors' surgery: this was initially Dr Fred Fisher, who had started in a practice in the West Walks; then from 1911 Dr Gowring, who took Dr Nash Worthram into partnership in 1920; on Dr Gowring's retirement in 1923 he was succeeded by Dr Mann. Dr Mann attended Hardy during his last illness and Dr Nash Worthram removed his heart postmortem.

Turn left into Glyde Path Road. The two houses on your left (Nos 56 and 57) mark the site of the Trenchard Mansion. This is the Elizabethan house, that 'smiled the long street down for near a mile', mentioned by Hardy in his speech accepting the Freedom of the Borough in November 1910 and the basis of the poem 'A Man' (CP 123). Part of the balustrade mentioned in the poem was incorporated in the present building and can be seen on the left-hand side of the narrow street. In 1884–5, whilst Max Gate was being built,

Hardy lived just behind this building in a house also now demolished and here wrote *The Mayor of Casterbridge*. On your right as you enter the lane is the sombre Portland stone Shire Hall, the original County Hall and site, until 1955, of the Assizes and Quarter Sessions. Here 'the red-robed judge, when he condemned a sheep-stealer, pronounced sentence to the tune of Baa, that floated in at the window from the remainder of the flock browsing hard by' in *The Mayor of Casterbridge*.

The courtroom within is now principally remembered for the trial of the so-called Tolpuddle Martyrs, whose crime was to form a 'Friendly Society of Farm Workers'. On the transfer of the Crown Court to the new County Hall building in Colliton Park, Shire Hall was purchased by the Trades Union Congress as a memorial to the six men who were so harshly treated by nineteenth-century justice. Incised in the stonework on the eastern end of this building are the distances to Hyde Park Corner, Blandford and Bridport, recalled by Hardy in that same first paragraph of 'A Changed Man' where 'the white riband of road disappeared over Grey's Bridge ... to plunge into innumerable rustic windings ... for 120 miles till it exhibited itself at Hyde Park Corner'. Across the High Street from Shire Hall is the Ship Inn, setting of the poem 'Leipzig' (CP 24), which was accompanied in *Wessex Poems* by Hardy's drawing of a fiddler outside the bay window of the old inn.

As Glyde Path Lane opens out into the County Hall complex, the substantial building on your left is Colliton House, an irregular L-plan, stone-faced, seventeenth-century house with arcaded chimney stacks – the model for High Place Hall, which Hardy transposed from this site to the corner of South Street (see p.103). The home of the Churchill family, whose coat of arms can still be seen over the entrance porch, its extensive park stretched north and west to the Roman boundaries. On Elizabeth-Jane's first visit to the house she is unsettled by a mask exhibiting a comic leer in an arch above a studded doorway, a leer greatly distorted by stone-throwing boys whose 'blows thereon had chipped off the lips and jaws as if they had been eaten away by disease'. This arch with its distorted mask now adorns the doorway of the County Museum library. Colliton House is the setting of the poem 'The Burghers' (CP 23), the action of which effectively maps out Hardy's *Casterbridge*.

Turn right opposite Colliton House down Colliton Street, a delightful and unspoilt remnant of old Dorchester; halfway down this street turn right into Grey School Passage. This alleyway opens up into the garden of Holy Trinity on the left. The timbered shop on the right, opposite the church itself, is the 'little retail seed and grain shop' which some members of the town council acquired for Henchard after his bankruptcy. Holy Trinity is regarded as the mother church of the town as it is the only one mentioned in Domesday. The present building – the third, at least, on this site – dates from

1876; it was returned to the original owners, the Roman Catholic Church, one hundred years later. **Turn left down High West Street**. The fine half-timbered house (now Prezzo) on your right is a magnificent late sixteenth-century survivor from the fire; in 1865 it was here that Lord Chief Justice Jeffreys lodged, with four other judges, whilst conducting the Bloody Assizes, in the Oak Room at the back of the Antelope Hotel.

Behind the bus stop just below Holy Trinity is the Dorset County Museum. This was built for the Dorset Field and Antiquarian Club in 1883 to the design of George Rackstrow Crickmay, the Weymouth architect for whom Hardy had worked after returning to Dorset from London. Hardy was actively involved with the club and museum, of which his friend Henry Moule was curator. The museum library is the setting for the telling of the tales of A *Group of Noble Dames*. The museum, which remains in the private ownership of Dorset Natural History and Archaeological Society, has an extensive Hardy archive and contains a reconstruction of Hardy's Max Gate study, the contents of which were gifted to the museum by his sister Kate. Immediately beyond the museum is the statue to the writer and poet William Barnes, both more glorious in itself and more happily situated than Hardy's seated memorial at Top-o'-Town.

Behind Barnes rises the equally glorious St Peter's Church, sole ecclesiastical survivor of the Great Fire, hemmed in on all sides by buildings; it is mainly fifteenth-century although the entrance doorway is Norman in origin. This is the church, 'whose massive square tower rose unbroken into the darkening sky, the lower parts being illuminated by the nearest lamps sufficiently to show how completely the mortar from the joints of the stonework had been nibbled out by time and weather, which had planted in the crevices thus made little tufts of stone-crop and grass almost as far up as the very battlements'. Hardy had first-hand experience of this decay because Hicks was engaged in restoring St Peter's when Hardy started his apprenticeship in 1856. Here, at the start of *The Mayor of Casterbridge*, Henchard's wife and daughter observe the curfew being rung – a custom which continued until 1939. This is also where the bells subsequently broke forth in full peal to celebrate the wedding of Farfrae and Lucetta. St Peter's features in a number of poems including 'At the Altar-Rail' (CP 345), 'The Chimes' (CP 415), 'The Peace Peal' (CP 774), 'Inscriptions for a Peal of Eight Bells' (CP 777) and 'In the Evening' (CP 802), Hardy's poem in memory of Sir Frederick Treves.

Cross the road at Barnes's statue and then turn right into Cornhill. Lloyds bank on the corner was Hardy's bank. The stone obelisk nearby marks the remains of the town pump – that original fount of pure water where Mother Cuxsom delivered her eulogy to Susan Henchard. The long iron handle, on which Lucetta saw a boy swinging, faced towards the bank, whilst the spout protruded towards High Street, below the plaque which informs us that this is the site of the old cupola or market house. **Pass the few residual market stalls to reach the Antelope Hotel**. This was once Dorchester's principal coaching inn, now reduced to an arcade of shops. The early nineteenth-century twin-bowed front obscures a fifteenth-century core. It was here that Henchard waited in vain to hand over Lucetta's *billet-doux*. Durngate Street on your left is another unspoilt slice of nineteenth-century Dorchester. Just beyond this stood the old Greyhound Inn, where Bob Loveday stabled his horse in *The Trumpet-Major*, and in the yard of which stood Isaac Last's Non-Conformist School, where Hardy obtained his secondary education. All that now remains of the Greyhound is an arched sixteenth-century doorway which was saved at Hardy's request and now spans the rear entrance to the 'Tudor Arcade'.

Fifty yards (forty-five metres) further down South Street, set back behind a flower-festooned lamp post, you stumble upon Henchard's house, now doing service as Barclays Bank (plate 4.5). This fine late eighteenth-century building sports a blue plaque confirming the status of its fictional occupants. It was described by Hardy as 'one of the best-faced with dull red-and-grey old brick', a view endorsed more recently by Pevsner who confirms its 'unmistakeable air of superiority ... faced with nothing but vitrified headers'. Through the open front door Elizabeth-Jane 'could see through the passage to the end of the garden – nearly a quarter of a mile off'.

4.5 Henchard's house

Further down on your right, at No. 44, an undistinguished brick building (currently occupied by New Look) has replaced the Central Temperance Hotel run by Arthur and Augusta Bugler. Their daughter Gertrude became the star of the Hardy Players, with her young sister Augusta (Norrie) eventually taking minor roles. Hardy frequently attended rehearsals here. Next door a coffee bar has taken over the Baroque former post office building, from which Hardy's memorial to the Postmen killed in the First World War has been safely transposed round the corner into Trinity Street. Diagonally opposite stands Napper's Mite, founded as an Almshouse in 1615 as an act of penance following the Great Fire. The ancient clock on the bracket over the entrance was the cause of Hardy's first appearance in print – 'an anonymous skit in a Dorchester paper on the disappearance of the clock ... in the form of a plaintive letter from the ghost of the clock'. The clock was immediately replaced and received further mention from Hardy in both *Far From the Madding Crowd* and *The Mayor of Casterbridge*.

Adjoining the almshouses was Hardye's Grammar School, founded in 1569, rebuilt by Crickmay in 1879, and finally demolished in 1966. This was *Casterbridge* Grammar School to which young Troy was sent 'for years and years'. Across the road note the first-storey plaque on No. 40 (Fox's Estate Agency) marking William Barnes's occupation of this house, from which he ran a school, attended by Sir Frederick Treves, amongst others, and often visited by Thomas Hardy when working next door for Hicks – a fact which is also recorded on a similar plaque above the Gorge Café. The founders of the Hardy Players were active members of the Congregational (now United) Church diagonally opposite on your left.

Follow the newly pedestrianized lower South Street towards its junction with the Walks. It was here at the bottom of 'Corn Street', 'where the last tree of the engirding avenue flanked the last house', that Elizabeth-Jane intercepted Farfrae in the foggy dawn to warn him about Henchard's threatening behaviour. Glance to your right across the end of Trinity Street into the walled Bowling Alley Walk; this was 'the dark dense old avenue', mainly sycamore, where Farfrae almost proposed to Elizabeth-Jane after the excitement of their dance in the 'pavilion'.

Turn left past the war memorial into South Walks. Like the adjoining Salisbury Walk, these are composed entirely of horse chestnut, forming an enchanting canopy in early May – as on that 'fine spring morning' when Henchard meeting Farfrae by chance in the 'chestnut-walk' told him that Lucetta had refused his offer of marriage. Charles Street on your left is Hardy's 'Back Street' where Abel Whittle lived.

Glance back across the first car park. The projecting stone barn at the far end of Charles Street marks the current back end of Henchard's property (10

South Street), far short of the near quarter mile described in the text. **Cross Acland Road and again glance behind to your left.** In front of the spire of All Saints Church can be seen the roof of the Waitrose complex; the tall triangular gable marks the site of Henchard's corn store at the far end of his long garden and grain yards. The drawing in *The Graphic* (which published the serial version of the novel) clearly shows, through the open door of a loft, a building closely resembling Wollaston House, standing, as now, on the other side of Acland Road. This is the granary in which Henchard intended to fight Farfrae to the death; where from the door below the cathead, there was a drop 'of thirty or forty feet to the ground' and where, from this elevated perch, 'his eyes could sweep the roofs round about, the upper parts of the luxurious chestnut trees, now delicate in leaves of a week's age, and the drooping boughs of the limes; Farfrae's garden and the green door leading therefrom'.

Follow South Walks onward. As the chestnuts come to an end, you reach Gallows Hill and Elizabeth Frink's bronze group of two martyrs facing Death – a memorial to twenty Catholic men who died for their faith in sixteenth- and seventeenth-century Dorchester. This too was the end point for the seventy-four rebels executed after the Bloody Assizes. **Cross Icen Way and take the path straight ahead into Salisbury Fields.** The tree-lined walk to your left is the 'deserted avenue of chestnuts' up which Fanny Robin struggled, supported by the dog, in order to reach the union without entering the town.

Do not enter this walk but keep straight ahead along the southern boundary of the fields. Note the beacon and the fine views behind of the prison and churches. You are on *Durnover* Hill, where in *The Dynasts* Napoleon's effigy was hung on a rough gallows and then set alight.

Follow the path to the alleyway beside Victoria Buildings. Behind the wall on your right stood Fordington Vicarage, home of the evangelical Revd Henry Moule, whose tireless local efforts and public campaigning during the 1854 cholera epidemic brought him to national prominence. Moule was the inspiration for Maumbry in 'A Changed Man' and can be seen as a model for the Revd Clare in *Tess of the D'Urbervilles*. Hardy was on friendly terms with Moule's seven sons, most especially Horace, who was Hardy's close friend and mentor from 1857 until his untimely death in 1873.

Turn right at the end of the alleyway. Note the blue plaque set high in the wall, commemorating Henry Moule's forty-one years at Fordington: in 'this house close to the most infected street', where he 'was occupied morn, noon, and night in endeavours to stamp out the plague and in alleviating the sufferings of the victims'.

Continue past Moule Terrace and Cottage to Fordington Green. This is a surprising tree-lined oasis with a distinct New England feel. It is dominated by St George's, the largest church in Dorchester and, as such, an early twentieth-century reconstruction of its former medieval glory. Hardy strongly opposed this restoration because it involved demolishing the Georgian chancel, but subsequently relented enough to design new Gothic pillars for the north aisle. St George's is the setting of the ballad 'No Bell-Ringing' (CP 901). At the back of the nave beside the tower door is a memorial stone 'For Carinus Roman Citizen, aged 50 years'. Archaeologists have suggested that a Roman temple stood at this site, just outside the walls of the town. What is more definite is that the cemetery behind the church has been in use since Roman times, 200 graves being unearthed in 1747 and fifty more in the year before Hardy was born.

Pass round the church to the green behind it and follow the path diagonally left across the grass to the gate into the cemetery. This is the spot where Elizabeth-Jane, whilst visiting her mother's grave, encountered Lucetta about the same purpose: 'the still-used burial ground of the old Roman-British city, whose curious feature was this, its continuity as a place of sepulchre. Mrs. Henchard's dust mingled with the dust of women who lay ornamented with glass hair-pins and amber necklaces, and men who held in their mouths coins of Hadrian, Posthumus, and the Constantines'.

If, on entering the graveyard, you continue to walk ahead on the same diagonal, you soon find yourself on the top of a bank overlooking the roofs and chimney stacks of Holloway Road. In the empty space to the right of these cottages and in front of the mill stood *Durnover* Barton. The overgrown boundary wall is the successor to Hardy's 'ancient thatched mud wall whose eaves overhung as much as one or two feet. At the back of the wall was a cornyard with its granary and barns – the place wherein Elizabeth-Jane had met Farfrae many months earlier.' From this point there are extensive views northward over *Durnover* Moor, where during the cholera epidemic Maumbry (Moule) supervised giant bonfires of infected, excrement-soaked bedding and clothing in an attempt to halt the spread of the contagion. As a child, Hardy witnessed, from the safe distance of Higher Bockhampton, the 'lurid glare' in the night sky caused by these conflagrations on Fordington Fields. It was also on *Durnover* Moor, in 1884, that Hardy attended the circus recalled in the poem 'Circus-Rider to Ringmaster' (CP 672). The moor itself – now bisected by the buzzing by-pass – features in the poems 'She Hears the Storm' (CP 228), 'A Wet Night' (CP 229) and the ballad 'The Fight on Durnover Moor' (CP 729). In *Durnover* cemetery the two 'wives' of Sergeant Clark unexpectedly encounter each other over their husband's grave ('Enter a Dragoon').

Turn round to pick up the main tarmaced path along the top edge of the cemetery. Admire the fine views across the moor towards the wood-engirdled Stinsford Church, with *Egdon* rising behind it – a magnificent burial spot, especially for an admirer of Thomas Hardy!

Follow the path down to the gate and onto King's Road and then turn left

along the pavement. Bear half-left to cross the Frome by the now-redundant Standfast Bridge. Note the further Ffooks injunction and pause on the bridge. Straight ahead upstream is *Durnover* Mill (now flats); its Georgian structure has repeatedly been altered, and its history is detailed on the plaque facing you, above which is an effigy dated 1590. To the left of the mill rises Holloway Row, still containing some nineteenth-century terraced cottages – as close as you can get now to the feel of that 'Adullam of all the surrounding villages'. It was in a cottage in Holloway Road – then known as Cuckolds' Row – that the 1854 cholera epidemic started. The narrow opening to the right, between the mill and the Swan Inn, is the eastern end of Mill Lane – Hardy's *Mixen Lane*:

> … the hiding-place of those who were in distress, and in debt, and trouble of every kind. Farm-labourers and other peasants, who combined a little poaching with their farming, and a little brawling and bibbing with their poaching, found themselves sooner or later in Mixen Lane. Rural mechanics too idle to mechanize, rural servants too rebellious to serve, drifted or were forced into Mixen Lane.

Even at the time of writing *The Mayor of Casterbridge* (1885), Hardy admits that it was 'now in great part pulled down'; piecemeal redevelopment of the area has continued ever since, especially at the hands of the Mill Street Housing Society (MSHS). **Walk past the Swan and then a further hundred yards (ninety metres) along King's Road.** Here you will find an engraved foundation stone on the corner of the third cream-coloured housing block stating that it was laid by Mrs Thomas Hardy JP, Chairman of the MSHS, on 1 June 1932 – the eve of Hardy's ninety-second birthday.

Turn into Mill Street, passing Durnover Court and Hardy Avenue. This is no longer 'an altar to disease', nor seemingly the red-light district of Dorchester, but a pleasant enough lane bordered by one or two Victorian cottages amongst the modern development narrowing down into a delightful shady path beside the Frome, which remains stubbornly on the side away from the moor: so how could a plank be lowered over the water to allow Charl or Newson in the *Mayor of Casterbridge* access to *Peter's Finger* from the open heath? The answer is that the brook that 'divided the moor from the tenements' was a small stream behind the houses long-since covered over. Before the London Road ribbon development, a returning householder would cross Grey's Bridge then strike out left across open moorland until encountering the stream which separated him from the cottages on *Mixen Lane*. *Peter's Finger* has also vanished without trace and was replaced by the Swan Inn, now also, in turn, defunct.

Follow *Mixen Lane* to its Dorford end, emerging opposite the White Hart. Your circumnavigation of *Casterbridge* is complete.

Outer *Casterbridge*: Earthworks and Houses

Maumbury Rings, *Mai-Dun*, *Pummery* and the Union

By foot, bicycle or car (seven miles/eleven kilometres)

There are a number of other sites of Hardyan interest outside the immediate Roman centre. They are all within walking distance, but here once more a bicycle or, for the more peripheral ones, a motor car could be advantageous.

Maumbury Rings

Head due south from the town centre on Weymouth Avenue (signposted Dorchester South Station). The market (open Wednesdays and Sundays) appears on your right, and to your left is the old Eldridge Pope Brewery, the work of Weymouth architect G.R. Crickmay. The brewery, originally established in 1837 by Charles Eldridge, licensee of the Antelope, did not survive into the twenty-first century. In its stead, ambitious redevelopment in the form of luxury apartments, shops, an hotel and a cinema is on the drawing board along with a scheme to convert the old maltings into a theatre-cum-arts centre and rebuild the railway station and talk of an open-air arena and a statue of Hardy gazing across the square. Time will tell, but global recession is unlikely to bear favourably on such proposals, which are liable to have a negative effect on the present town centre and especially on the few remaining High Street businesses. As for the open-air arena, did the developers not notice that it is already there, just beyond the station, nearly 2,000 years old, and an underused resource? That 'vast Arena where men once bled' – 'the Cirque of the Gladiators which faced that haggard mark of Imperial Rome' (CP 27).

Hardy called Maumbury Rings 'one of the finest Roman amphitheatres … remaining in Britain'. The 'dismal privacy which the earthen circle enforced' rendered it ideal for clandestine meetings; here Henchard first re-encounters Susan, Lucetta comes to beg the return of her letters, and Henchard spies upon Farfrae and Elizabeth-Jane in *The Mayor of Casterbridge*. At his meeting with Susan, the mayor enters 'by the south path' – the spot where the gallows stood in the eighteenth century and where on 21 March 1705 the eighteen-year-old Mary Channing was half-strangled and then burnt at the stake in front of 10,000 spectators. The barbarous execution of such a young girl was legally justified on the grounds that she had committed not just mariticide but *petit treason* by such an act of flagrant disdain for a husband's authority.

Hardy describes the terrible death of this young girl in chapter XI of *The*

Mayor of Casterbridge, giving the story in detail in 'The Mock Wife' (CP 728) and in an article entitled 'Maumbury Ring', published in *The Times* on 9 October 1908; in *The Times* article he argues strongly that Mary Channing was wholly innocent of the murder of her husband. Is he implying that she is another 'Pure Woman', with shades of Tess? The newspaper commissioned the article after recent archaeological excavations had revealed that Maumbury was originally a Neolithic hilltop henge, extensively adapted by the Romans for use as an amphitheatre, and subsequently further modified by the Parliamentarians in the Civil War as a gun emplacement to guard the Weymouth road. In 1767, the gallows were again moved further away from the town, to Bradford Down on the Bridport Road, before returning in the nineteenth century to their final site, within the prison. As a child, Hardy witnessed the December 1850 'No Popery' riots, including the 'execution' and burning of effigies of the Pope and Cardinal Wiseman in the centre of the rings.

Kay-Robinson considered Maumbury to be 'the grimmest spot in Dorchester', a description that belies its modern role as a leafy and grassy oasis in an ever-expanding, noisy and polluted suburbia. The rings retain their historical role as the town's major site of public assembly for events of both national and local importance – from Royal jubilees and visits to military memorial services, political rallies and more popular entertainments (plate 4.6). They remain

4.6 Maumbury Rings

an ideal spot for readings of Hardy's poetry; they are never grim, no longer dark (thanks to the ubiquitous street lamp), but able to retain a cool central chill on a summer's day – perhaps wafting from subterranean Roman chambers. From the elevated walk around the ridge of the henge there are extensive views over *Casterbridge* (Dorchester) and to the south towards *Mai-Dun*.

Mai-Dun: *An Ancient Earthwork*

Leave Maumbury Rings by the south-western exit and negotiate the road crossing to continue south along the tree-lined Weymouth Avenue. Dorchester Cemetery is on your left, another Roman burial site, and features in the poem 'Her Death and After' (CP 27), considered by Hardy to be, along with 'The Dance at the Phoenix' (CP 28), 'as two good stories as I ever told'. In his speech accepting the freedom of the town in November 1910, Hardy said that here lay the Dorchester which he knew best: 'names on white stones one after another, names that recall the voices, cheerful and sad, anxious and indifferent, that are missing from the dwellings and pavements'. Hardy provided an illustration for *Wessex Poems*, showing the cemetery in the foreground with Maumbury Rings over the wall and *Casterbridge* and the downs in the background – a view now obscured by housing development along Maumbury Road that followed the engirdling of the rings by railway lines.

Opposite the cemetery gates, turn right into Maiden Castle Road. After an unpromising start, the way becomes increasingly attractive, especially beyond the intriguing Prince of Wales School, and once over the by-pass 'at one's every step forward *Mai-Dun* rises higher against the south sky, with an obtrusive personality that compels the senses to regard it and consider' ('A Tryst in an Ancient Earthwork'). Hardy's short story is a comprehensive and evocative portrait of Maiden Castle, as explored on a stormy winter night; the earthwork serving, as Michael Irwin has observed, as a metaphor for the larger world in its state of permanent conflict, motion, change and decay. After 2,000 years of erosion, it remains an awe-inspiring place. It is a fitting memorial to those ancient Britons who, with primitive flint tools, constructed the largest Iron Age hill fort in Europe – extending over half a mile (800 metres) in length and enclosing within its five miles (eight kilometres) of multiple ramparts an area of forty-seven acres (nineteen hectares). A walk around the circumference of the inner rampart is most rewarding and best approached from the diagonal path that scales the ramparts, starting from the far left corner of the car park. Once atop this grassy parapet, the wind whistling through your hair, you imbibe the true spirit of this Wessex Height – 'for thinking, dreaming, dying on'. With skylarks as your only companions, the realization dawns that 'mind-chains do not clank where one's next neighbour is the sky' (CP 261).

In Hardy's lifetime, the Roman temple had been uncovered, but detailed archaeological analysis had to await the arrival of Sir Mortimer Wheeler in the 1930s – hence the somewhat Roman bias of Hardy's short story. An account of these discoveries with artefacts from the excavations, including human skeletons, is displayed in the County Museum. In calling the castle 'Mai-Dun' rather than the contemporary corruption 'Maiden', Hardy was following his consistent habit of reverting to old place names wherever possible – 'Mai-Dun', as he informs us, is Celtic for 'great hill'. From the great hill, there are fine views across Dorchester to the north-east. To the south-east runs 'the hedgeless Via – the original track laid out by the legions of the Empire' (now the A354) which Henchard frequently scanned with his telescope to observe Elizabeth-Jane and Farfrae and where, one fateful day, his lens instead revealed Newson in *The Mayor of Casterbridge*. To the south lies Winterbourne St Martin and the downs, and to the west Blackdown topped by the Hardy Monument – all little changed since Henchard's day.

To the north, however, the horizon is very different; the skyline is filled by an extensive display of irregular modern housing, bearing a close resemblance to Disneyland, with turrets and towers and all the mock-medieval apparatus of a pantomime set (plate 4.7). Prince Charles's so-called 'Vision of Britain'

4.7 'Disneyland' from *Mai-Dun*

appears no less than a hilltop abomination when viewed from the hilltop home of the ancient Britons.

Pummery *and the Union*

Head back from *Mai-Dun*, bearing left at the rings into Maumbury Road and left again into Damer's Road. After passing under the railway, the Dorset County Hospital looms on your right. This new development took place within the grounds of Damer's Road Hospital, formerly the workhouse. Indeed the first building you encounter on your right, with a chapel attached, is the front of the Union. It is little changed since Fanny Robin in *Far From the Madding Crowd* struggled to reach it, this 'stone edifice, consisting of a central mass and two wings', 'a picturesque building' which 'looked like an abbey' and commanded 'one of the most magnificent views in the county' (plate 4.8). The elevated coffin door is no longer discernible. Hardy's poem 'To an Unborn Pauper Child' (CP 91) enjoins a foetus, whose mother has been committed to the Union, to follow the example of Fanny's infant and 'Breathe not, hid heart: cease silently'. *Casterbridge Union* is also the destination of the protagonists in the 'The Curate's Kindness' (CP 159) and 'Christmastide' (CP 829).

From the Union, retrace your steps back under the railway, then turn left up Cornwall Road and cross the Bridport Road to Poundbury Road

4.8 The Union

opposite (by car this involves a diversion via Top-o'-Town). The monumental gatehouse on your left, now the military museum, is an example of late-Victorian excess and probably the only building left in Dorchester which would not be out of place in Charlie's Poundbury. It served as the entrance to the Infantry and Militia Barracks, now mainly demolished and all of a later date than Hardy's military fiction. The barracks where Billy Smallbury searched in vain for the missing Fanny Robin in *Far From the Madding Crowd*, where Captain Maumbry was stationed in 'A Changed Man', and from where 'The King's-Own Cavalry' strode forth to their memorable 'Dance at the Phoenix' (CP 28) still survive to the side of Poundbury Road, just round the first bend and still backing onto the football pitch. The football pitch is all that remains of the once extensive grass square known as barrack-green, 'that promenade of a great many towns-people cheerfully inclined' when the band played there on Sunday afternoons ('A Changed Man'). The old soldier in 'The Revisitation' (CP 152) and Luke Holway of 'The Grave by the Handpost' were also quartered in these barracks. Here, on the night of 2 November 1899, Hardy watched the troops departing for the Boer War, recorded in 'The Going of the Battery' (CP 57).

Pursue Poundbury Road uphill. Just beyond the last industrial outpost, a display board and gate in the fence indicate that you have reached Pummery. Hardy described *Pummery* as, that:

> ... elevated green spot surrounded by an ancient square earthwork ... whereon the Casterbridge people usually held any kind of merry-making, meeting, or sheep-fair that required more space than the streets would afford. On one side it sloped to the river Froom, and from any point a view was obtained of the country round for many miles. This pleasant upland was to be the scene of Henchard's exploit – his grand entertainment which ended in miserable failure.

Having trudged uphill, you may dispute Henchard's claim that it is 'close to the town' and sympathize with the townsfolk who preferred Farfrae's 'little affair' in the West Walks. Poundbury is an Iron Age hill fort with double ramparts except on the north, where the ground drops dramatically away. In the valley below was 'Pummery' where the old man in 'The Curate's Kindness' thought to drown himself. Over the years, the Poundbury enclosure was put to a number of uses – Hardy remained consistently sympathetic to the suffering of the occupants, whether saturated sheep ('A Sheep Fair' CP 700) or German prisoners of war. As described in *The Mayor of Casterbridge*, *Pummery* remains a spectacular viewpoint, although the views to the south and east are mainly of twentieth-century Dorchester and not Henchard's

Casterbridge at all. In contrast, the north-east prospect discloses a pleasant expanse of *Egdon* with Rainbarrow dominant. To the south-west Charlie's cemetery serves as a fitting foreground to the Poundbury Farm estate, which obliterates the more distant horizon. To the north-west the course of the Roman aqueduct, constructed in the first century to supply the town with clean water, can still be seen, snaking its way around the hillsides. Across the Frome, to the right of the aqueduct and part shrouded in trees, stands Wolveton, the home of Lady Penelope – Hardy's eighth Noble Dame. This sixteenth-century 'ivied manor-house, flanked by battlemented towers' belonged to the Trenchard family, one of whom became Lady Penelope's first husband in that unfortunate sequence which led to her untimely death from anorexia nervosa. This romantic dwelling, with its large mullioned windows, rises above the lush water meadows, their osier-surrounded streams rich in wildlife, and with buzzards casually circling over the grazing sheep; an appropriate image, for the original Trenchard fortune was founded on wool. Wolfeton House is regularly open to the public during the summer months and well worth inspection.

A Walk to Max Gate and Winterborne Came

By foot (four-and-a-half miles/seven kilometres)

'I mean to build a hall anon, And shape two turrets there ...' (CP 295)

Max Gate is about a fifteen-minute walk from the centre of Dorchester. The simplest route is along Prince of Wales Road from opposite the lower end of South Street, and then turning right onto Alington Road.

Max Gate, Hardy's home from 29 June 1885 until he died there on 11 January 1928, stands isolated at the south-western corner of Dorchester. The plot Hardy acquired in 1883 from the Duchy of Cornwall was an open, exposed field, just below Conquer Barrow, cut off from the rest of the town by the Southampton railway line. As described in the poem 'Everything Comes' (CP 457) the site was 'bleak and cold', searched through by 'all the winds upon the wold', so the poet planted 'some two or three thousand small trees, mostly Austrian Pines' and beech as a screen 'both from winds, and eyes that tease'. One of the pines survives, and plenty of the beech. The poem 'At Day-Close in November' (CP 274) beautifully counterpoises youth and age, the trees then and trees now. In the twentieth century, the Syward Road and Came View estates sprang up, destroying the splendid isolation to the east, but in 1988 the Department of Transport cut a deep gully along the north-western boundary of the house leaving it perched as on a cliff-top above an endless tide of noisy polluting motor traffic. By way of compensation, Alington Avenue was realigned, so that Max Gate no longer stands on the Wareham Road but is approached by a private cul-de-sac. Hardy's town gained what has proved to be no more than a temporary peace from the by-pass – traffic flow statistics for the High Street in 2008 show the same volume as in 1988 – and his house an unpleasant kind of solitude.

The house, designed by Hardy and built by his brother and father, has never won aesthetic approval. Pevsner succinctly summarizes this view: 'Unfortunately the house has no architectural qualities whatever.' He does, however, concede that, 'the environs speak more eloquently of Hardy's personality than the house itself'. Max Gate is a typical brick villa of the 1880s, comfortable and functional; Hardy needed space in which to write and Emma needed rooms in which to entertain. It grew organically as his income increased, the house accurately reflecting Hardy's status as a middle-class professional.

Fortunately for us, the house and garden have been preserved and remain a family home. This is thanks to the foresight of Hardy's sister Kate. She bought the house at auction on Florence's death and donated it to the National Trust on the condition that it was let by the Trust to provide income to maintain the Bockhampton Cottage. As the house was not to be open to the public, the contents of Hardy's study were donated to the County Museum, where the room has been faithfully reconstructed. However, since a change of tenancy in 1993, Max Gate (the front garden, conservatory, hall and reception rooms) has been open to the public on three afternoons per week in the summer (plate 4.9). This is a great boon. The visitor can sit on a bench ('The Garden Seat' CP 518) and absorb the atmosphere of the garden, wander along Hardy's favourite 'Nut Walk' between the rows of beech trees (which he planted), and visit the Pets' Cemetery – last resting place of, amongst others, Snowdove ('Last Words to a Dumb Friend' CP 619), Wessex ('A Popular Personage at Home' CP 776 and 'Dead "Wessex" the Dog to the Household' CP 907) and Kitsey ('The Roman Gravemounds' CP 329).

Max Gate is built on a Roman burial ground, which occupied an earlier Bronze Age site. Whilst the footings were being dug for the new house, a whole series of Roman graves were exposed. Not surprisingly these found their way into the text of the novel which Hardy was then writing, *The Mayor of Casterbridge*:

> It was impossible to dig more than a foot or two deep about the town fields and gardens without coming upon some tall soldier or other of the Empire, who had lain there in his silent unobtrusive rest for a space of fifteen hundred years. He was mostly found lying on his side, in an oval scoop in the chalk, like a chicken in its shell; his knees drawn up to his chest.

4.9 Max Gate

This is an exact description of the first three graves unearthed at Max Gate. Covering another of the skeletons was a large sarsen stone, which Hardy labelled the 'Druid Stone' and which remains on view where he set it in an alcove in the hedge at the start of the Nut Walk ('The Shadow on the Stone' CP 483). Hardy kept various fragments of pottery and other artefacts from these graves, displaying them in his study, where they can still be inspected in the Dorset County Museum – on 'The Little Old Table' (CP 609).

From the garden, the visitor can see the windows of the three different upstairs rooms that served in turn as Hardy's study, the first of which, above the drawing room, subsequently became the bedroom in which he died. Inside the house, you are assured of a warm welcome from Andrew and Marilyn Leah and their team of volunteer helpers. The Leahs have accumulated for display a wealth of information concerning Hardy and his life at Max Gate and the many famous visitors who called in the 1920s, when Hardy had become the grand old man of English literature.

Max Gate resonates with Hardy's poetry from the well known 'An August Midnight' (CP 113), 'The Going' (CP 277), 'Timing Her' (CP 373) and 'The Spell of the Rose' (CP 295), to a whole host of poems concerning marriage, memory, moonlight and mortality including 'Looking Across' (CP 446), 'At Moonrise and Onwards' (CP 517), 'Shut Out that Moon' (CP 164), 'At the

Piano' (CP 482), 'The Last Performance' (CP 430), 'Lost Love' (CP 259), 'Lament' (CP 283), 'The House of Silence' (CP 413), 'Ten Years Since' (CP 691), 'The Strange House' (CP 537), 'His Visitor' (CP 286), 'Nobody Comes' (CP 715) and 'The Aging House' (CP 435).

In the brick boundary wall to the left of the Druid Stone you will find a small wooden door; this is the 'little green gate' through which Hardy would escape for his walks, secreted both from both the eyes of prying admirers, loitering by the main entrance, or from unwanted visitors knocking on his front door. The gate is no longer in use, but its outer side in Syward Road (a little brown door behind a yew tree) is the proper starting pointing to follow Hardy's footsteps on his walks to Winterborne Came – 'to the hill-top tree by the gated ways' ('The Walk' CP 279).

Head for the 'Max Gate Roundabout' and bear diagonally across it to take the signposted path through the scrub opposite. Head up the left-hand edge of the field. You are on the path as Hardy knew it. **After about 300 yards (275 metres), a stile in the hedge on your left marks the path to Came Rectory**. This was William Barnes's home from 1862 until his death in 1886. Hardy is known to have used this path to reach the rectory, in preference to walking along the road. Unfortunately, the path is now rather poorly defined and the traffic fairly treacherous when you reach the highway. It does, however, afford glimpses of the delightful early nineteenth-century 'thatched cottage with wide eves and wider verandah, on whose rustic pillars roses, clematis and honeysuckle entwine'.

Retrace your steps and follow your original path up the hill towards the wood on the horizon. Hardy climbed this path on his way to Barnes's funeral on 11 October 1886; as the coffin was wheeled out into the road from the rectory, the sun reflecting off the brass fittings caught Hardy's eye: 'Thus a farewell to me he signalled on his grave-way, as with a wave of his hand' ('The Last Signal' CP 412). Hardy also remembers Barnes in 'The Collector Cleans his Picture' (CP 573) and 'The Old Neighbour and the New' (CP 640).

Turn around at the entrance to the wood to admire the views all over Dorchester. To your right (in winter), the clump of trees at the edge of the Came View estate marks the remains of Conquer Barrow, the setting of 'The Death of Regret' (CP 327), 'The Clasped Skeletons' (CP 858) and 'Evening Shadows' (CP 833), whilst the hill behind the rectory rises to Frome Hill tumulus, where Angel paused to look across the *Valley of the Great Dairies* towards *Talbothays*.

Follow the path straight through the wood and down to the gate onto the lane below. Here Hardy waited for the bier carrying Barnes's coffin which he then followed to St Peter's Church. **To reach the church, follow the drive straight ahead over the winterbourne, taking the middle metalled track**

ahead. Follow this drive round towards Winterborne Came House and eventually a sign on your right will direct you round high stone walls to St Peter's. This is a well proportioned little parish church, now sadly redundant. Barnes is buried under a Celtic cross, just to the south of the tower.

Behind his grave there are clear views of Came House, built by John Damer (whose older brother, Joseph, was the creator of Milton Abbey) and described by Pevsner as, 'a mid-eighteenth-century masterpiece'. Hardy's uncollected story 'The Doctor's Legend' is based on the history of the Damer family and is set here at Came. Lady Cicely has all the attributes of an eleventh 'Noble Dame'; it seems likely that Hardy excluded the story from this sequence for fear of alienating his near neighbours. The cottage 'outside his garden wall, near the entrance to the park', where the poor woman with the 'Death's Head' daughter lived, can be easily identified on the corner of the high garden wall as you head back along the main drive. The area still has a hostile, alienating feel 250 years after the time of this story – its tall excluding walls and absence of direction signs generating an ambiguous, unfriendly atmosphere. As you retrace your steps up the young wind-warped beech avenue towards the wood above Max Gate, look back for further views of the Damer's house – then follow Hardy's homeward.

Review: From the age of ten until just before his twenty-first birthday, Hardy walked daily from the rural isolation of his parents' *Egdon* cottage to the centre of Dorchester. Although it was a county town of 'assizes, railways, telegraphs and daily London papers', it remained somewhat a municipality in miniature, still confined within old Roman boundaries. The sharp contrast between two such diverse environments lent a cutting edge to his subsequent creativity. His novels were further enhanced by his intense awareness of local history, including the recent hang fairs, the cholera epidemic and papal riots, and more distantly the Monmouth rebellion, the Great Fire, Roman skeletons, and evidence of human occupation stretching back 5,000 years.

Exploring *Casterbridge* in the footsteps of Henchard and Elizabeth-Jane, it rapidly becomes apparent that this is a landscape more real than imagined, for Hardy has placed his personal stamp on so many of the places visited. The first impression of *Casterbridge* from Stinsford Hill is the view of Dorchester obtained by the young Hardy on his daily walk to school; at the White Hart he used to stop for a drink; he paid for the sign at the Bow; from these Fromeside meadows he watched an execution; here is his statue; here he was living whilst he wrote *The Mayor of Casterbridge*; he was a founder member of this county museum, which now contains so many of his artefacts; in this cemetery the population of his Victorian Dorchester are buried.

As we walk around Dorchester, these memories run in parallel with the experiences of his fictional and poetic characters: here Henchard nearly drowned; here Maumbry preached; here Bathsheba was Queen; here Lucetta gazed out upon the *carrefour*. In many such places fiction and the recoverable past meld in his poems about real people in real places: 'The Chapel Organist' at Dorford; 'The Casterbridge Captains' at All Saints; 'The Mock Wife' at Maumbury Rings. This process intensifies further at Max Gate where Hardy lived for the last forty years of his life. Hardy's 'fictional' *Casterbridge* is a dramatized presentation of the history of a town and the lives of its real citizens in the nineteenth century and back through the remembered (or recoverable) past. Hardy's careful melding of the real with the imagined in his depiction of this urban landscape and its population lends both authority and authenticity to his 'tentative philosophy' – his poetic portrayal of the human predicament.

CHAPTER FIVE

West of Wessex

'When I set out for Lyonnesse, / A hundred miles away' (CP 254)

IN EARLY FEBRUARY 1870 Hardy, who had retreated from lodgings in Weymouth back home to *Egdon* in order to complete *Desperate Remedies*, was disturbed by a request from Crickmay to travel 'next week' to North Cornwall to 'take a plan and particulars' of the dilapidated church at St Juliot, with a view to its rebuilding. Hardy, somewhat reluctant to undertake further architectural work, particularly at such a distance from home, postponed the trip until he had sent the finished manuscript of his first published novel to Alexander Macmillan (who in fact rejected it). As faithfully recorded in *The Life* on Monday 7 March Hardy rose at 4 a.m. and made his way to Dorchester to undertake a complex railway journey, which eventually deposited him at Launceston station at 4.03 p.m. Approximately three hours later he arrived at St Juliot Rectory to be 'received by (a) young lady in brown'. This was the start of a three-day visit, the details of which were carefully documented in the diaries of both parties – for by the time Hardy departed at dawn on Friday 11 March, they were undoubtedly in love.

In Hardyan terms 'this wild weird western shore' (CP 291) is a very special landscape. It was here that he fell in love with the most influential woman in his life. After she had died he returned and fell in love with her *and the landscape* all over again, in the process generating his *veteris vestigia flammae* – the most profound sequence of poems charting love and loss in the English language. And it was here more than anywhere – away from his true Wessex – that fiction and fantasy, story-telling and autobiography, poetry and the landscape merge in a single visionary continuum. Hardy recurrently denied the possibility of *any* autobiographical content in his fiction, but in *A Pair of Blue Eyes* we have a faithful reproduction of his meeting with and courtship of Emma. Stephen Smith, an architect's assistant, arrives one evening at the rectory, after a long journey, to draw up plans for the restoration of the decrepit and isolated church. At the moment of his arrival the rector is in bed with gout. Smith (Hardy), who does not ride, walks along the cliff-tops beside Elfride (Emma) who is mounted on her Pansy (Fanny). They fall in love, but their beautiful courtship is disrupted by Parson Swancourt's (John Gifford's) discovery that Smith (Hardy) is not a gentleman by birth at all, but the son of a stonemason i.e. 'a low-born churl', to use Gifford's own words. In this special landscape, surely the dream far outpaces the reality?

Hardy, who had set off for Cornwall reluctantly, 'came back from Lyonnesse / With magic in my eyes'. He was transformed in four nights and three days, by the magic of the landscape, by the magic of a woman – who at this stage in her life, though happy to play the organ in church, held views more pagan than Christian – by the magic of valleys where witchcraft still held sway, and by the magic of the historic heritage. Tintagel and King Arthur had recently been popularized by Tennyson, who had revived the term Lyonnesse, just as Hardy was to subsequently resurrect Wessex, the territory of King Alfred. Of these various forms of magic that enchanted the bearded young poet from Dorset, I believe that the landscape was the most important. Happily – and uniquely for a Hardyan landscape – St Juliot, the Valency Valley, Boscastle Harbour and the wild cliff-tops are virtually unchanged in the 140 years since Hardy first set foot on them. We can therefore follow directly in the footsteps of Hardy and Emma, Stephen and Elfride ...

Lyonnesse: The Walk

St Juliot, Boscastle and Beeny Cliff

By foot (seven miles/eleven kilometres)

After breakfast on the Tuesday morning, Smith (Hardy) sets off accompanied by Elfride (Emma) and the rector to inspect the church. **The ideal starting point for this walk must therefore be the rectory, but unless you happen, like Smith (Hardy), to be staying there, then the next best starting point is St Juliot's church. Alternatively, and more practically for most people, start from the village car park in Boscastle, just upstream from the harbour (p.130).**

From the rectory, the narrow grass-embossed lane gently curves down past a house called Endelstowe towards the 'pinnacled tower' of St Julitta's (also known as St Julietta's). The church as seen by Hardy was a venerable building, the earliest parts of which were Saxon; its massive fourteenth-century tower was on the verge of collapse – the bells already having been removed for safekeeping – and, with the exception of the fine fifteenth-century south aisle and porch, the rest of the church was beyond salvation. Today you see the results of Hardy's and Crickmay's sympathetic restoration, in which they re-used parts of the old fabric wherever possible. Pause for a moment to admire the magical setting of this typical Cornish churchyard – in spring asparkle with snowdrops and daffodils – as Smith observed, an integral part of the wild hillside and 'a delightful place to be buried in' (plate 5.1). Just inside the church door are copies of drawings of the church made by Hardy and Emma. On the north wall are three memorial tablets, the first to the Revd Caddell Holder (Hardy's brother-in-law), the second erected by Hardy in memory of Emma and the third to Hardy himself. This erroneously states that he 'is buried in Westminster Abbey' and is based upon his own template, but 'Westminster Abbey' has been substituted for the original wording, 'Stinsford Dorset', which matched Emma's memorial.

Hardy revisited Emma at St Juliot an extra six times over the ensuing three years although neither of them was to visit St Juliot during their thirty-eight year marriage. In March 1913, almost forty-three years to the day from his original visit to Cornwall, the recently widowed Hardy returned to St Juliot, supported by his brother Henry – see 'Seven Times' (CP 652). On 8 September 1916, Hardy, accompanied by his second wife Florence, made his

5.1 St Julitta's Church

final visit to St Juliot's church – forty-six-and-a-half years to the day from his first visit there on that Tuesday morning with Emma. This late visit is recorded in the poems 'The Marble Tablet' (CP 617), 'The Monument-Maker' (CP 671), 'Apostrophe to an Old Psalm Tune' (CP 359), 'Quid Hic Agis' (CP 371) and 'They Would Not Come' (CP 598). Opposite the Hardy memorial tablet is the Simon Whistler engraved-glass window, depicting scenes illustrating Hardy's Cornish poetry, installed in 2003 at the instigation of the Thomas Hardy Society.

From the church door, take the path straight ahead over the slate stile beside the Celtic cross and into the field. Bear half-right and follow the waymarked route along the field boundaries towards the wooded Valency Valley, of which there are fine views ahead as it curves its way down to the sea. Through the open gateway at the fourth field boundary, beside a 'wind-warpt' blue cedar, you cross at right-angles the path which runs from the Old Rectory – that leafy oasis on your right, still 'a little paradise of flowers and trees' – to Lesnewth Church, the *East Endelstow* of *A Pair of Blue Eyes*. In the novel, the two churches for which Parson Swancourt has responsibility are named *East* and *West Endelstow*, although on the ground they lie on a north–south axis divided by the Valency Valley. This is because Hardy in the text transposed St Juliot (*West Endelstow*) to a position much nearer the coast, the site of Forrabury church, on the headland above Boscastle, where 'not a tree could exist up there; nothing but the monotonous grey-green grass'.

The rather well presented, isolated stone house on your right as you approach the wood is probably Widow Jethway's cottage, which Hardy describes as 'some way down the valley, and under a row of scrubby oaks … absolutely alone'. The widow obtains her water supply from 'a streamlet … hollowed into a basin' beside the house, which 'was rather large'. The size, the isolation and the presence of the 'streamlet' make this cottage the most likely model for Mrs Jethway's home. However, Hardy may well have merged its appearance with that of the now completely ruined Penventon Cottage, which you encounter on your left shortly after entering the wood.

The path climbs through the trees, then descends to the hamlet of New Mills. The mill has now been replaced by a trout fishery. Here, the second cottage on your left, with its gable-end chimney angled towards the path, is the model for Stephen Smith's parental home, the disguising 'huge cloak of ivy' trimmed away. From the front of the house a path leads over a 'little wood bridge' to ascend to Treworld Farm and Lesnewth.

Just below New Mills, the tributary stream from Lesnewth joins the Valency, increasing the velocity of the river and producing a series of small waterfalls. This is the area that enchanted Knight in *A Pair of Blue Eyes*:

'Elfride, I never saw such a sight!' he exclaimed. 'The hazels overhang the river's course in a perfect arch, and the floor is beautifully paved.' Here they walked together to 'a tiny cascade about a foot wide and high, and sat down beside it on the flags that for nine months in the year were submerged beneath a gushing bourne'. This autobiographical passage recalls Hardy and Emma's stream-side picnic in August 1870, during the course of which a drinking-glass slipped from her hand and was lost ('Under the Waterfall' CP 276). Hardy sketched Emma, all breast and bottom, as she knelt beside the brook, and later remembered these moments as their 'Best Times' (CP 646). The stream is here overhung by both hazel and oak. The drinking-glass is perhaps still wedged under a boulder, awaiting discovery, although more likely it has long-since disintegrated or been swept out to sea in the periodical flash floods which devastate this steep valley – of which there have been four major examples since Friday 19 August 1870. The flagstones and waterfalls end near the footbridge which carries one of two paths up through ancient woodland to Minster (the second path is reached by stepping stones further downstream) – a diversion to this mystic church set deep in a woody glade is well worth the extra thirty minutes.

Continue downstream to reach the car park at Boscastle, where toilets and other refreshments are on hand. No remnant survives of the Norman Bottreaux Castle, from which the village name is derived, but the quayside dwellings remain untouched in their stony, uneven timelessness – the enchanted heart of Hardy's 'region of dream and mystery'.

Cross the Valency River by means of the road bridge. Note the 'overshot watermill' admired by Hardy and ahead the tower of the Wellington – at present the only hotel surviving in Boscastle. Hardy stayed here with his brother Henry in March 1913. A climb up Old Road straight ahead leads to the composition of what is arguably his greatest poem, 'At Castle Boterel' based on a 'dry March' day forty-three years previously:

> What we did as we climbed, and what we talked of
> Matters not much, nor to what it led, –
> Something that life will not be balked of
> Without rude reason till hope is dead,
> And feeling fled.
>
> It filled but a minute. But was there ever
> A time of such quality, since or before,
> In that hill's story? To one mind never,
> Though it has been climbed, foot-swift, foot-sore,
> By thousands more.

Primaeval rocks form the road's steep border,
And much have they faced there, first and last,
Of the transitory in Earth's long order;
But what they record in colour and cast
Is – that we two passed. (CP 292)

The primaeval rocks, wholly unchanged in the interim, still form 'the road's steep border' (plate 5.2). **Retrace your steps back to the harbour or continue to the top of the road, bearing left into Forrabury Hill to reach St Symphorian's Church.** The isolated hilltop position of the church, against a background of 'the serene impassive sea', was used by Hardy as the setting for St Juliot as *West Endelstow Church*, but transported to a cliff-top two miles (three kilometres) westward.

Back in Boscastle, follow the riverbank towards the sea, turning right up the waymarked coastal path just beyond the visitor centre. Climb the steep path up Penally Hill. There are fine views over the harbour – a mixture of natural haven, medieval breakwater and reconstructed sixteenth-century jetty – and beyond that 'the headland, vulturine' where the

5.2 Primaeval rocks form the road's steep border

5.3 *Castle Boterel*

blow hole 'snores like old Skrymer in his sleep' ('The Wind's Prophecy' CP 440) (plate 5.3). Further up, the views extend along the coast to the south, with Forrabury Church prominent and the cleft of the Jordan Valley stretching inland.

The view soon switches northward as you head around the cliff-edge towards Pentargon Bay. The next two miles (three kilometres) of coastal path form the magical heartland of both *A Pair of Blue Eyes* and 'The Poems of 1912–13', in particular the four poems which immediately precede 'At Castle Boterel' (CP 288–291):

Beeny Cliff

March 1870–March 1913

I

O the opal and the sapphire of that wandering western sea,
And the woman riding high above with bright hair flapping free –
The woman whom I loved so, and who loyally loved me.

II

The pale mews plained below us, and the waves seemed far away
In a nether sky, engrossed in saying their ceaseless babbling say,
As we laughed light-heartedly aloft on that clear-sunned March day.

III

A little cloud then cloaked us, and there flew an irised rain,
And the Atlantic dyed its levels with a dull misfeatured stain,
And then the sun burst out again, and purples prinked the main.

IV

– Still in all its chasmal beauty bulks old Beeny to the sky,
And shall she and I not go there once again now March is nigh,
And the sweet things said in that March say anew there by and by?

V

What if still in chasmal beauty looms that wild weird western shore,
The woman now is – elsewhere   whom the ambling pony bore,
And nor knows nor cares for Beeny, and will laugh there nevermore.

In *A Pair of Blue Eyes*, Elfride guides Knight along the footpath from the rectory towards Beeny Farm, following exactly the same route which we shall use to walk away from the coast. However, at the point where the footpath joins the lane, just east of the farm, 'Elfride came to a small stream', which she used 'as a guide to the coast' along a narrow valley which suddenly vanishes:

> In its place was sky and boundless atmosphere; and perpendicularly down beneath them – small and far off – lay the corrugated surface of the Atlantic. The small stream here found its death. Running over the precipice it was dispersed in spray before it was half-way down, and falling like rain upon projecting ledges, made minute grassy meadows of them. At the bottom the water-drops soaked away amid the debris of the cliff. This was the inglorious end of the river.

It is no longer possible to follow the small stream from Beeny along the valley towards the precipice, mainly because lack of grazing has rendered it wilder, but the valley remains and the stream continues to disappear in its 'flounce flinging mist', 'the waterfall, above which the mist-bow shone' (CP 288 and 289). This second poem 'After a Journey' gives a detailed description of Pentargon Bay in the form of a monologue addressed to Emma's 'voiceless ghost'; the bay with its deep adjoining caves was accessible on foot in Hardy's time but now, due to landslips, can only be reached by boat (plate 5.4).

5.4 Pentargon – the valley's end at the upward waterfall

5.5 The 'Cliff Without a Name'

Head towards the little footbridge over Elfride's stream. The black cliff on your left, 'a vast stratification of blackish-grey slate, unvaried in its whole height by a single change of shade', is Hardy's 'Cliff Without a Name' (plate 5.5). To the lovers Elfride and Knight, approaching beside the stream, it was the cliff 'on the right hand' which 'terminated in a clearly-defined edge against the light'; this was, in fact, the southern end of Beeny, with which Hardy eventually identified it. Here, where the wind whips up the waterfall, hurling it back inland, Knight conducted the foolish experiment with his hat, which left him suspended over the cliff-edge, confronting a trilobite – like himself, seemingly, frozen in death. It is indeed a cliff whose 'sheer perpendicularity' lends it 'a presence not necessarily proportionate to its actual bulk', but Hardy's careful geographical researches have limited basis in fact. His 'Cliff Without a Name' is approximately 400 feet (120 metres) high, the top of Beeny is equivalent to Beachy Head at 530 feet (160 metres), Buckator peaks at approximately 600 feet (180 metres) and High Cliff, beyond, 730 feet (220 metres), which way outstrips Great Orme's Head at 390 feet (115 metres) – his designated highest point on the western seaboard; as usual topography is being adapted to suit narrative purpose.

As you approach Beeny, a signboard cautions that these are 'Steep and Crumbling Cliffs' with a black-and-yellow illustration of a latter-day Knight falling to his death – modern underclothes, alas, would offer no salvation! Geologists state that these rocks are carboniferous and therefore, in theory, could contain one of those fossilized 'early crustaceans called Trilobites' – but none have been found, as yet, north of Boscastle.

After rounding the summit of the 'Cliff Without a Name' the narrow path continues outside the fence along the edge of Beeny for about half a mile (800 metres), slowly ascending the summit at Fire Beacon Point. Hardy first visited here on 10 March 1870, walking beside Emma who was mounted on her 'beloved Fanny' – Emma was to become Elfride and later 'The Phantom Horsewoman' (CP 294). As you follow the narrow, enclosed paths and head from stile to stile over stony field boundaries, it is not easy to imagine 'the woman riding high above with bright hair flapping free', but the landscape was almost certainly less enclosed in Emma's time and Fanny was perhaps adept at clearing those stone walls. On the young lovers' return visit to Beeny on a wet Monday in August 1870, Emma remarked that 'It never looks like summer here' – this became the opening line of a poem dated 8 March 1913 (CP 456). On that rainy day Hardy sketched 'Beeny'; his drawing shows Gull Rock and Buckator, the cliff immediately north of Beeny (see 'The Figure in the Scene' CP 417 and 'Why Did I Sketch' CP 417). On a clear day there are magnificent views along the coast from Fire Beacon Point as far as Pentire to the south and Hartland Point in the north.

Follow the path ahead along the edge of the next three fields. **Cross the fourth stile to sit on the cliff-edge seat just beyond and admire Buckator and the heavily populated gull island. To continue on the circular walk, return over this stile and turn left inland, following the path to the road. However, if you have the time and the energy and the weather is set fair, keep northward on the coastal path 'up the cliff, down' and up again towards Buckator.** The point at which Hardy sketched the cliffs is about 250 yards (230 metres) beyond the cliff-top seat. Not surprisingly, Buckator features in *A Pair of Blue Eyes* as *Windy Beak*, 'the second cliff in height along that coast' (which it actually is) and 'the cliff to which Elfride had ridden with Stephen Smith, on a well-remembered morning of his summer visit'. The seat where Elfride lost an earring whilst kissing Smith, only to find it again whilst kissing Knight, was located here. Although the western side of Buckator, like Beeny, presents a sheer black precipice, the northern side declines more gently and is pockmarked with old slate workings connected by a network of steep meandering paths. On this slope Kenneth Phelps found a stone seat, which, although man-made, could certainly serve as the original for the lovers' trysting place. Indeed, when Knight is frostily cross-questioning Elfride about her previous experiences on the seat, she tries to deflect him by observing that 'we ought to be off this ledge before it gets too dark to let us see our footing. I daresay the horse is impatient'; this statement both fits with lower Buckator and implies that Emma was not foolhardy enough to take her horse right to the cliff-edge. Beyond here the path leads to Rusey, behind which rises the gently declining slope of the highest point on the south-west coastal path: High Cliff. A mile (one-and-a-half kilometres) beyond this you reach the cliffs above the beautifully wild and unspoilt beach of Strangles, visited by Hardy and Emma during their courtship and unchanged to this day.

For St Juliot, cross back over the stile beside the seat and head inland along the field edge and then a narrow, often muddy, holloway to reach the tarmaced lane. Turn right along the lane and follow it downhill and across Emma's Pentargon-bound stream. From here take the footpath straight ahead (ignore the signposted path on left) and follow it along the left-hand edge of two fields to a farm drive and the main Boscastle Road. Cross straight over to steps up to a stile opposite. Follow this path straight ahead across five fields via a variety of ancient stiles; in practice, this means slightly left across the first two fields, slightly right across the third and fourth fields, then along the top boundary of the final field. This is the exact route, unaltered in 140 years, which Emma and Hardy took on their walks to and from the rectory. Ahead, to your right, is that 'little paradise of flowers and trees', the rectory of St Juliot. **On reaching the farm lane, turn left, then right to return to the church; alternatively turn right downhill**

for a view of the rectory. This stone building, sitting under a slate roof and with a large walled garden, magnificent flowering shrubs, formal lawns and flower-beds dropping down the hill into a wild wooded paradise, remains virtually unchanged from that windy March night in 1870, when Emma first greeted Hardy at the front door in the porch which stands before you.

The Old Rectory, built in 1847, is currently an award-winning, environmentally friendly bed and breakfast, seeped in Hardyan details and run by the most congenial and informative hosts (plate 5.6). A stay there is a must for any true Hardy enthusiast; on offer is the rector's bedroom, Emma's room (complete with original 'thunderbox') or the guest room in which the young architect's assistant slept and dreamt as he fell in love with 'a pair of blue eyes'. Here, far more than at Max Gate, you will imbibe a true feeling for Hardy and the world which he inhabited. In the garden rests a seat on which Hardy used to sit with Emma – from here and the nearby platform there are extensive views across the Valency Valley. The couple were reading Tennyson on this spot on 18 August 1870 whilst the battle of Gravelotte was being fought in north-eastern France and a ploughman was harrowing the fields on the hillside opposite the rectory; forty-five years later these combined memories resurfaced as 'In Time of "The Breaking of Nations"' (CP 500), written in the darkest days of an even bloodier conflict. More of Hardy's poems are associated with the Old Rectory than with any other single building; the total is at least thirty-five, prominent amongst which are 'She Opened the Door' (CP 740), 'A Week'

5.6 St Juliot Rectory

(CP 312), 'A Duettist to Her Pianoforte' (CP 543), 'At the Word Farewell' (CP 360), 'The Seven Times' (CP 652), 'The Frozen Greenhouse' (CP 706) and 'A Dream or No' (CP 288).

The track to the east of the rectory is the footpath which links the two churches under Parson Swancourt's care and was the route taken by Hardy and Emma when they attended Evening Prayer at Lesnewth Church on 14 August 1870. The path runs muddily straight down to a footbridge over the Valency River and then up past Halamiling Farm to reach Lesnewth. This is another Cornish gem nestling in a wooded garden against a hillside beside a stream, the church roof lower than the nearby road. Lesnewth is the setting of the poem 'The Young Churchwarden' (CP 386), written in disillusioned retrospect by the successful suitor. Hardy's rival was Henry Jose, who never married and whose grave stands to the right of the path as it curves down towards the church. The Jose family still flourish locally, for the great-grandson of Henry's nephew was reglazing the greenhouse at the Old Rectory when I visited in March 2009. The road from St Juliot to Lesnewth crosses a ford beyond which 'primaeval rocks form the road's steep border'. The continuation to Minster has a one in four gradient as it ascends the wooded valley which separates the two parishes – this is the 'depression' of 'great steepness' described in *A Pair of Blue Eyes*. To this day the road remains so quiet that a passing car is enough of an event for the farm dogs to come out to see what is happening.

'A Man Was Drawing Near to Me'

Hardy's First Journey to St Juliot

By car (twenty-two miles/thirty-five kilometres)

The poem 'A Man Was Drawing Near to Me' (CP 536) is based upon material from Emma's *Some Recollections*, describing Hardy's first fateful journey to St Juliot from her perspective. It is still possible and rewarding to retrace this journey, although sadly one can no longer arrive at Launceston by train – the line and its extension, the North Cornwall Railway, fell victim to the Beeching axe in 1967.

On 7 March 1870, Hardy, who had risen at 4 a.m. to catch the first train from Dorchester West, eventually arrived 'after changing trains many times' at Launceston station just after 4 p.m. The station at which he arrived is today an empty tarmaced space guarded by a forlorn semaphore signal, plus one stone workshed; however, its memory lives on in the Railway Inn. (The nearby narrow-gauge steam railway station belonged to the North Cornwall extension.)

Hardy walked up the steep track past the remains of the Norman castle to the Market Square where he stopped at the White Hart Inn for refreshment and to hire the dogcart plus driver for the onward journey to St Juliot. The White Hart survives, though robbed of much of its former glory, its extensive stabling converted into a rather dingy shopping arcade. This is 'the inn / smiling nigh' of 'St Launces Revisited' (CP 296) and also the Falcon where Elfride stabled Pansy en route to Plymouth and London during her abortive elopement with Stephen Smith. Emma had fond associations with the town, which was home to various aunts and cousins and where her 'much-loved uncle' was bank manager.

To follow the route taken to St Juliot by Smith (Hardy), **leave Launceston on the main western road (A30) – now a busy dual carriageway – and exit at the first opportunity (A395). As you head off the slip road onto the roundabout there are striking views ahead of Cornwall's two highest points:** Brown Willy (to the left) and the lower, but more prominent, Rough Tor. **This turnpike road, little changed over the last century, is soon crossing open moorland,** which is quite reminiscent of *Egdon* although described in *A Pair of Blue Eyes* as a 'whole dreary distance of open country'. Only those giant silent propellers, the wind-turbines, are new; I suspect that Hardy would have held a sneaking sympathy for these ghostly eco-friendly power sources, as tall as cathedral spires and to an 'impercipient' perhaps more useful.

'The Face at the Casement' (CP 258) is a poetic account of a visit made by Hardy and Emma in May 1871 to William Serjeant, the consumptive son of the curate of St Clether – and one-time contender for Emma's hand. **A short deviation from the main road leads by holloways to the (unaltered) Old Rectory directly opposite the church**. Here Serjeant's tomb is marked by a stone cross in the south-east corner of yet another delightfully wild grave-garden. **A footpath from the far side of the graveyard leads across open moorland to St Clether's Holy Well and Chapel, through which the baptismal stream flows unhindered.**

'By Halworthy' bear right onto the B3262 just beyond the Wilsey Down Hotel. Continue across the semi-cultivated moorland to the A39(T), then turn right 'where Otterham lay', through Otterham Parish rather than village (the junction is at Otterham Station which did not exist in 1870). Take the third left (B3263) then turn left again at 'Tresparrett Posts', then right for Tresparrett itself. Head straight on and steeply down – you are at the top of the Valency Valley. Just before the ford, take a sharp right for St Juliot, past Anderton Byre, 'then hard at hand by Hennett Byre' (on your right). Then imagine Hardy's arrival as described in the poem: 'There was a rumble at the door, / A draught disturbed the drapery ... The man revealed himself to me.'

If you look at the map to contemplate this journey, you will immediately wonder why Hardy was driven by such a devious route from Otterham Station to the crossroads at Tresparrett; the direct route via Marshgate is two-and-a-quarter miles (three-and-a-half kilometres) whereas the route described by Hardy is just under six miles (nine-and-a-half kilometres). Three explanations seem likely. The first and more probable is that he was actually driven along the direct route – and the roads have not changed since 1870 – but used 'Tresparrett Posts' in the poem because of the useful rhyme with 'coasts' and 'ghosts'. Alternatively, the driver may not have known the best route or may just have been a cabman spinning out the journey to increase his income. It is important, however, not to forget that this is a 'partly real, partly dream country'. Tresparrett Posts was also named by Hardy as the setting for that sorrowful retrospect 'When Three Roads Joined' (CP 544).

'Those places that once we visited' (CP 277)

> Sometimes we all drove to Tintagel and Trebarwith Strand where donkeys were employed to carry seaweed to the farmers; Strangles Beach also, Bossiney, Bude and other places on the coast. Lovely drives they were with sea-views all along ...

Much of the content of Hardy's *Poems of 1912–13* is based upon Emma's *Some Recollections*, written in her attic eyrie at Max Gate during 1911, recalling those far-off days of their courtship. If you visit out of season and turn a blind eye to the motor cars and tourist tack, you can experience this coast much as Hardy first saw it in March 1870. A seven-mile (eleven-kilometre) walk along the coastal path from south-east of Boscastle to Trebarwith takes in the Rocky Valley, Bossiney and Tintagel, some beautiful coastal scenery and a fair chance of spotting seals, basking sharks and plentiful seabirds. Alternatively, follow Elfride and Knight by taking a drive 'along a road by neutral green hills, upon which hedgerows lay trailing like ropes on a quay' to that 'local lion, Barwith Strand' (B3263) (plate 5.7).

To reach Bossiney Haven, park by the red telephone box on the right as you are just about to enter the village and from here a footpath leads to the beach. Bossiney village marks the beginning of the extensive down-market sprawl which constitutes the day-tripper's Tintagel. Blinker your eyes, suppress your nausea and make your way straight to Tintagel Head, the Castle and Island. Here, on 'Dundagel's famed head', you will escape the crowds. The island is a magnificent, enchanting, magical place, the essence of the whole 'wild weird western shore' where 'the unseen waters' ejaculations awe me' whilst 'the waked birds preen and the seals flop lazily' (CP 289 and 291) (plate 5.8). It is small wonder that Castel Dyntagell was the setting for both Emma's

5.7 High tide at Trebarwith

5.8 Tintagel: *The Island*

unpublished novel *The Maid on the Shore* and Hardy's poetic drama *The Famous Tragedy of the Queen of Cornwall*, written in memory of that 'Iseult of my own', the Emma of 'I found Her Out There' (CP 281).

Sadly, there are two blots on this otherwise enchanted horizon. Firstly, King Arthur's Castle Hotel, that monstrous, solid late-Victorian eyesore which dominates the adjoining Barras Head and which does not seem to have mellowed one iota since the day of its construction. Blame Alfred, Lord Tennyson, whose *Morte d'Arthur* and *Idylls of the King* started a tourist trail to the once remote and unspoilt village of Trevena. The building is a colossus, so wholly out of keeping with its environs that it dominates the landscape for miles around and constantly intrudes upon the coastal walker. The only positive note is that the outcry caused by its original construction launched the National Trust on its policy of purchasing vulnerable stretches of coastland.

The second blot on the horizon is a poetic one and can be found in 'The Interloper' (CP 432). This poem describes Hardy's drive with Emma and her sister Helen 'to Boscastle, Tintagel and Penpethy slate-quarries with a view to the church roofing' on 8 March 1870. They are accompanied on this drive by 'another' 'whom I like not to be there'; this 'interloper' is the hereditary tendency to mental instability which ran in the Gifford family. The poem's subtitle graphically states, 'And I saw the figure and visage of Madness seeking for a home'. This unwanted guest 'is that under which best lives corrode' and was the cause of much of the poet's subsequent marital unhappiness.

Hardy married Emma in September 1874. However, the bliss of their Cornish courtship appears to have rapidly turned sour – see 'We Sat at the Window' (CP 355). After their 'happiest time' at Sturminster Newton, the childless couple became increasingly estranged. With time Emma's agnosticism turned to extreme evangelism and her dress and behaviour became increasingly inappropriate. She had always believed that she had compromised her social status by marrying a man of lowly origins and could never accept Hardy's literary success. In old age, many considered her to be mentally ill; there was certainly a significant family history of psychiatric illness – this being 'The Interloper' of Hardy's poem. In medical terms, she was probably suffering from a schizoid personality disorder. Emma died in November 1912 and Hardy married Florence Dugdale in February 1914. (For more information see Michael Millgate's book, *Thomas Hardy: A Biography*, and Tony Fincham's *Hardy the Physician*.)

The Penpethy slate quarries, the setting of 'Green Slates' (CP 678), are still being worked. They lie about three miles (five kilometres) south-east of *Dundagel* and visitors are welcome at several of the quarries.

At Trewarmett, just before Penpethy, a narrow lane leads steeply down

5.9 Trebarwith Strand

to Trebarwith Strand. It is wise to consult the tide tables before visiting
because the extensive sands are only exposed during a narrow three-hour
window around low tide. At the right moment the beautiful bay will burst
upon you, very much as described by Hardy in *A Pair of Blue Eyes* (plate 5.9).
No donkeys to be found now but the Surf Shop on your right is the 'little
cottage with shed attached' where Mrs Swancourt stabled her carriage.

The coastal path from Tintagel to Trebarwith is peppered with abandoned slate works. It affords beautiful views back towards 'Dundagel's famed
head' and also a chance to inspect St Merteriana's Church in solitary splendour on the exposed Glebe Cliff. It is of Norman origin and thus
contemporaneous with the nearby castle. Emma, whose sister Helen lived in
Trevena prior to her marriage, painted a watercolour of the church interior.
Hardy attended a service here on his last visit to Cornwall with Florence in
September 1916 – and took such offence at being asked to move pew to
make way for the choir, that the couple marched out during the sermon,
never to return. The final stanza of 'The Voice of Things' (CP 353) makes
direct reference to this incident. In 1913 the magical landscape had rekin-
dled a fantasy; *Lyonnesse* revisited with a demanding, new young wife in
1916 was a far more prosaic reality.

Bodmin: 'I Rose and Went to Rou'tor Town' (CP 468)

This poem, which is the dark doppelganger to the bright 'When I Set Out for Lyonnesse', tells the story of Hardy's rejection as a suitable son-in-law by Emma's parents. *Rou'tor*, named after Rough Tor, the second-highest and most spectacular peak on Bodmin Moor, is an appropriate name for Bodmin, the town where Hardy received such rough treatment.

The family home which Hardy and Emma visited 'with gaiety and good heart' in August 1872 was Kirland Manor. **It is situated on a leafy public footpath off Crabtree Lane just south of Bodmin.** This isolated Regency house facing due south across open farmland appears much as Emma described it in the 1860s, including the large garden, rookery and stream full of fish. After his summary dismissal, Hardy retreated to the nearby home of some friends of Emma's, St Benet's Abbey on the A389, just south of Lanivet. This was originally built in the fifteenth century by the Benedictines as a Lazar House and is now a bed and breakfast and tearoom. A summerhouse stood in the garden of St Benet's (now sadly vanished without trace) and it was here that Hardy wrote the second instalment of *A Pair of Blue Eyes* with Emma's assistance. I believe this to be the model for the summerhouse at *West Endelstow* and the one referred to in the poems 'Where They Lived' (CP 392) and 'The Man Who Forgot' (CP 490). A number of authorities have tried in vain to locate this building at St Juliot but there is absolutely no evidence of there ever having been a summerhouse at the Old Rectory.

A short walk south-east from St Benet's brings one (under or over the A30) to Repery Cross, where five lanes meet. An old wooden finger-post stood here, against which Emma stretched out her arms as they returned from a walk one evening in August 1872 – 'Her white-clothed form at this dim-lit cease of day / Made her look as one crucified' – in a foreboding, tragic vision of things to come ('Near Lanivet, 1872' CP 366).

A lane, once the main highway, runs due east from Repery to Lanhydrock, the model for *Endelstow House* – relocated seventeen miles (twenty-seven kilometres) north-west for the purposes of *A Pair of Blue Eyes*. At Lanhydrock (now in the care of the National Trust) you can still pass through 'an ancient gateway of dun-coloured stone' to reach 'a spacious court, closed by a facade on each of its three sides'. Here is the long, barrel-vaulted picture gallery explored by Elfride and Stephen and a church adjoining the mansion – there being no 'division between God's Acre and Lord Luxellian's' – the carefully tended graveyard forming 'virtually a part of the manor-house lawn'. But, as Kay-Robinson observed, most of the rest of the detail of *Endelstow House* is a description of Athelhampton, on the edge of *Egdon* Heath and intimately known to Hardy. Similarly, the depiction of the opening of the Luxellian family vault is based upon Hardy's knowledge of the O'Briens' tomb at Stinsford. **As you return up the drive from Lanhydrock**, note the estate cottages tucked away in the trees to your left – the family homes of real-life Smiths.

Plymouth: 'The Marble-Streeted Town' (CP 643)

In March 1913, Thomas and Henry Hardy returned from Boscastle to Dorchester via Plymouth, where Emma had spent her childhood. This gave rise to a number of poems of memory and regret, prime amongst which is 'During Wind and Rain' (CP 441), an imaginative development of scenes from Emma's childhood based upon her *Some Recollections*. Of that nineteenth-century Plymouth, the Hoe and the sea remain, but the rest has fallen victim to time and the Luftwaffe. Of the various Gifford homes, the only one still standing is 9 Bedford Terrace – the 'high new house' of 'During Wind and Rain'. It remains a grand house in a rather scruffy cul-de-sac in what is generally an area of student lodgings. 'The West-of-Wessex Girl' (CP 526), 'Places' (CP 293) and 'Lonely Days' (CP 614) are also rooted in this Plymouth visit.

Devon: *The Romantic Adventures of a Milkmaid*

In the novella *The Romantic Adventures of a Milkmaid* Margery lives and works with her father at *Silverthorn Dairy-House*, which Pitfield has reasonably identified with Upexe Farm, situated deep in the valley of the Exe, just west of Silverton and five miles (eight kilometres) due north of Exeter. The baron's home, *Mount Lodge*, is modelled on Killerton House, a National Trust estate south-east of Silverton. Within the grounds of Killerton stands 'The Bear's Hut', a quaint thatched summerhouse – the spot where Margery first encounters the suicidal nobleman. In the adjoining woodland are several large and ancient chestnut trees, within the hollow trunk of one of which Margery changed into her ballgown. Ultimately, the baron takes her to his yacht, anchored in an inlet near *Idmouth* (Sidmouth), which remains a picturesque and genteel resort. Here Margery decides to return to her long-suffering husband, Jim, rather than flee abroad with her mysterious bipolar admirer.

Devon: 'The Honourable Laura' (*A Group of Noble Dames*)

'The Honourable Laura' is the only Hardy story to be set in North Devon and one where he engages in his common trick of telescoping distances and transposing locations. However, 'the wild north coast of Lower Wessex' can certainly be identified with the inaccessible, unspoilt area around Woody Bay, between Lynton and Coombe Martin, traversed by the South West Coast Path. The *Prospect Hotel* is based upon the isolated Hunters Inn but relocated in the story from its secluded inland position at the top of the Heddon's Mouth gorge to a more exposed position near Inkerman Bridge above Woody Bay, where a much smaller hotel survives to this day. The outlook seaward from here is indeed 'wild and picturesque in the extreme', and from the wooded cliff-top the cascade still plunges down 'vertically to a depth of eighty or a hundred feet before losing itself' on the rocks below. Hardy has moved the 'chasm in the cliff' from Heddon's Mouth to Woody Bay, and the whole area is so isolated and far from any highway that it is unlikely that even an eloping couple would chance upon it by accident on a dark December night.

Cornwall: *A Mere Interlude*

The action of A *Mere Interlude* is set in south-west Cornwall and on the Scilly Islands. As Hardy uses a minimal number of descriptive passages and there is no evidence that he ever visited these places, mere entry of their names in the Hardy Glossary (see pp.260–5) should suffice.

Somerset: *A Laodicean*

A *Laodicean* is the only Hardy novel for which the Thomas Hardy Society failed to produce a tour pamphlet; the reason for this is that there is minimal evidence that Hardy ever visited the novel's alleged Somerset location and a strong case in favour of the argument that the descriptions of *Stancy Castle* are based on Corfe Castle rather than Dunster Castle (with the paintings borrowed from Kingston Lacy), that *Markton* is based on the village of Corfe, and *Sleeping Green* upon nearby Slepe, which until the late nineteenth century was actually called Sleeping Green. Hardy can be excused for this, his least topographically intact novel, on the grounds that it was written under the pressure of serial deadlines whilst he was seriously ill, confined to his Tooting home in a reclining position with his feet on the mantelpiece and forced to dictate his text to Emma. The expansion of Wessex into north-western Somerset, a mere stone's throw from a Wessex Height, was part of his deliberate centrifugal policy to push the boundaries of his literary territory far away from their Bockhampton heart and at the same time provided a useful connection towards their most western Cornish extremity, thus giving the impression that his Wessex was a unified, continuous territory. Despite all these provisos, a visit to Dunster is well worthwhile and can be taken as part of a tour through western Wessex, heading from *Casterbridge* to *Narrobourne*, *Ivell*, *Ivelchester*, *Glaston*, Sedgemoor, Wills Neck and thence onto *Cliff Martin* and that 'wild weird western shore' beyond.

Dunster Castle retains a fairytale magic, especially from a distance as first glimpsed from the approaching A358. It is a National Trust property; the park and gardens are open throughout the year and the castle is closed only during the winter (plate 5.10). The village, with its early seventeenth-century yarn market and Conygar tower, is well preserved in a twee home-counties way, counterbalanced by the relentless irregular tourist tide. The partly fifteenth-century Luttrell Arms Hotel could represent the principal inn of *Markton*, that 'rambling edifice of stagecoach memories' where George Somerset stays, but an equally good case can be made for the wholly sixteenth-century Bankes Arms in Corfe. Paula Power is fascinated by the de Stancy monuments in *Markton* Church, which could indeed be the Luttrell tombs at Dunster. Leaving Dunster Castle by the north gate to enter the village you are confronted by a well preserved Baptist Chapel (now a craft shop and tearooms); though no longer 'alone in a field', its proximity to the castle matches Hardy's description. Whilst both Dunster and Corfe can still boast a working steam railway, and one must not underestimate the phallic significance of the train thrusting

5.10 Dunster Castle

through the Power's tunnel in Hardy's 'Story of Today', sadly neither railway line is endowed with a single tunnel (see the section on Upwey, p.174).

Somerset: *A Tragedy of Two Ambitions*

The footpath beside the mill-stream at *Narrobourne*, where the inebriated Halborough drowned in front of his two clerical sons in A *Tragedy of Two Ambitions*, can easily be identified at Hollywell between East and West Coker, to the south-west of Yeovil. **Follow the footpath, which starts from the A30 (Hendford Hill), past the Foresters Arms (which has car parking) and over the old mill and sluice, then along a bank across the water meadows beside the Coker stream towards the manor house and church at West Coker.** This walk will give a strong sense of the setting of this tragic tale, even if minor topographical details do not exactly match.

'A Trampwoman's Tragedy'

Hardy considered 'A Trampwoman's Tragedy' (CP 153) to be 'upon the whole, his most successful poem'. He started writing it in the autumn of 1901 following a bicycle ride from Dorchester over the Polden Hills to Glastonbury. The tale is based upon the life of Mary-Ann Taylor and the events occurred in 1827.

The ballad begins with the Trampwoman setting out 'From Wynyard's Gap'. This 'cosy house' remains a thriving inn on a spectacular wooded view-point on the A356 north of Beaminster. Here several long-distance paths still converge, including: the Brit Way, waymarked all the way to the South Coast, passing en route the long-demolished 'Hut renowned on Bredy Knap'; and the River Parrett Trail which, 'by fosseway, fields, and turnpike tracks', leads to the Bristol Channel, skirting en route 'sad Sedge-Moor'. To the modern 'Trampwoman', the Bussex battlefield approached along Monmouth Road, Westonzoyland, appears no more than a stretch of flat fertile farmland bisected by narrow dykes.

Old drovers' tracks still lead from the Parrett north-eastward towards 'the toilsome Polden Crest' (stanza 2) and 'the inn that beamed thereby', 'far-famed as Marshal's Elm' (stanza 6). As Hardy describes in his footnotes, the building is no longer an inn but it is readily identifiable at the eastern edge of the Polden ridge beside the crossroads on the B3151. The northward views extending 'from Mendip to the western sea' with *Glaston* Tor dominating the foreground are as magnificent as the Trampwoman contends.

Stanza 3 is a self-explanatory reminiscence of their previous trudgings across

Hardy's Wessex: the midges inhabit Marshwood Vale, that stretch of rich agricultural land lying between Pilsdon Pen and the coastal cliffs. The 'Lone inns
we loved' are scattered across Wessex. 'King's Stag' on the B3143 north of
Alton Pancras was burnt down in 1910, bequeathing its name to the rather
dull surviving hamlet. 'Windwhistle high and dry' remains a free house on the
'beautiful spot' described in Hardy's footnotes – the ridge on the A30 midway
between Chard and Crewkerne. 'The Horse on Hintock Green' is a popular
woodland tavern below High Stoy on the A37 at Middlemarsh, although its
name has changed from the White Horse to Hunter's Moon. Overall, therefore, three of the Trampwoman's six favourite 'wayside taps' remain in business.
The rest of the poem describes the murder of one of the Trampwoman's
companions by her jealous 'sweetheart' and its consequences. Hardy's endnotes
deal with both Blue Jimmy and *Ivelchester* Jail. The Trampwoman ends her days
'haunting the Western Moor' – in other words, Exmoor.

Review: Hardy's 'wild weird western shore', a landscape virtually unchanged
since he first set foot there, acts as a catalyst to accentuate and further develop
that melding of autobiography with fiction, fantasy, poetry and story-telling.
The supernatural scenery of *Lyonnesse* acts as an image-intensifier, magnifying
emotions; it is a vast, untamed open-air arena which dramatizes love, loss and
betrayal. Here Hardy fell in love with both the landscape and Emma,
returning forty-three years later to fall in love again with the landscape and a
'ghost-girl rider'. Today, the walker can follow the footsteps of the courting
couple as described in detail in *A Pair of Blue Eyes* and revisited in the *Poems
of 1912–13*; trace their steps from the rectory to the magic churchyard, to the
picnic site under the waterfall, *Castle Boterel*, Pentargon and the 'Cliff
Without a Name'. The magical landscape spreads further afield to Tintagel, St
Clether and *Rou'tor Town* and thence out into Devon and Somerset, finally
retracing the footsteps of the Trampwoman and her companions to the three
of her six favourite 'wayside taps' which remain in business.

CHAPTER SIX

South to the Channel Coast

And citizens dream of the south and west,
And so do I. (CP 512)

THIS CHAPTER EXPLORES Hardy's coastal landscape, which extends from Bridport in the west to Worthing in the east. It is a glorious stretch of untamed downland, tumbling cliffs, secret bays and long shingle beaches set against a rich blue sea and sky. In part this landscape coincides with that 'jewel in the crown of textbook geology' (1), the Jurassic coast – the only natural landscape in Great Britain to be designated a World Heritage Site – but Hardy's landscape is broader, deeper and more personal and hence I have avoided that designation here. This chapter moves from west to east in a series of short walks around focal Hardyan sites, which are themselves linked by a series of long-distance walks, most especially the South West Coast Path.

A Walk Around *Port-Bredy*

From Bridport to West Bay

By foot (two miles/three kilometres)

We will start at *Port-Bredy* (Bridport), where 'The shepherd on the east hill could shout out lambing intelligence to the shepherd on the west hill, over the intervening town chimneys.' Although Bridport has engulfed much surrounding meadow-land since Hardy wrote *Fellow-Townsmen* (1880), the town is still engirdled by a semicircle of hills; the most prominent of these, Colmer's Hill, with its crowning circle of separated trees, distinctively visible for many miles around, still encloses the High Street to the west (plate 6.1).

6.1 Colmer's Hill

Start from Bridport's eighteenth-century town hall. This is where Barnet attended council meetings, and past which Barnet and Downe drive at the start of *Fellow-Townsmen*. **Follow East Street down to the relatively unscathed 'Black Bull Hotel'.** No. 36, now a solicitors', was once the town's Savings Bank of which Barnet was a trustee. Beside this stood 'Barnet's old habitation', which was 'bought by the Congregational Baptist body, who pulled down the time-honoured dwelling and built a new chapel on its site', now itself mellowed into Bridport United Church. **Shortly beyond the church turn into** 'a small street on the right, consisting of a row of those two-and-two brick residences of no particular age, which are exactly alike wherever found, except in the people they contain'; this is King Street, where Downe lived with his loving wife and children.

Escape the traffic noise and bustle of East Street by following this road on into Church Street, which curves round to join 'a long street leading due southward'. Turn left into South Street. This is little changed since Hardy's time, composed of curving terraces of brick- and stone-built cottages with broad pavements, once the centre of the local rope- and net-making industry. On your right is the mellowed sandstone of St Mary's Church where Downe and Lucy were married, as also were Farfrae and Lucetta in *The Mayor of Casterbridge*, following Bathsheba's example of heading west for a clandestine wedding in *Far From the Madding Crowd*. Opposite the church stood the Five Bells, still distinguishable by the tiled sign on its upper storey, most probably the 'Ring of Bells' in 'The Whalers Wife' (CP 836).

South Street feeds into Westbay Road, which is industrial then heavily residential – there is no trace of the lonely silent road which Barnet followed. Beyond the roundabout, an estate of bungalows (Wanderwell) covers the empty knoll on which 'Chateau Ringdale' was constructed. At the southern end of the knoll the Edwardian Roundham House Hotel is a solitary reminder of more elegant days. Lucy's cottage, a few hundred yards further on, is untraceable. West Bay, 'a little haven, seemingly a beginning made by Nature herself of a perfect harbour', has the usual summer coating of tourist froth, but on a winter's day it is still a fair match for Hardy's description, with the thatched Bridport Arms Hotel being the 'Harbour Inn'. To the left, the 'vertical cliff coloured a burning orange by the sunlight' composed of golden Bridport sand alternating with calcareous sandstone, forms a glorious start to the coastal footpath leading on to *Budmouth* (Weymouth) (plate 6.2). In the crowded summer time, escape to tranquillity up the footpath beside the Brit estuary.

En route to Weymouth, the coastal path goes through Abbotsbury, where the fourteenth-century Abbey Barn (one of the largest barns in England) served Hardy as a model for Bathsheba's Shearing Barn. Beside the road

6.2 East Cliff, *Port-Bredy*

6.3 The Fleet and Portland

junction in nearby Portesham 'the old-fashioned house which was the family residence of the Hardys' still stands unchanged – this is the manor where Bob Loveday in *The Trumpet-Major* volunteered for naval service. Above Portesham rises Blackdown, surmounted by its solidly Victorian phallic memorial to Admiral Hardy (not our Thomas Hardy). Without climbing the tower, which is locked except on summer weekends, there are still fine views over the fleet towards *Budmouth* and *Slingers*. The best views of all, over Chesil Beach, are to be had on a clear windy day from Abbotsbury Hill, one mile (one-and-a-half kilometres) west of the village (plate 6.3).

A Walk Around *Budmouth* (Weymouth)

'The Boats, the sands, the esplanade' (CP 447)

By foot (two miles/three kilometres)

Starting from Weymouth railway station yard, turn left past the magnificent Somerset pub towards Queen Victoria's (fiftieth) Jubilee Clock. On reaching the esplanade, you are confronted by the beautiful blue bay stretching from the Cliffs of White Nose on your left to Nothe Fort on your right.

Turn left past Royal Crescent to Belvidere Terrace. At the far end of this stood the Belvidere Hotel (now probably the Langham) where Miss Aldclyffe interviewed Cytherea in *Desperate Remedies* (plate 6.4). The far grander Victoria

Terrace follows, occupied mainly by the magnificent Hotel Prince Regent (formerly the Hotel Burdon). Ahead in Waterloo Place stands the forlorn figure of Queen Victoria. Cross the road to the pier bandstand. Hardy records how in April 1869, having just been interviewed by Crickmay, who had absorbed Hicks's architectural practice on the latter's death, he stood 'opposite the Burdon Hotel on the Esplanade, facing the beautiful sunlit bay' listening to the band playing a Strauss Waltz. Forty-eight years later this 'spot of time' resurfaced in a poem entitled 'At a Seaside Town in 1869 (Young Lover's Reverie)' (CP 447):

> The boats, the sands, the esplanade,
> The laughing crowd;
> Light-hearted, loud
> Greetings from some not ill-endowed;
>
> The evening sunlit cliffs, the talk
> Hailings and halts,
> The keen sea-salts,
> The band, the Morgenblatter Waltz

6.4 Melcombe Regis

Whilst working for Crickmay, Hardy enjoyed all the pleasures of a summer seaside resort: swimming in the mornings from the shingle beach to the north of the bandstand towards Preston and rowing in the bay in the evenings.

Retrace your steps along the front or on the beach. Look at the views ahead of the harbour, with Portland behind, topped by the Verne Prison. Throughout Hardy's fiction, if characters travel abroad, they invariably depart from *Budmouth*; for example, in *The Return of the Native*, Eustacia Vye was heading for the steamer on that fateful November night which ended tragically at *Shadwater Weir*. Hardy himself took the ferry to Cherbourg en route to Paris on two of his French expeditions. Beyond the Jubilee Clock, stands the Royal Hotel, a Victorian rebuilding of the original Old Royal Hotel, past whose 'two semi-circular bays' Dick drives Fancy in *Under the Greenwood Tree*. In the assembly rooms here King George III and his daughters used to dance during their many visits to Weymouth, a red cord separating the royal party from the townsfolk.

On reaching the Tea Cabin, cross the road to inspect the recently restored statue of King George III, the lion and the unicorn, and his adjoining bathing-machine (plate 6.5). In *The Trumpet-Major*, Bob Loveday, disappointed in love, walks disconsolately along the esplanade when an episode occurs which Hardy had carefully transcribed from a contemporary newspaper report:

> The royal bathing-machine had been drawn out just as Bob reached Gloucester Buildings … immediately that the King's machine had entered the water a group of florid men with fiddles, violoncellos, a trombone, and a drum, came forward, packed themselves into another machine that was in waiting, and were drawn out into the waves in the King's rear. All that was to be heard for a few minutes were the slow pulsations of the sea; and then a deafening noise burst from the interior of the second machine … the condensed mass of musicians inside, striking up the strains of 'God Save the King,' as his Majesty's head rose from the water … a performance … possibly in the watery circumstances tolerated rather than desired by that dripping monarch.

6.5 King George and his bathing machine

Bear diagonally right to the corner of Westham Road, then turn around to envisage the opening scene of Book Three of *Under the Greenwood Tree*:

> The scene was the corner of Mary Street in Budmouth-Regis, near the King's statue, at which point the white angle of the last house in the row cut perpendicularly an embayed and nearly motionless expanse of salt water projected from the outer ocean – to-day lit in bright tones of green and opal. Dick and Smart had just emerged from the street, and there on the right, against the brilliant sheet of liquid colour, stood Fancy Day; and she recognised him.

The scene is unchanged to this day (motor traffic excepted) with St Aldhelm's Head still 'closing the bay' (plate 6.6).

Walk down Westham Road, turning right into Park Street. The castellated Salvation Army citadel on the corner occupies the site of No. 1 West Parade, where Hardy lodged in 1872. **Turn left into Wooperton Street.** Hardy lodged intermittently at No. 3 (see plate on wall) between 1869 and 1871, here writing most of *Desperate Remedies* and many poems. No. 3 Wooperton Street, like many of its neighbours, has a bay window on the first floor, suggesting that Hardy, like Newson at the end of *The Mayor of Casterbridge*, could thus obtain 'a glimpse of a vertical strip of blue sea' by 'leaning forward far enough to look through a narrow lane of tall intervening houses'. New building on Park Street has rendered this feat impossible today. In Hardy's time, the car park was an extension of the Backwater, so the window would have definitely afforded views of the sun setting over the Radipole lakes.

6.6 St Aldhelm's Head enclosing the bay

Continue past Hardy's lodging towards Westham Bridge, bearing left along the quayside path beside the marina – admire the boats and their names! On reaching the car park, follow the old railway track as it curves towards the bulk of Holy Trinity Church, then past the Sailor's Return, under the bridge and up the steps on your left onto 'The Harbour Bridge' (CP 742). Here Mlle V. collapses at the sight of Monsieur G. in 'A Committee-Man of the Terror', thus starting a troubled liaison. The Bridge also forms the setting for a relationship based on mistaken identity in 'The Contretemps' (CP 539):

> One pairing is as good as another
> Where all is venture! Take each other,
> And scrap the oaths that you have aforetime made …

Weymouth harbour forms the likely setting for 'The Newcomers Wife', the tale of another Matilda Johnson and her naive lover (CP 304).

Cross the Opening Bridge with extensive views over the harbour and follow the path along the further quayside. You are now in Weymouth proper, having until now (historically speaking at least) been in the separate resort of Melcombe Regis. Note the boat trips on offer, including a whitewater ride to Lulworth and back, but sadly not stopping there. Hardy's first definite reference to Weymouth is a diary entry dated 26 August 1868:

> To Weymouth with Mary [his sister]. Found it was Weymouth Races. To Lulworth by Steamboat. A woman on the paddle-box steps: all laughter: then part illness and remainder laughter. M and I alighted at Lulworth Cove: she did not, but went back to Weymouth with the steamer. Saw her for the last time standing on the deck as the boat moved off. White feather in her hat, brown dress, Classic features, short upper lip. A woman I would have married offhand, with probable disastrous results.

A typically Hardyan encounter! In *Desperate Remedies* Cytherea and her brother Owen make the same trip from *Budmouth* to *Lulwind Cove* by steamer. They land 'by the primitive plan of a narrow plank on two wheels'; this device, or its successor, can still be seen, gathering rust at Lulworth. Steamer trips lasted well into the twentieth century. An enterprising Weymouth sailor revived a motor-boat passenger service to Lulworth in 2006, sadly having to abandon the exercise after three years, mainly because of lack of co-operation from the current owner of the 'narrow plank on two wheels'!

From the Quay bear first-right up Trinity Street. To your right admire the beautiful Hope Congregational Chapel, which Pevsner describes as 'a painful thing to see'! Opposite stands an early seventeenth-century house (see plaque), Hardy's *Old Rooms Inn*, a popular drinking place in *The Dynasts*. Here boatmen and burghers discuss Nelson's death at Trafalgar and the journey of many weeks back to England, his body preserved 'so that he could lie in state afterwards to the naked eye'. The boatman explain that he was preserved 'in a case of sper-rits' but 'they were a long time coming owing to contrary winds, and the *Victory* being little more than a wreck. And the grog ran short because they'd used near all they had to peckle his body in. So they broached the Adm'l!' Thus Nelson 'was their salvation after death as he had been in the fight'.

Continue past the old cottages, left across the top end of Hope Square – past Brewers Quay – and straight on up the path ahead (Hill Lane) between the walls, across Horsford Street, then up Look Out to the Nothe Gardens. This 'unique blend of recreation and wildlife areas' forms a wonderful and unexpected antidote to the bustling pressure of the town. Pause to breathe in the scenery. In the cove below you, Christoph waited with the boat he had stolen from the harbour to rendezvous with Matthaus Tina, on that fateful evening when Phyllis changed her mind in 'The Melancholy Hussar of the German Legion'. Beyond, in Portland Harbour, the sailing events of the 2012 Olympics are scheduled to occur.

From the cove, a diversion of one mile (one-and-a-half kilometres) south along the coastal path – now shamefully temporarily diverted inland – brings you to the ruins of Sandsfoot Castle. This is *Henry VIII's Castle*, where Pierston and Avice failed to meet to 'carry out island custom in our courting' i.e. to ensure that Avice was pregnant before matrimony in *The Well-Beloved*. The castle is a picturesque cliff-top ruin, much eroded, and so securely fenced off as to render it virtually impregnable to the casual visitor – certainly no place to attempt 'island custom'!

Otherwise, turn left, following the seaward path, then curving up to the greensward above Nothe Fort. This was originally commissioned in 1872 and is now a Museum of Coastal Defence.

Head inland, still on the upper (wooded) path above Barrack Road. From here there are fine views across *Budmouth* Harbour towards grey King George III on his charger above the Bowleaze Holiday Park.

On reaching the car park, turn right down steps to the quayside, where you can pick up the rowing boat ferry across the harbour. This is the orig-inal means of crossing the harbour; the ferrymen believe that their charter was granted by Queen Elizabeth I for services in the war against the Spanish.

Once safely across, head straight to the beach and esplanade. You pass the Pavilion Theatre on your right where in September 1927 Hardy received a standing ovation at a dramatization of *The Mayor of Casterbridge*. To your left admire Esplanade Terrace leading round to the Baptist Chapel; ahead the beautiful curving sands are paralleled by the curving façades of the houses. On this southern beach dogs are permitted all year round, there is sand sculpting, donkey rides and a funfair (plate 6.7). This is the bright and lively seaside resort which throughout Hardy's writings appears as the antithesis to sombre, lonely *Egdon*. In the preface to *The Return of the Native*, Hardy wrote:

> The date at which the following events are assumed to have occurred may be set down as between 1840 and 1850, when the old watering place herein called 'Budmouth' still retained sufficient afterglow from its Georgian gaiety and prestige to lend it an absorbing attractiveness to the romantic and imaginative soul of a lonely dweller inland.

This is the *Budmouth* of the Hussar's Song from *The Dynasts*:

> When we lay where Budmouth Beach is,
> O, the girls were fresh as peaches,
> With their tall and tossing figures and their eyes of blue and brown!
> And our hearts would ache with longing
> As we paced from our sing-songing,
> With a smart *Clink! Clink!* up the Esplanade and down. (CP 930)

6.7 *Budmouth* beaches

And which found its most powerful advocate in Diggory Venn as he tried to manipulate Eustacia in *The Return of the Native*:

> And in my travels I go near Budmouth. Now Budmouth is a wonderful place – wonderful – a great salt sheening sea bending into the land like a bow – thousands of gentlepeople walking up and down – bands of music playing – officers by sea and officers by land walking among the rest – out of every ten folks you meet nine of 'em in love.

In *Budmouth-Regis* the young Pierston falls madly in love with a girl on horseback who rides past and happens to smile at him in *The Well-Beloved*; this is a reflection of Hardy's own experience aged fourteen, recounted in *The Early Life*. A number of poems recall Hardy's life as a young man (aged thirty) in Weymouth including 'Her Father' (CP 173), 'At Waking' (CP 174), 'The Dawn after the Dance' (CP 182), 'At a Watering Place' (CP 341), 'An Ancient to Ancients' (CP 660), 'On the Esplanade' (CP 682) and 'Singing Lovers' (CP 688). The latter two poems refer to boating on Weymouth Bay; 'On the Esplanade' is one of a number of early poems which first surfaced as prose in *Desperate Remedies*. A boating accident at *Budmouth-Regis* is the sad conclusion to 'The History of the Hardcombes'; the bodies of the two lovers, mismatched in marriage, are washed up at *Lulwind* 'tightly locked in each other's arms, his lips upon hers … in their death they were not divided'.

Turn away from the waterfront and cross the road to the further pavement. Note Banus and the Dream On Tea Room on the corner of Bond Street; these mark the site of the Theatre Royal, which was visited by King George III and is where Matilda Johnson appears on stage in *The Trumpet-Major*. The rear night-club entrance to Banus in Bond Street still shows clear signs of the building's original purpose.

Continue past King George III to Moby Dick's Pub and Eating Place. This is Gloucester Lodge built by George III's brother in 1870 and used by the king as his regular summer residence for many years (see plaque). Hardy records in *The Trumpet-Major* how, 'The fear of invasion was such that six frigates lay in the roads to ensure the safety of the royal family, and from the regiments of horse and foot quartered at the barracks, or encamped on the hills round about, a picket of a thousand men mounted guard every day in front of Gloucester Lodge, where the King resided.' No doubt he obtained this detail from contemporary sources, but a guard of 1,000 men on the esplanade might prove more cumbersome and obstructive than useful! High Limit Slots now links Gloucester Lodge to the Royal Hotel (see plaque); the old assembly rooms here are the setting for 'The Ballad of Love's Skeleton' (CP 915).

Turn left beside Edward's Fish and Chips and then turn right after

the Registered Firearms Dealer to the station. Alternatively, to complete your walk by unwinding in a more natural environment, carry straight ahead and across the Swannery Car Park to the RSPB Radipole Reserve; here a series of footpaths lead you amongst the reeds and through the lagoons to an oasis of wildlife, far removed from the 'urban roar'.

The Isle of Slingers (The Isle of Portland)

A Circular Coastal Walk

By foot (nine miles/fourteen kilometres)

'The peninsula carved by Time out of a single stone'

To reach Portland, take the (clearly signposted) South West Coast Path from Nothe Gardens (p.158) to Sandsfoot Castle, continuing on to cross Ferrybridge and then along Chesil Beach to Chiswell. Once upon this 'Gibraltar of Wessex', you have, like Pierston at the start of *The Well-Beloved*, 'a laborious clamber' to 'reach the top'. Alternatively, in season, a ferry service operates from Weymouth Quay to Portland Castle, the well preserved twin of Sandsfoot. Thirdly, a crossing by car conveniently places you at the car park in New Ground (behind the Heights Hotel), where the walk starts. The knoll just south of the car park is Hardy's *Top-o'-Hill*; from here there are superb views over the entire length of Chesil Beach, Portland Harbour and West Bay (*Deadman's Bay*) and ahead the coastline tapers away beyond Lyme towards Exmouth. Immediately below you are the combined towns of Chiswell and Fortuneswell: the *Street of the Wells* in *The Well-Beloved*, where stand 'the houses above houses, one man's doorstep rising behind his neighbour's chimney, the gardens hung up by one edge to the sky, the vegetables growing on apparently almost vertical planes, the unity of the whole island as a solid and single block of limestone four miles long ... all now dazzlingly unique and white against the tinted sea'.

To start the walk, follow the waymarked footpath beside and then along the road (New Ground) until you come to the entrance to the Verne Prison, approached by a 'drawbridge' over a deep moat. The Verne was origially a naval fortification built in the 1850s by prisoners from the nearby Grove Prison; they were used as hard labour to quarry stone for both the citadel, which destroyed an Iron Age earthwork, and for the breakwater in construction of the harbour (hence the deep fosse). In 1948, the Verne ceased to be a military fortress and became the island prison, the original prison at the Grove having become the Portland Borstal, or Young Offenders Institution, as it is now known. Two of Hardy's first cousins (sons of James Hardy) were warders at the prison and hence formed his main Portland connection. As a young man Hardy was also friendly with the three Cozens sisters, who grew up at Lewell Mill on the edge of the heath and who ran a Ladies School on Portland at the time when Hardy was lodging in Weymouth; here he attended dancing classes which involved 'a gay gathering for dances and love-making by adepts of both sexes'!

Avice II, who suffers from Pierston's susceptibility to multiple simultaneous 'Well-Beloveds', takes in washing for the fortress, where a soldier has caught her eye. This leads to a typical Hardyan scene in which Pierston is watching Avice watch the soldier:

> She did not see him, and abandoning the right-hand course he slowly ascended the incline she had taken. He observed that her attention was absorbed by something aloft. He followed the direction of her gaze. Above them towered the green-grey mountain of grassy stone, here levelled at the top by military art. The skyline was broken every now and then by a little peg-like object – a sentry-box; and near one of these a small red spot kept creeping backwards and forwards monotonously against the heavy sky. Then he divined that she had a soldier-lover.

Follow the track past the Verne entrance and, as intermittently waymarked, curve southward to pass to the seaward site of the Grove, where high barbed-wire fences have taken the role played by the fosse at the Verne. Once clear of the prison, admire the seaward view along the Jurassic coast to St Aldhelm's Head. Inland is Yeoman's Quarry, now in part a nature reserve. At the start of *The Well-Beloved*, Pierston 'stretched out his hand upon the rock beside him. It felt warm. That was the island's personal temperature when in its afternoon sleep as now. He listened, and heard sounds: whirr-whirr, saw-saw-saw. Those were the island's snores – the noises of the quarrymen and stone-sawyers.'

Portland Stone has been quarried since Roman times and the industry peaked in the second half of the nineteenth century, at the time of the setting of *The Well-Beloved*. In the final months of his life, Hardy was still taking his daily 'melancholy little walk' alongside the railway line behind Max Gate, timed to coincide with the daily passing trainload of Portland Rock. Portland Stone was first brought to London in 1620 by Inigo Jones to grace the Banqueting Hall of Whitehall Palace for Charles I. Following Wren's rebuilding of St Paul's Cathedral and the other City churches, Portland Stone became the premium material for public buildings in London and most major cities of Great Britain and Ireland. It was used for many war and other memorials, ranging from the façade of Waterloo Station (p.239) to the Menin Gate at Ypres, to the stones in the Pets Cemetery at Max Gate. In *The Well-Beloved*, Pierston encounters Avice II on a London wharf, to where she has travelled 'just for a trip' accompanying blocks of stone on 'a lumpy craft'.

Marcel Proust in *A la Recherche* talked of the 'stonemason's geometry in the novels of Thomas Hardy'. Proust thought that the theory of love espoused by Hardy in *The Well-Beloved* closely resembled his own ideas: 'I've just read something really beautiful,' he wrote in a letter to a friend in 1909, 'which unfortunately resembles just the least little bit, though it's a thousand times better, my own work: Thomas Hardy's *The Well-Beloved*. It even has that slight touch of the grotesque which belongs to great works of art.' Proust had had to wait until 1909 for a French translation of *The Well-Beloved*; but Hardy read Proust in French and it seems likely that he read this passage from Proust's posthumously published *La Prisonniere*:

> Do you remember the stonemasons in *Jude the Obscure*, and in *The Well-Beloved* the blocks of stone which the father hews out of the island coming in boats to be piled up in the son's work-shop where they are turned into statues; and in *A Pair of Blue Eyes* the parallelism of the tombs, and also the parallel line of the boat and the nearby railway coaches containing the lovers and the dead woman; and the parallel between *The Well-Beloved*, where the man loves three women, and *A Pair of Blue Eyes*, where the woman loves three men, and in short all those novels which can be superimposed on one another like the houses piled up vertically on the rocky soil of the island? (2)

It seems an appropriately Hardyesque experience to be reading a review of your book written, so to speak, by a ghost!

As the path approaches Church Ope Cove turn left away from the coast under the archway of Red King's Castle. These are the remains of a fifteenth-century addition to an original eleventh-century castle built by William Rufus.

Follow the lane to Avice's Cottage, twice briefly described in The Well-Beloved: 'Opposite to the spot on which he sat was a roomy cottage or homestead. Like the island it was all of stone, not only in walls but in window-frames, roof, chimneys, fence, stile, pigsty and stable, almost door', and later, 'A few steps further revealed the cottage which with its quaint and massive stone features of two or three centuries' antiquity, was capable even now of longer resistance to the rasp of Time than ordinary new erections.' The thatched roof, though picturesque, is in fact a twentieth-century addition.

It is here that Pierston, the twenty-year-old returning native, first re-encounters the blossoming Avice I; here that the forty-year-old Pierston spies on Ann-Avice through her un-curtained window on the day of Avice I's funeral; and here, on an 'evening early in the subsequent winter', he paced up and down the lane whilst the moans of the sea were 'accompanied by an equally periodic moan from the interior of the cottage chamber' as Ann-Avice is delivered of Avice III. During Hardy's lifetime the cottage fell into serious disrepair, but it was purchased, along with its immediate neighbour, rehabilitated and presented to the local council to serve as a museum by Dr Marie Stopes, the pioneer of family planning. She holidayed for many years in one of the two original Portland lighthouses, and Thomas and Florence Hardy visited her in 1923. Today the museum is run by the independent Portland Museum Trust.

From the museum turn left along the road and then left back towards the sea, down the footpath beside *Sylvania* **Castle.** This was described by Hardy as 'a private mansion of comparatively modern date, in whose grounds stood the single plantation of trees of which the isle could boast'; this is still largely true. The house was originally built in 1800 by John Penn, a descendant of William Penn, who founded the state of Pennsylvania. It was rented by Pierston during the summer of his courtship of Ann-Avice, who was employed here as a laundress, whilst her *Sandbourne*-educated daughter, Avice III, subsequently works at *Sylvania* as a governess.

The wooded footpath leads into the churchyard. This contains the remains of the fourteenth-century St Andrew's church (the original twelfth-century building having been incinerated by the French), abandoned in 1753 because of its precarious position and poor state of repair. As the young Pierston courts Avice, the pair wander in the darkness 'so far as to the old Hope Churchyard, which lay in a ravine formed by a landslip ages ago. The church had slipped down with the rest of the cliff, and had long been a ruin. It seemed to say that in this last local stronghold of the Pagan divinities, where Pagan customs lingered yet, Christianity had established itself precariously at best. In that solemn spot Pierston kissed her.'

Remember that Hardy also described *Egdon* Heath as a final pagan stronghold; on Portland there is some historical backing for his view, for in 1816 fifty Methodists were expelled from their Fortuneswell Chapel because they refused to give up their belief in witchcraft. They retaliated by setting up their own chapel, known as Conjuror's Lodge, which still stands in Chiswell.

Take the path from the far (northern) end of the churchyard down the steps towards the beach, bearing right back onto the coastal path. As you climb back up the cliff, pause to admire this secluded cove, the only proper beach on Portland. *Hope Cove* – as well as being the site of Pierston's first kiss with the grown-up Avice I – was the place where he subsequently observed Avice II 'spreading white linen (to dry) upon the pebbly strand'. It was also here that beneath the faint light of a new moon he freed Avice III when her boot had become 'jammed in a crevice of the rock'. From this cove Avice III subsequently eloped with Henri Leverre in a stolen oarless ketch on the morning of her intended wedding to Pierston. In *The Well-Beloved*, Hardy states that the stones used to build St Paul's Cathedral started their perilous sea journey at *Hope Cove*. In *The Trumpet-Major* Anne Garland, exhausted by her walk from *Overcombe* to the *Beal*, is rowed homeward from here in a lerret (a type of boat), across the bay to *Budmouth* Harbour.

The path climbs through Southwell Landslip and then follows the road for about 300 yards (275 metres) before returning down a track to the cliff-edge. On regaining the sea, look behind to Cheyne House, thought to be the model for Pierston's parental home – 'the furthest house out there on the cliff'. When 'the young man of sixty' responds to Avice II's requests to call upon her, he finds that 'she had long ceased to live in the little freehold cottage she had occupied of old' but was now resident in the 'very house that had once been his own home. There it stood as of yore, facing up the Channel, a comfortable roomy structure, the euonymus and other shrubs, which alone would stand in the teeth of the salt wind, living on at about the same stature in front of it.' This is also the house where she dies.

Follow the path towards the *Beal*. Look out for 'the treacherous cavern known as Cave Hole, into which the sea roared and splashed now as it had done when they [Pierston and Avice I] visited it together as children'; it is to be found near the sea, just before the first two huts. Of the three lighthouses near the *Beal*, the two more northerly date from 1716. The present (tall) lighthouse came into commission 190 years later, in 1906. It is automatic and controlled from Harwich, so sadly there is no lighthouse keeper! The lower lighthouse is a bird observatory. The squat upper lighthouse, once the home of Marie Stopes, remains a holiday let.

In 1805, Anne Garland, in *The Trumpet-Major*, followed 'the central track' down the island, 'the wide sea prospect extending' on both sides, 'she approached and gazed at Portland Bill, or Beal, as it was in those days more correctly called':

> The wild, herbless, weather-worn promontory was quite a solitude, and, saving the one old lighthouse about fifty yards up the slope, scarce a mark was visible to show that humanity had ever been near the spot. Anne found herself a seat on a stone, and swept with her eyes the tremulous expanse of water around her that seemed to utter a ceaseless unintelligible incantation.

To experience, in part, that solitude in the twenty-first century, visit on a winter weekday and make your way to the obelisk, which projects above a lunar landscape whilst the waves crash around Pulpit Rock. (The large TH engraved on the obelisk stands for Trinity House.) Here Anne watches the *Victory* sail past until the ship is absorbed into the main, 'no more than a dead fly's wing on a sheet of spider's web'.

Hardy first described the treacherous waters and complicated currents of the Race in *A Pair of Blue Eyes*, as Knight and Elfride pass by on their steamer trip from London to Plymouth. He reiterated the description in *The Well-Beloved*, when Avice III and Henri are swept out to sea in their oarless ketch. Henri's flare, made of their combined handkerchiefs and his umbrella, is enough to draw the attention of the crew of the *Shambles* lightship – now redundant and replaced by an automatic buoy. Here 'the confluence of three currents makes the surface of the sea boil like a pot even in the calmest weather'. In 'The Souls of the Slain' the poet, brooding alone 'with darkness and silence' on the *Beal* at night, hears the spirits of the men slain by the Boers returning to their homes like migrating birds, using this southernmost promontory as a navigational aid (CP 62) (plate 6.8).

Head north from this exposed headland, taking the coastal path up the greensward to the west of the pub and passing to the seaward side of the Stopes's lighthouse. The next two miles (three kilometres) are straightforward cliff-top walking with fine views over Chesil Beach and along the

6.8 The *Beal*

western shore, passing on your right the Southwell Business Park and then the housing estates of Weston. Level with the northern end of these you reach a cliff-top defence converted into a dwelling; here take the footpath inland (see if you can spot the Hardy Way sign: these things spring up in the most bizarre places!). Follow the path half-left round the edge of Bowers Quarries (climb the bank to inspect this massive hole in the ground – the heart of the island is still being ripped asunder for export) and left beyond the cemetery to enter the graveyard of St George's Church, Reforne.

This wonderful building, 'the most impressive eighteenth-century church in Dorset', (3) was built in 1753 to replace the unstable St Andrew's Church above Ope Cove. Unfortunately this church too was made redundant after only 150 years to be replaced by All Saints in the centre of Easton. The original £2,100 required to build this church was raised largely by the 'sale of the right to sit in pews'; in the census of 1851, there were only 20 free sittings as opposed to 622 paid-up sittings, the result being that there was nowhere for newcomers to sit. At All Saints, the third island Anglican church at Easton, consecrated in 1917, all seats were free. St George's, in the care of the Churches Conservation Trust, is open every afternoon in the summer; its glorious interior is well worth inspection (plate 6.9).

6.9 St George's, Reforne

Pierston, on receiving the news of Avice I's death, realizes that he loves 'the woman dead and inaccessible as he never loved her in life' and speeds posthaste back to his native peninsula:

> Ascending the steep incline … he looked southward towards the Beal. The level line of the sea horizon rose above the surface of the isle, a ruffled patch in mid-distance as usual marking the Race … Against the stretch of water, where a school of mackerel twinkled in the afternoon light, was defined, in addition to the distant lighthouse, a church with its tower, standing about a quarter of a mile off, near the edge of the cliff. The churchyard gravestones could be seen in profile against the same vast spread of watery babble and unrest.
>
> Among the graves moved the form of a man clothed in a white sheet, which the wind blew and flapped coldly every now and then. Near him moved six men bearing a long box, and two or three persons in black followed. The coffin, with its twelve legs, crawled across the isle, while around and beneath it the flashing lights from the sea and the school of mackerel were reflected; a fishing-boat, far out in the Channel, being momentarily discernible under the coffin also.
>
> The procession wandered round to a particular corner, and halted, and paused there a long while in the wind, the sea behind them, the surplice of the priest still blowing. Jocelyn stood with his hat off: he was present, though he was a quarter of a mile off; and he seemed to hear the words that were being said, though nothing but the wind was audible.

Hardy is at his descriptive cinematic best on this magical island; in *The Well-Beloved*, his final completed novel, he offers the essence of his understanding of the inter-relationship between man and the natural environment.

Hardy avoids describing the church itself, although Pierston subsequently attends a service here whilst stalking Avice II, at the same time encountering Nichola Pine-Avon, who is effectively stalking him. Hardy's observation that there are only 'half-a-dozen Christian and surnames in the whole island' is readily confirmed by an inspection of the gravestones in this churchyard. Two of the most common are Pearce and Stone, which Hardy combined into the name of his protagonist; not forgetting that 'Pierre' is also the French for 'rock'.

Follow the path to the northern end of the graveyard. Note how the Grove Prison dominates the eastern skyline. **Then bear left along the path which curves back to West Cliff.** The rocky debris below is called West Weares and the bay locally known as Alleluia Bay after a certain Nuncle Hiram, who used to paint biblical texts on the cliffs. To Pierston this was *Deadman's Bay*, where the sea at night produced 'a long-drawn rattling, as of bones between huge canine jaws', and where the night winds were charged with a 'huge composite ghost' of all 'those who had gone down in vessels of war, East Indiamen, barges, brigs, and ships of the Armada' in a precursor of 'The Souls of the Slain'.

On your right several paths lead into Tout Quarry Sculpture Park, 'an international venue for art in the environment and sculpture in stone' – Pierston's twenty-first-century successors – which is rewarding to explore. Ahead is the *Street of the Wells* where Pierston, his artistic sense having left him after the severe illness precipitated by his third successive failure to marry an Avice, occupies himself in destructive good works: closing 'the old natural fountains ... because of their possible contamination, and supplying the townlet with water from pipes' and pulling down 'mullioned Elizabethan cottages' to replace them with 'new ones with hollow walls, and full of ventilators'.

Follow the path to the derrick. Here cross the main road and take the steep path up the bank opposite back to the war memorial and New Ground.

The Trumpet-Major and 'The Melancholy Hussar of the German Legion'

A Downland Walk

By foot (five miles/eight kilometres)

Heading east from Weymouth, the coastal path and highway run together past Lodmoor Nature Reserve to Preston. This is *Creston*, 'the place of safety' to which Laura Maumbury was sent to avoid the cholera whilst 'her husband was slaving in the slums' in 'A Changed Man'. Here she became acquainted with Lieutenant Vannicock, stationed at the *Budmouth* infantry barracks. **From Preston the suburban sprawl continues along the road leading due north towards Sutton Poyntz and the Downs to abruptly cease beside a tree-lined duck-laden millpond surrounded by nineteenth-century cottages:** Hardy's *Overcombe*. Kay-Robinson's detailed exposition on the *Overcombe* Mills must stand as the definitive interpretation. In summary, the Loveday's Mill in *The Trumpet-Major* was an imaginative creation combining features of both the upper and lower mills at Sutton Poyntz plus the mill at Upwey. The great pool was always here beside the Springhead but Hardy transferred it to the garden site of the upper mill, which was demolished in 1856 to make way for the Weymouth Waterworks, where the mill house alone survives (map 6.1).

> Immediately before her was the large, smooth millpond, over-full, and intruding into the hedge and into the road. The water, with its flowing leaves and spots of froth, was stealing away, like Time, under the dark arch, to

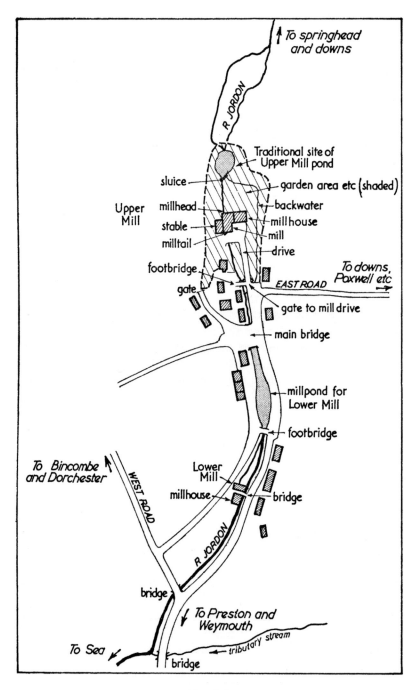

Map 6.1

tumble over the great slimy wheel within. On the other side of the mill-pond was an open place called the Cross, because it was three-quarters of one, two lanes and a cattle-drive meeting there. It was the general rendezvous and arena of the surrounding village. Behind this a steep slope rose high into the sky, merging in a wide and open down, now littered with sheep newly shorn.

From the Springhead, walk round the northern end of the millpond, the Cross, then follow the path down the west side of the pond and past the lower mill to rejoin Sutton Road. Head south, turning right into Puddledock Lane. After the farm on your right, take the footpath straight ahead along the upper boundary of two fields (ignoring the path to the right). Then turn sharply right, uphill, and follow the obvious waymarked track through downland pasture to reach a stile at Coombe Valley Road. Cross the road and follow the waymarked path ahead over a rough, steep field to pick up the South West Coast Path across a field and along an easy chalk track to Bincombe. Your tranquillity will be disturbed by the builders of the Weymouth Relief Road, determined to defy Hardy's assertion that 'Here stretch the downs, high and breezy and green, absolutely unchanged since those eventful days. A plough has never disturbed the turf, and the sod that was uppermost then is uppermost now'!

As the track descends into Bincombe to a gate under some trees, the irregular plot on your right is all that remains of Dr Grove's house and garden where Phyllis sat on the wall, awaiting Matthaus Tina in 'The Melancholy Hussar of the German Legion'. Remember Hardy's statement that, 'Phyllis told me the story with her own lips. She was then an old lady of seventy-five, and her auditor a lad of fifteen.'

Bincombe, unlike its neighbours, has managed to keep the modern world at bay; there are no hideous developments here. It remains a jewel, a tiny tranquil piece of old Dorset, with a church, farm, cottages and village square. Although half a mile (800 metres) away, the monstrous earth-movers have destroyed the downland to construct another highway to nowhere, Bincombe remains safely hidden behind its protective knoll. The church and tree-lined graveyard diffuse a true religious serenity, calming and restorative. The registers record two burials:

Matth: Tina (Corpl.) in His Majesty's Regmt. of York Hussars, and Shot for Desertion, was Buried June 30th, 1801, aged 22 years. Born in the town of Sarrbruk, Germany.
Christoph Bless, belonging to His Majesty's Regmt. of York Hussars, who was Shot for Desertion, was Buried June 30th, 1801, aged 22 years. Born at Lothaargen, Alsatia.

6.10 Bincombe – the Hussar's graves

Hardy reports that 'their graves were dug at the back of the little church, near the wall. There is no memorial to mark the spot, but Phyllis pointed it out to me', adding that 'Phyllis lies near'. Despite Hardy's assertion that the graves are unmarked, two small flat slabs of Purbeck stone to the south-east of the graveyard near the wall are believed to mark the soldiers' graves (plate 6.10). Archaeologists, however, date these stones from the twelfth century. Phyllis's last resting place cannot be identified.

From Bincombe Church retrace your steps to the stile onto Coombe Valley Road. Cross over, but now take the path on your left, round the southern side of Green Hill. Cross Plaisters Lane on an uphill diagonal to take the South West Coast Path, which is straight ahead. Admire the horned cattle though watch for the bull! Climb the ridge with the path to join the track from Came. The ruined barn to your left here could well have been the hospital barn pointed out by John Loveday in *The Trumpet-Major*.

Two hundred yards (180 metres) beyond this junction divert left to the tumulus in the middle of the field. This is the summit of East Hill (520 feet (160 metres)); on 'a clear day' with 'a little wind stirring' it is one of the best viewpoints in the county, as witnessed by Anne Garland:

The eye of any observer who cared for such things swept over the wave-washed town, and the bay beyond, and the Isle, with its pebble bank, lying on the sea to the left of these, like a great crouching animal tethered to the mainland. On the extreme east of the marine horizon, St Aldhelm's Head closed the scene, the sea to the southward of that point glaring like a mirror under the sun. Inland could be seen Badbury Rings, where a beacon had been recently erected; and nearer, Rainbarrow, on Egdon Heath, where another stood: farther to the left Bulbarrow, where there was yet another. Not far from this came Nettlecombe Tout; to the west, Dogberry Hill, and Black'on near to the foreground, the beacon thereon being built of furze faggots thatched with straw, and standing on the spot where the monument now raises its head.

In the next field turn right down the permissive path beside the right-hand boundary. Pause again to admire the view and remember Hardy's account:

Here stood the camp; here are distinct traces of the banks thrown up for the horses of the cavalry, and spots where the midden-heaps lay are still to be observed. At night, when I walk across the lonely place, it is impossible to avoid hearing, amid the scourings of the wind over the grass-bents and this-tles, the old trumpet and bugle calls, the rattle of the halters; to help seeing rows of spectral tents and the impedimenta of the soldiery. From within the canvases come guttural syllables of foreign tongues, and broken songs of the fatherland; for they were mainly regiments of the King's German Legion that slept round the tent-poles hereabout at that time.

As you descend from the Ridgeway you encounter King George III on horse-back, riding away from his troops. The once white image is now sadly grey, following a misguided restoration attempt by the television presenter Anneka Rice using grey chipstone, and in certain lights no longer visible from *Budmouth*. Towards the end of *The Trumpet-Major*, John Loveday tells Anne that men are 'cutting out a huge picture of the king on horseback in the earth of the hill. The King's head is to be as big as our mill-pond and his body as big as this garden.'

Walk down with care over carved horse and rider or take the rather irregular footpath descending to the east of the down, rejoining the well defined path through the trees at the south-western corner of the field. Follow this diagonally straight across the next field (watching out for deer) to a junction of paths in the far corner. Carry straight on towards Overcombe. The path joining from your right is the 'zigzag path down the incline from the camp to the river-head at the back of the house' built rapidly by squads of soldiers on the day the cavalry arrived. This was in order to give their horses access to the millpond where 'the thirsty animals drank, stamped, flounced, and drank again, letting the clear, cool water dribble luxuriously from their mouths'. **Your footpath becomes White Horse Lane, which joins Sutton Road, where the waterworks and old mill house are to your right, the Springhead and millpond on your left.**

Along the Ridgeway

West from Bincombe lies Upwey. Here at the junction of the Ridgeway and the straight old Roman road (the current hairpin dates from 1824) the local population (Anne Garland included) gathered to catch a glimpse of the Royal carriages on their way to *Budmouth*. The old road can still be followed; a chalky byway through the trees leading down to that original 'good inn', the Ship, where in *Under the Greenwood Tree* Dick rested his horses 'going and coming, and not troubling the Budmouth stables at all' and where on that memorable Sunday he and Fancy became engaged. Here Hardy also was inclined to break his journey:

> Sweet cyder is a great thing,
> A great thing to me,
> Spinning down to Weymouth town
> By Ridgway thirstily,
> And maid and mistress summoning
> Who tend the hostelry:
> O cyder is a great thing,
> A great thing to me! (CP 414)

Although in the poem 'Old Excursions', dated April 1913, Hardy questions 'What's the good of going to Ridgeway?' (CP 472).

Where the current Dorchester Road bridges the railway there is a clear view back to the Bincombe Tunnel in a deep cutting, probably the original model for the tunnel in *A Laodicean*, where Paula fears that Somerset has been crushed by a passing train. Upwey Station, just south from here, is the setting of 'At the Railway Station, Upway' (CP 563). A diversion into old Upwey takes you to the Mill and Wishing-Well Tearoom, a Victorian afternoon attraction, which amazingly survives in the twenty-first century. There is a Hardyan link in that Edward Prince of Wales visited the Wishing-Well after lunching at Max Gate in July 1923. In *The Trumpet-Major*, Anne Garland, returning from watching the *Victory* sail towards Trafalgar, 'turned into a little lane' and rested near 'a little spring of water, having a stone margin round it',

Here she is surprised by 'two elderly gentlemen', the King and his Physician, who have been tasting the sulphuric waters. This was Nottington Well, just south of Upwey, long-since abandoned as a health resort, although the octagonal spa house survives.

East from White Horse Hill, the Ridgeway leads to Poxwell (*Oxwell*), where Squire Derriman's manor house, depicted in the final stages of decay in *The Trumpet-Major*, is now restored to its original early seventeenth-century glory. How the miserly Derriman would have baulked at such wanton extravagance! From *Oxwell*, it is but a short walk to Warmell Cross (CP 556) (now a roundabout, its central island graced by elegant beeches). The ambush of the Revenue men in 'The Distracted Preacher' took place in the wood just north of the current junction.

'The Distracted Preacher'

A Smuggler's Walk

By foot (up to eleven miles/eighteen kilometres)

Nether-Moynton (Owermoigne) is a pleasant surprise to the uninitiated. Despite significant modern development and its proximity to the main road, it remains a beautiful, tranquil little village. The church is, as described in 'The Distracted Preacher', set higher than the adjoining gardens. In season, 'the living churchyard' is rich in wild flowers. The tower has little to show for its smuggling past since the loft, which secreted the smugglers, is securely locked. Mrs Newberry's house might have been any of the three substantial cottages in the terrace immediately adjoining the graveyard or possibly the grander thatched 'Dairy Cottage', which was her abode according to village legend. Direct access to the churchyard from any of these cottages has been obstructed by modern development along East Farm Lane. On the textual grounds of proximity to the graveyard wall, I opt for the cottage nearest to the church as most likely to be Lizzie Newberry's. Glebe Field, opposite the cottages, could well have been the orchard which housed Owlett's contraband tree. To the west of the church, the first house on the right on Hollands Mead Avenue incorporates the remains of the village smithy. The gravel track to the left (Pollards Lane) leads to the beautifully restored, thatched Chilbury Cottage, where Methodist services were held in the nineteenth century. Hardy does not state that Stockdale had his own chapel in the village, merely that 'the village was a local centre from which he was to radiate at once to the different small chapels in the neighbourhood'.

In 'The Distracted Preacher' Lizzie and her crew make two forays to the coast to land their tubs. Hardy gives clear details of both routes and it is possible to combine them in a single circular walk through some of Dorset's most spectacular coastal scenery.

Start from Lizzie's house beside the church, bear left into Kit Lane, crossing the main road to ascend Gallow's Hill opposite. Pause beside the crossing on the first hilltop (Owermoigne Down) for superb views across the Frome Valley to *Egdon* Heath with *Weatherbury* (Puddletown) prominent on your left.

Continue down through North Holworth Farm, where you lose the tarmac, up and then gently down towards the sea, passing a magnificent thatched barn below to the left to reach the South West Coast Path near Holworth House. Here bear left and pause on the cliff-top after about 200 yards (180 metres). You are on the summit of Burning Cliff, where Lizzie 'kindled a bough of furze', which ignited a bush, to warn off the waiting lugger because of the proximity of the Revenue men (plate 6.11). An irregular path leads down Burning Cliff to the beach below. At this point Stockdale, who has been stalking Lizzie, turns tail and flees home across the open country. Alternatively, by turning in an eastward direction along the coastal path, you can join the smugglers at the second night's rendezvous point and then return to *Nether-Moynton* in their company.

6.11 Burning Cliff and Ringstead Bay from White Nothe

From Holworth, the path climbs to Whitenothe cottages, once the home of the writer Llewelyn Powys. From the 'nose' itself (correct Hardyan pronunciation) there are superb views along the coast in both directions, especially over the long unspoilt curve of Ringstead (*Ringsworth*) Bay.

Follow the coastal path on its rollercoaster route towards Durdle Door. At Scratchy Bottom, below Swyre Head, which overlooks the Door, there is a typical smugglers' path to the beach down a semi-vertical slit in the chalk.

Immediately past Durdle Door (provided it is not high tide) descend the steps to Man-o'-War Beach and walk along the beach round the minor headland to St Oswald's Bay beyond. At the rocky far end of this beach 'not many hundred yards from Lulwind Cove' (the site of the successful drop on the second night) you will find a narrow path leading up a gully inland. Make your way up this public right of way, taking care as it has a tendency to erosion (plate 6.12). When a house appears on your right, turn left onto a marked footpath, which soon descends into a field, the furthermost overflow car park for Lulworth Cove. As you are not laden with 'tubs of spirits that have accidentally come over in the dark from France', this is a good point to divert for rest and refreshment – and give *Lulwind* due consideration.

6.12 The smugglers' path, St Oswald's Bay

6.13 *Lulwind Cove*

I have already referred to Hardy's detailed account of Lulworth in *Desperate Remedies* (see p.157). Troy takes a swim 'between the two projecting spurs of rock which formed the pillars of Hercules to this miniature Mediterranean' to find himself contemplating death as he is swept out to sea. In 'A Tradition of 1804' 'Bonaparty ... the Corsican ogre' lands at *Lulwind Cove* to espy the land in preparation for invasion. 'At Lulworth Cove a Century Back' (CP 556) is based on Keats's friend Joseph Severn's account of their brief anchoring at Lulworth on his route 'to Rome – to death, despair'. Hardy believed that Keats was of Dorset stock, an idea supported by Severn's statement that Keats was already familiar with the Dorset coastline. The best views of *Lulwind* are obtained from the footpath which climbs steeply to the east towards the army ranges (plate 6.13). There are fine views eastward from here towards Kimmeridge, Clavell Tower and St Alban's Head.

The return route to *Nether-Moynton* is a challenge because the smugglers deliberately struck across country in order to elude the excisemen. Therefore, this route is a close approximation, using existing trackways, not all of which are designated public rights of way.

Follow the well defined path from the Lulworth car park westward, turning right at the first gate along the field boundary, then bearing left to join the track heading uphill behind Hanbury Tout. Bear right along the waymarked path through the caravan park. At the T-junction just before the road (near 'Daggers Grave'), turn left away from the road past

Newlands Farmhouse along a field-boundary track, which gives superb views out to sea. After just over a mile, turn right at a signstone inscribed 'East Chaldon Permissive Path' along a fenced track. Follow this down to Chideock Farm, once a stronghold of the Powys clan (to your right is 'the ancient earthwork called *Round Pound*'). Take the left fork at the farm. After about 600 yards (550 metres) turn left to ascend Chaldon (*Shaldon*) Down where the tracks are better defined. You will come to a T-junction where a track leads steadily down to the road at West Chaldon (*Shaldon*); you have, as directed in the text, kept south of *East Shaldon*. From *West Shaldon* Lizzie stuck to the road, over *Lord's Barrow* to turn left along the Wareham Road before taking the footpath on the right back to *Nether-Moynton*. For the modern walker the footpath from West Chaldon to Holworth then Gallow's Hill provides a quieter alternative route.

A Walk Around Purbeck Heights and Heaven's Gate

Ethelberta and Eliza-Bright

By foot (one-and-a-half miles/two-and-a-half kilometres)

This is a short walk with several potential extensions. On a clear day, the views are probably the best in Dorset and the ideal start for an exploration of Hardy's Purbeck. **The B3069 leads from Corfe up wooded Kingston Hill. Turn right beside the heavily ivied Scott Arms (the beer house in *Little Enckworth* patronized by Julian), past the magnificent St James' Church (1880), along this narrow lane through open fields to reach 'Sheep Pens' car park in some trees on your left.**

Now on foot, continue in your original direction along the lane which soon becomes a stony track. As you climb, look behind and to your left for views over Poole Harbour and Brownsea Island with Corfe Castle dramatically poised in the foreground, and Nine Barrow Down to the east.

At the end of the third field you find yourself at Heaven's Gate on the top of Smedmore Hill (plate 6.14). The views now extend for fifteen miles (twenty-four kilometres) westward, with the sweep of Weymouth Bay curving around to Portland in the distance, the Jurassic Coast extending before you and Kimmeridge Bay at your feet. Most of the land in the middle-distance is within the MOD firing ranges and therefore beautifully conserved but inaccessible. **A right turn here along waymarked footpaths will lead you down to the bay, from where you can pick up the coastal path past Clavell Tower and along to Chapman's Pool, where a track leads back to Kingston.**

6.14 Heaven's Gate – Smedmore House, Clavell Tower
and Kimmeridge Bay

Clavell Tower, a folly dating from 1830, was recently dismantled and re-erected eighty-five feet (twenty-five metres) back from the cliff-edge to postpone that inevitable tumble into the sea (it is now converted into a holiday cottage). Hardy made a drawing of a courting couple approaching the tower at sunset to illustrate the 'She, to Him' sequence in *Wessex Poems*. The 'she' was Eliza-Bright Nicholls, who lived in coastguard's cottages as a child on the cliff beside Kimmeridge Bay. Millgate describes Eliza as 'the most important figure in Hardy's early emotional life', the couple being 'more or less formally engaged from 1863 until 1867'.

Hardy and Eliza may have originally met at Kimmeridge, but their full relationship dates from Hardy's time in London (1862–7), where Eliza was in service with the family from Smedmore Hall – the country house below your feet. Sketches by Hardy survive dated 3 September 1863 indicating at least that he visited Kimmeridge on that day with Eliza. As well as the 'She, to Him' poems (CP 14–17), here read 'The Musing Maiden' (CP 892) and 'The Wind's Prophecy' (CP 440). The latter refers to Emma replacing Eliza, or quite likely her younger sister, Mary, in Hardy's affections.

Eliza and her father, George, were major sources for Hardy's interest in the South Dorset coast and smuggling ('The Distracted Preacher'). Eliza believed that she was the model for Cytherea in *Desperate Remedies* and it seems likely that *A Pair of Blue Eyes* was originally conceived as being set on the Purbeck coast with Eliza as the heroine.

Follow the path left from Heaven's Gate to the viewpoint on the tumulus at Swyre Head for further stunning perspectives, the coast now opening up to the east. From here bear left again along an easy ridgeway track and thence beside a wood and across a field back to Sheep Pens.

The panorama before you extends across Egmont Bight towards St Aldhelm's Head. The eighteenth-century mansion in such a beautiful setting is Encombe House, the model for Lord Mountclere's *Enckworth* in *The Hand of Ethelberta*. The detailed descriptions of the house, given by Hardy, are entirely spurious, although based in part upon his knowledge of Kingston Maurward. Just north of Kimmeridge is Steeple – the *Kingscreech* of 'Old Mrs Chundle'. And between the two lies Blackmanston Farm – surely the name-source for the evil protagonist of *Desperate Remedies*? From Egmont Bight it is nearly ten miles (sixteen kilometres) along the coastal path to Swanage, where Hardy lived with Emma between July 1875 and March 1876 and where most of *The Hand of Ethelberta* was written. The approach to *Knollsea*, past Purbeck Quarrs, is round Durlston Head, from where the path opens out into the gardens above Peverill Point, that 'sinister ledge of limestones jutting from the water like crocodile's teeth'. From here, *Knollsea* appears 'a seaside village lying snug within two head-lands as between a finger and thumb'. On a clear day, the Isle of Wight is dominant ahead with Old Harry Rocks and the towers of *Sandbourne* to the north. Local poems are 'To a Sea-Cliff' (CP 768), 'The Sunshade' (CP 434) and 'Once at Swanage' (CP 753).

Head across the gardens towards the town, keeping above the car park to reach a small gate onto Seymer Road. Opposite this is Belvedere Road, an unmetalled cul-de-sac flanked by tall Georgian houses. The furthest semi-detached cottage up this lane is West End Cottage, where the Hardys lodged as guests of Captain Masters, who became Captain Flowers for Ethelberta, who stayed there also. Despite the loss to development of 'the orchard of aged trees' on the slope below the cottage, there are still clear views across the bay to Old Harry, especially from the front bedroom occupied by Hardy and Emma. Hardy, characteristically, was later to write posthumous poems recalling both 'Mrs Masters's Fuchsias' (CP 584) and his coastal walks with Emma (CP 792). A snicket, called Piggy Lane, leads from just below the cottage down to the seafront and pier, from where Ethelberta sailed for Cherbourg whilst the Hardys contented themselves with a trip around the Isle of Wight.

Corvsgate (Corfe)

A Ride With Ethelberta

By ass or foot (seven miles/eleven kilometres)

Due to economic necessity – and following biblical precedent – Ethelberta rides into *Corvsgate* (the original Saxon name for Corfe) upon a 'sad-looking' donkey in *The Hand of Ethelberta*. **Retrace her route, by following the coastal path northward from Swanage and then climbing Ballard Down to the ghostly signpost and stone seat which mark the junction with the Purbeck Way.** Pause and admire Studland Heath, that most easterly remnant of *Egdon*, Sandbanks to the north, with Swanage Bay laid out to the south.

Head west along the Purbeck Way, dipping down to cross the valley at Ulwell and then straight on over Nine Barrow Down, that 'huge cemetery of barrows', to Corfe. To your right on the top of the hill above Ulwell stands the Giant's Grave where Ethelberta stood and beheld 'two sorts of weather pervading Nature at the same time. Far below on the right hand it was a fine day, and the silver sunbeams lighted ... the broad Channel ... as fair under the sun as a New Jerusalem ...' whilst on her left it 'was dark and cloudy weather ... a zinc sky met a leaden sea ... the low wind groaned and whined, and not a bird sang'. 'The ridge along which Ethelberta rode divided these two climates like a wall.' Whilst you are unlikely to encounter such a marked dichotomy in the weather, you will find *Corvsgate Castle* very much as described by Ethelberta from its first appearance as towers rising out 'of the furthermost shoulder of the upland' onward.

Modern Corfe bears more than a passing resemblance to Dunster; both are best visited well out of season, when the besieging tourist hordes are held somewhat at bay, although then the castles are locked up and the steam railway, which is the best way of returning to Swanage, out of service. It is likely that Corfe was the original model for *Castle de Stancy* in *A Laodicean*, anticipating the ruined state caused by the fire, and the Bankes family are the model for the de Stancys (pp.146–7). Hardy both anticipates and parodies the Thomas Hardy Society in his description of the meeting of the Imperial Archaeological Association at *Corvsgate* where Dr Yore delivers his paper:

> ... under the dozens of bright eyes that were there converged upon him, like the sticks of a fan, from the ladies who sat round him in a semicircle upon the grass. However, he went on calmly, and the women sheltered themselves from the heat with their umbrellas and sunshades, their ears lulled by the hum of insects, and by the drone of the doctor's voice.

The lecturer renders an accurate potted history of the castle, but an account which he increasingly romanticizes, permitting him the opportunity to look deeply into 'those fair concentrated eyes, when the sunshades were thrown back, and complexions forgotten – in the interest of the history'! The castle built by William the Conqueror in 'an extraordinary natural position' on a mound in a cleft in the Purbeck Hills – and as such the first secular masonry structure in Dorset – remains remarkably unchanged since being 'slighted' by the Puritan forces in 1646. Over this dramatic, romantic ruin, the worlds of Thomas Hardy and Enid Blyton touch hands (plate 6.15) (Blyton holidayed in Purbeck up to three times a year from 1931 to the 1960s and Corfe Castle appears as Kirrin Castle in the *Famous Five* books).

If you follow Ethelberta's 'ascent on foot' to the top of the mound, you will be greeted by the descendants of 'the tribe of daws' who peered invidiously upon her. Admire the fine views to the north as far as Win Green in Wiltshire and to the south over Corfe towards wooded Kingston Hill, both dominated by disproportionately large Victorian churches. The railway line and station demarcate the eastern boundary of Corfe; the Castle Inn in East Street remains much as it was when Picotee and Julian waited there for Sol.

6.15 *Corvsgate Castle*

Havenpool (Poole)

'To Please His Wife' is set in *Havenpool* (Poole), which has altered considerably even since Kay-Robinson wrote about it. The town hall from which Jolliffe escorted Emily home survives unscathed as the Guildhall (1761), with its distinctive external steps, at the top of Market Street. Head from here down towards St James Church, which is where the story begins; these streets form a tranquil oasis amidst a bustling twenty-first-century shopping centre. This maritime church (1821), where Joliffe came to offer a prayer of thanksgiving for deliverance from shipwreck, is unaltered since Hardy's time except in terms of access; it is permanently locked, admission only being granted by the church office 9.30 a.m.–1 p.m. Tuesday–Friday. So if you wish to admire its pillars made from Newfoundland timber and find the names of the four protagonists on the church walls, make sure you plan well in advance!

The church stands in an enclave of Georgian Mansions. Nos 7–11 Thames Street (currently the Hotel du Vin), former home of the real-life Lesters, is probably as near as you can get to finding Emily's marital home. To the north-east of the church, St James House offers a viable alternative and does have the advantage of being 'nearly opposite' (down an alleyway) a much more humble abode, Lower House, which would serve for Joanna's house and shop. When indoors, Joanna's hopes were raised by hearing 'a shout or excitement ... at the corner of the Town Cellar'; these are at least within earshot, to be found lower down Thames Street. In the story, 'the worthy merchant's home' is a 'substantial brick mansion' 'faced directly on the High Street'; this has led to it being identified with No. 100 (now Barclays Bank, long ago rebuilt in Ashlar Stone). I recommend avoiding the High Street, except perhaps to visit No. 14: 'Hardy's Restaurant'!

'The Sailor's Mother' (CP 625) is a poetic rendition of the ending of 'To Please His Wife'. The 'paved wharf-side' of *Havenpool* is the setting for that heart-rending poem 'The Mongrel' (CP 861).

Sandbourne (Bournemouth)

Sandbourne is best remembered as the setting for that poem of early marital disharmony 'We Sat at the Window (Bournemouth 1875)' (CP 355). Although one or two brave people claim to have positively identified 'The Herons' – the guest-house where Tess slaughtered Alec in *Tess of the D'Urbervilles* – with minimal information provided by Hardy and the exponential growth of this town of shifting population, such identification is not truly possible (p.19). In her flight from the murder scene, Tess caught up with Angel somewhere west of the main station on an open highway which 'dipped into a valley' i.e. in the Talbot Woods/Wither Moor area, just south of the current university and now entirely built over. From here, it is a fifteen-mile (twenty-four-kilometre) walk to 'that old brick building' within a wooded glade 'behind a brook and a bridge': Moyles Court (*Bramshurst Manor*). 'Their footpath which had taken them into the depths of the New Forest', north-east of Ringwood, is today part of the Avon Valley Way, which conveniently continues from Moyles Court to Salisbury! 'Throwing a Tree' (CP 837) is set in the *Great* (New) *Forest*.

'An Imaginative Woman' in *Solentsea* (Southsea)

On 19 July 1893, Hardy visited Florence Henniker in Southsea, where she was living whilst her husband was stationed in Portsmouth. These were the intense early days of their friendship. On 14 September 1893, Hardy sent the manuscript of 'An Imaginative Woman' to his publisher: the story of a romance that never was between a published poet and an 'impressionable palpitating' young married woman with literary ambitions of her own. The story is set in *Solentsea*. Beyond this, facts are few: it has proved impossible to identify where the Hennikers lived in Southsea or the exact location of *Coburg House* which Ella Marchmill rented and the railway extension to Southsea which Hardy carefully added in red crayon to his map of Hampshire was 'Beechinged' long ago. Despite these drawbacks, I would still recommend a visit to the esplanade at Southsea; the front has a certain genteel tranquillity, absent from its larger and more boisterous neighbour.

The South Parade Pier is a Victorian gem; the Isle of Wight is a mere stone's throw away, the Ryde is spread out in front of you and the obelisk on Culver Down clearly visible. Ella catches a steamer from the pier to the *Island* in search of the elusive Robert Trewe (called in the manuscript Crewe, the maiden name of Mrs Henniker's mother). As to *Coburg House*, it 'stood in a terrace facing the sea, and was fronted by a small garden of wind-proof and salt-proof evergreens, stone steps leading up to a porch'. The most likely candidate is a smart brick-built house called St Helens, facing the sea, a short distance east of the pier. Three poems relating to Florence Henniker are 'At an Inn' (CP 45), 'A Broken Appointment' (CP 99) and 'The Division' (CP 169).

The Sussex Connection

A walk from Tolmare to Nepcote

By foot (one-and-a-half miles/two-and-a-half kilometres)

In January 1867, Hardy's relationship with Eliza Nicholls finally disintegrated. He had given her a ring and a portrait of himself, both of which she treasured for the rest of her life; whatever Hardy's thoughts, Eliza had regarded herself as engaged to be married. As far as can be surmised from the available evidence, their separation, which was in part the result of Hardy's infatuation with Eliza's younger sister, Mary, occurred beside Tolmare Pond at the top of Longfurlong. Until the advent of the motor car, this was a beautiful wild valley sweeping through the downland escarpment to the north of Worthing. **Today Tolmare sits beside a bend in the busy A280 at the point where it is crossed by Honeysuckle Lane, an ancient drover's track. This is the starting point of the walk.**

Tolmare was a large dew pond beside ancient lime kilns. Sadly, it was damaged by a tank during the Second World War and subsequently finished off by a farmer in the 1950s; it is now a rubble-filled, overgrown pit (plate 6.16). Car parking is available beside the pond, which is on the Monarch's Way.

6.16 Tolmare Pond (2008)

Neutral Tones

We stood by a pond that winter day,
And the sun was white, as though chidden of God,
And a few leaves lay on the starving sod;
– They had fallen from an ash, and were grey.

Your eyes on me were as eyes that rove
Over tedious riddles of years ago;
And some words played between us to and fro
On which lost the more by our love.

The smile on your mouth was the deadest thing
Alive enough to have strength to die;
And a grin of bitterness swept thereby
Like an ominous bird a-wing. . . .

Since then, keen lessons that love deceives,
And wrings with wrong, have shaped to me
Your face, and the God-curst sun, and a tree,
And a pond edged with grayish leaves.

1867 (CP 9)

The pond still boasts a solitary ash tree.

Cross the road to take the middle path of the three on offer, diagonally right across a field to a stile. Follow the path downhill across irregular horse pasture to a further stile and onto a fenced path. The group of buildings diagonally across the field on your left constitute what is currently called the 'Huntsman's Dog and Cat Hotel'. In the nineteenth century 'great pieces of horseflesh' used to be hung here on a gibbet prior to being fed to the hounds, for these kennels were then the home of the local fox hounds. Hardy would have seen this macabre site, which is thought to be the source of the episode where Ethelberta encounters 'horses' skulls, ribs, quarters, legs, and other joints' suspended to form an offensive 'huge open-air larder', beside which stood 'numerous horses in the last stage of decrepitude', accompanied by the 'stygian howl' of a hundred confined hounds in *The Hand of Ethelberta*.

The path descends beside a wood to reach Findon Church. Hardy's sketches of Findon indicate that he was here in 1863, whilst his drawing of the church is dated Whitsun 1866. Just inside the churchyard to the right of the path is a curved red marble tombstone beneath which are buried three sisters, Eliza, Mary and Olive Nicholls, alongside their parents.

From the church, continue down the drive past Findon Place. Cross the dual carriageway with caution. Follow the track straight opposite to the High Street, then bear right then left up Steep Lane to emerge at Nepcote Green. The smart white house with blue shutters to the right of the green is the former Running Horse Inn (a skittle alley is still visible to the left of the house). Here George Nicholls settled in 1862, having been invalided out of the Coastguards. It was a lucrative living because the green was the site of a major annual downland sheep fair, which still survives in truncated form. Eliza, who continued to live at Nepcote with her widowed father, called on Hardy at Max Gate in 1913 in the hope that, after Emma's death, her long devotion might be rewarded. Having agreed to the visit, Hardy informed her on arrival that he was intending to marry Florence Dugdale, nearly forty years his junior. Eliza died in 1918, unmarried and still faithful to Hardy.

Emma and Florence in Worthing

Well into the twentieth century Worthing remained a small seaside town; its boundaries have since spread exponentially, engulfing Findon Valley and rendering Nepcote effectively a suburb of Worthing. Hardy and Emma spent the first night of their honeymoon in nearby Brighton. Once established at Max Gate, they were both in the habit of taking holidays on the Sussex coast to enjoy the benefits of 'the Sussex air'. As part of her policy of 'keeping separate', Emma increasingly stayed in Sussex alone; she seems to have particularly favoured Worthing. It was from Worthing in February 1893 that Emma sent her damning, paranoid epistle to Mary Hardy.

In July 1911, Emma spent two weeks in Worthing accompanied by Florence Dugdale whom she regarded in all innocence as her friend, completely unaware of any duplicity on Florence's part. They stayed in lodgings at 5 New Parade, a late Victorian terrace well preserved to this day. A postcard survives sent by Florence to Mary Hardy, describing how she daily crossed the promenade wall in her 'bathing dress' to reach the sea. New Parade can be found a quarter of a mile (400 metres) to the east of the pier, beyond Denton Gardens. Worthing Pier is worthy of inspection, for it still shows the signs of its original use as an embarkation point for the passenger ferries which used to ply their way along the English coast from seaside town to seaside town. In August 1872 Hardy travelled from London to Plymouth by steamer, an experience which, under the pressure of writing to serial deadlines, he rapidly recycled into the text of A Pair of Blue Eyes.

Review: Hardy's southern coastal landscape, encompassing some of the most spectacular and beautiful scenery in England, extends for a distance of 105 miles (169 kilometres) from Bridport in the west to Worthing in the east, involving in the process the text of eleven out of his fourteen novels (all except *Two on a Tower*, *The Woodlanders* and *Jude the Obscure*), eight short stories, *The Dynasts* and many poems. Along this coast, Hardy's cinematic technique is frequently in evidence; his descriptions start with a bird's-eye view of hills, coasts and homesteads and then focus sharply in on a particular scene and a particular character within that scene, the observer often remaining detached, watching from a window, over a hedge or through a gap in a fence. My text explores the coastal landscape through a dozen separate walks, ranging from one to eleven miles (one-and-a-half to eighteen kilometres) in length, in places highlighting Hardy's 'immediately recoverable past', most prominently in *Trumpet-Major* country; in places, especially on Purbeck, focussing on the beauty and wildness of the coastal scenery; and elsewhere, most particularly in *Budmouth* and Findon, looking predominantly at autobiographical factors.

CHAPTER SEVEN

Moving North

WHEN HARDY MOVED into Max Gate on 29 June 1885, he had published nine novels and was well on the way to completing his tenth, *The Mayor of Casterbridge*. Of these ten novels, all but two were set in or around *Egdon Heath*, Dorchester and the nearby Dorset Coast, in other words, the territory of Hardy's own childhood. The two exceptions are *A Pair of Blue Eyes*, based upon his Cornish courtship of Emma, and *A Laodicean*, set ostensibly in north-western Somerset. During that first decade at Max Gate, Hardy wrote his final four novels, moving south to the *Isle of Slingers* for *The Well-Beloved*, but travelling northward for his three more substantive texts. For *The Woodlanders* and *Tess of the D'Urbervilles* this was into the Vale of Blackmoor, the landscape of his mother's childhood and home territory for many generations of maternal ancestors. The restless, peripatetic *Jude the Obscure* begins at the Berkshire home of Hardy's paternal grandmother, Mary, but ends in the Midland city of *Christminster*, which Hardy set just north of the outer boundary of Wessex on the map of his 'part real part dream country'. The established, middle-aged novelist settled in his own substantial Victorian 'Villa' allowed his imagination to expand northward into the magical fertile country beyond the inhospitable hostile chalk downs which engirdled *Casterbridge*, *Egdon* and the Channel Coast.

To a significant extent Blackmoor Vale, like Wessex itself, appears to be Hardy's own construct; if nothing else, he certainly expanded and redefined its boundaries. Historically, Blackmoor was a Norman hunting ground. The name does not appear at all on nineteenth-century Ordnance Survey maps but has been consistently present on them ever since the publication of the definitive Wessex edition of Hardy's novels. The dialect poet William Barnes was born near Sturminster Newton and is now referred to as being from Blackmoor Vale. But the research trail invariably leads back to Hardy and his much-quoted definition from *Tess of the D'Urbervilles*:

This fertile and sheltered tract of country, in which the fields are never brown and the springs never dry, is bounded on the south by the bold chalk ridge that embraces the prominences of Hambledon Hill, Bulbarrow, Nettlecombe-Tout, Dogbury, High Stoy, and Bubb Down. The traveller from the coast, who, after plodding northward for a score of miles over calcareous downs and corn-lands, suddenly reaches the verge of one of these escarpments, is surprised and delighted to behold, extended like a map beneath him, a country differing absolutely from that which he has passed through. Behind him the hills are open, the sun blazes down upon fields so large as to give an unenclosed character to the landscape, the lanes are white, the hedges low and plashed, the atmosphere colourless. Here, in the valley, the world seems to be constructed upon a smaller and more delicate scale ...

This is Hardy's *Valley of the Little Dairies*, in former times the *Forest of White Hart*. Until recently it was a densely wooded country, where the medieval customs of the Green Man and his companions survived well into the nineteenth century. Lea defined these woodlands as 'a region inhabited by simple-minded people, where many old-fashioned ideas and superstitions still linger'. (1) Whilst Hardy wove the latter into his fiction, he could hardly have seen his mother as an example of the former.

The Woodlanders

The Woodlanders presents special problems to the student of Hardyan landscapes, for not only does one, as usual, have to balance Hardy's caution that 'it is an imaginative Wessex only' against his very clear descriptions of real places, but here, uniquely, he deliberately set out to obscure the evidence by subtly altering the location of the *Hintocks* with each revised edition. The end result is something of a muddle, for although *Great Hintock* has been moved from Melbury Osmund five-and-a-half miles (nine kilometres) south-east to Minterne Magna, much of the text still describes the former village and does not fit the latter, and *Little Hintock* has become lost in the process. In 1926 Hardy replied to a letter from Arthur Hind, who had made the not unreasonable assumption the Minterne Parva was now *Little Hintock*, by 'saying that I myself do not know where "Little Hintock" is! It has features which were to be found fifty years ago in the hamlets of Hermitage, Middlemarsh, Lyons-Gate, Revels Inn, Holnest, Melbury Bubb etc.' Hardy had moved the setting from the woodland region of the Melburys, through which passes the A37, that 'coach-road running almost in a meridional line from Bristol to the south shore of England', to the area around High Stoy Hill, which is skirted by that lesser highway, the A352.

On Hardy's list, last but not least is Melbury Bubb, the only place mentioned not within the vicinity of High Stoy because it lies immediately below the Wessex Height that forms the nodal point for the action of *The Woodlanders*, as it was originally conceived. Here Bubb Down, or as Hardy calls it *Rubdon* or *Rub-Down Hill*, stands 685 feet (210 metres) above sea level; it is 150 feet (forty-five metres) short of High Stoy but has a commanding viewpoint over the Melburys and Blackmoor Vale to the north. It is also the lonely spot where 'the forsaken coach-road' bisects the woods 'as the head of thick hair is bisected by the white line of its parting'. In later editions, Hardy gradually excised 'Rubdon' in favour of 'High-Stoy', passing through a transitional phase where the text read 'High-Stoy or Rubdon Hill'. In *Tess of the D'Urbervilles*, Hardy refers to Bubb Down by its real name, as in the description of Blackmoor Vale, cited above. *Quelle confusion!* Indeed, Ralph Pite has suggested in his biography of Hardy that Hardy was trying to portray elusiveness by means of confused geography! In order to make sense of 'the part real part imagined' landscape of *The Woodlanders*, it is best to stick to the text of the first edition (readily available in the *Penguin Classics* series) and that is what I shall do here. In this context Melbury Bubb is as near as one can get to *Little Hintock*, and Melbury Osmund, *Great Hintock*.

This raises the question, why was it necessary for Hardy to move the setting of *The Woodlanders* eastward, particularly because of his emotional attachment to the Melburys area, long the home of his maternal ancestors? The answer must be to avoid giving offence to the Ilchester family, owners of Melbury House and estate and much of the surrounding woodlands. Whilst the position of *Hintock House* and its immediate environs was undoubtedly that of Melbury House, the description of the building is wholly based on the now-demolished Turnworth House, many miles to the north-east near Blandford. Initially, *The Woodlanders* does not appear to have caused offence; in other words, the Ilchesters were not concerned that people might link Felice Charmond with themselves. However, when 'The First Countess of Wessex' appeared with illustrations in December 1889, there was no doubt that *King's Hintock Court* was also Melbury House. Hardy records that the Earl of Ilchester was angry that Hardy had had the audacity to put 'a legend of his family' into a book. Apocryphal stories tell that the Earl banned all Hardy's books from his house, even searching the servants' bedrooms for copies, and held a bonfire of them in the stable yard! I suspect that *A Group of Noble Dames* hit such a raw nerve at Melbury House because Hardy's mother had been raised on parish relief nearby and had been in service with the Ilchester family up until her marriage. If the living of Stinsford had not been in the Ilchesters' patronage, Jemima would have never gone there to work (for the Earl's brother-in-law) and would never have met Thomas Hardy II.

From Hardy's viewpoint, why did this noble disapproval cause him such concern that he set about rewriting (and in the process obscuring and confusing) the text of the novel which he regarded as his personal favourite? Why in this instance and no other? The answer, I believe, is because he did not wish to risk causing any further offence to the Ilchesters who were then (and remain now) the owners of Puddletown Heath, which surrounds the cottage in which his elderly parents were both then still living. Hardy's reference to the Earl's anger occurs in a footnote to a letter dated 21 December 1905, in which he comments on this, the fifth, Earl's recent demise. Relations between Hardy and the Ilchesters rapidly improved from then on; Hardy and Florence both dined and stayed at Melbury House on several occasions and in the twenty-first century the Ilchesters are proud of the association between their estate and the great Wessex novelist.

A *Woodlanders* Walk

Melbury Bubb to *Hintock* Park

By foot (seven miles/eleven kilometres)

The best way to get a true feel of *The Woodlanders* country is on foot. At any time of year it is a rewarding venture through beautiful countryside, and generally easy going. Start from the common at Evershot, the green at the bottom of East Hill (Holywell turning off the A37), where an ancient stone seat is shaded by an enormous holm oak.

Head north up Park Lane, bearing right where the road divides beside the tall Scot's Pine. Follow this track up and over the hill. As you descend, there are clear views of the wooded Bubb Down straight ahead. If a breeze is up, notice how the conifers in the plantation beyond the meadow on your right sigh, just as Marty South observes in 'The Pine Planters' (CP 225).

At the next division in the bridleway, again turn right, signposted A37. (A short diversion down the bridleway to the left will give you a view of Lucerne Lake, the largest in the park.) Follow the bridleway uphill beside Hazel Wood; then from the top corner of the wood continue at the same angle left across the field to the gate into the coppice. Pause at the gate and look back at *Hintock House* in its wooded glen; this is a hollow but not the deep, damp hole (of Turnworth) described by Grace on her visit to Mrs Charmond. You are joining the road by 'that obscure gate to the east' through which Charles Phelipson made off with Betty Dornell, later to become 'The First Countess of Wessex'. Sadly the late nineteenth-century boom in rail

travel did not persist and the A37 today bespeaks noise, danger and environmental disaster rather than the 'tomb-like stillness' of 'the deserted highway'
described on the first page of *The Woodlanders*.

**Cross this rat-run and take the bridleway opposite up through the wood,
turning left after a short distance along a contouring track through coppice.
Follow this for 600 yards (550 metres) until you meet another bridleway
at a T-junction. Turn left down to a wooden barrier, then right onto a
woodland track, to reach a gate into a large sloping meadow with a prominent trig point near its lower end.** The route should be easy to follow, despite
this being the wood where Grace and Felice spent the night huddled together
after becoming hopelessly lost, but if you happen to accidentally divert to the
upper edge of Bubb Down Wood, you will be rewarded by an aerial picture of
the hamlet of Melbury Bubb with extensive views over Blackmoor Vale
beyond (plate 7.1). At the field gate, you are rewarded on a clear day by a
similar magnificent panorama to the north and east; it was here that Grace
Melbury discovered her infatuated husband:

> … leaning over a gate on Rub-Down Hill … which opened on the brink of a
> steep, slanting down directly into Blackmoor Vale, or the Vale of the White
> Hart, extending beneath the eye at this point to a distance of many miles. His
> attention was fixed on the landscape far away, and Grace's approach was so
> noiseless that he did not hear her. When she came close she could see his lips
> moving unconsciously, as to some impassioned visionary theme.

Dr Fitzpiers disappears 'into the gorgeous autumn landscape' in pursuit of
Felice Charmond, to be replaced by Giles Winterbourne who:

> looked and smelt like Autumn's very brother, his face being sunburnt to
> wheat-colour, his eyes blue as corn-flowers, his boots and leggings dyed with
> fruit-stains, his hands clammy with the sweet juice of apples, his hat sprin-
> kled with pips, and everywhere about him that atmosphere of cider which at
> its first return each season has such an indescribable fascination for those
> who have been born and bred among the orchards…. Nature was bountiful,
> she thought. No sooner had she been starved off by Edred Fitzpiers than
> another being, impersonating bare and undiluted manliness, had arisen out
> of the earth, ready to hand.

**From the field gate, head straight down the slope, passing to the right of
the trig point, and then bear right beside the hedge and through a gate,
and follow the curving track downhill through two further gates and the
farmyard.** Behind the wall on your right is the Jacobean manor house and

7.1 George Melbury's house, *Little Hintock*

beside it the church, originally Saxon but wholly rebuilt in 1854 – the First World War memorial tablet inside (showing two dead) bears testimony to the limited population of this tiny parish. The church tower nestles neatly against the hillside, but look in vain for Dr Fitzpiers house on the slope behind, that 'comparatively modern' dwelling with its neat regular garden. The most likely candidate for Fitzpiers' lodging is the extended brick house on the corner of the lane just below the churchyard.

Retrace your steps from the church to admire the manor house. This is the model for the Melburys' home which lay at the 'end of Hintock Lane' and was roomy enough for the timber dealer to be able to set aside a disused wing for the exclusive occupation of Grace and Fitzpiers on return from their honeymoon, including a 'ground-floor room, with an independent outer door, fitted up as a surgery'. This house 'had, without doubt, been once the manorial residence appertaining to the snug and modest domain of Little Hintock', a house 'of no marked antiquity, yet of well-advanced age; older than a stale novelty, but no canonized antique; faded, not hoary; looking at you from the still distinct middle-distance of the early Georgian time'.

Further retrace your steps back through the farmyard. Survey the remains of the 'wagon-sheds' and 'many rambling out-houses' which surrounded 'Mr. Melbury's homestead'. **Continue all the way back to the trig point.** The extensive wood which encloses this pasture is the site of the revels on 'old Midsummer eve' when the girls 'attempt some spell or enchantment which would afford them a glimpse of their future partners for life'.

From the trig point follow the faint path across the meadow to your left. You will suddenly find yourself at the top of two steep terraced declivities of alpine gradient; here pick up the curving track which leads to a gate at the lower left corner of this surprising field. For ease of passage, go through the gate and follow the track through Stock Wood – still appropriately stocked with game – and across a cow pasture to reach Church Farm, Stockwood. Alternatively, to adhere to public rights of way, turn left at the gate to find a stile hidden in the far left corner of the field; follow this narrow, slippery and rather overgrown path down through marshy coppice, then ahead across a meadow to turn left onto a track.

This is another idyllic spot with the house and tiny St Edwold's church, tucked in below the wooded slopes of Bubb Down. Stockwood (originally Stoke-St-Edwold) is championed by some as *Little Hintock*. However, whilst the house and yard could be Mr Melbury's, there is nothing else there apart from the smallest church in Dorset, which is almost attached to the house; there is no village of woodlanders. And it is far too accessible, being five minutes' walk straight off the A37. In the search for *Little Hintock*, the church is actually a disadvantage, for in the novel only *Great Hintock* is so endowed.

Cross the brick bridge into the meadow and follow the farm drive to the road, here turn right and then take the signposted path over the stile in the hedge on your left. Follow the field boundary hedge on your right to another stile, cross this and now follow the left-hand field boundary. The farm to your right is Manor Farm, where Jemima Hardy lived with her mother and siblings after their father's death. When you reach a further stile in the hedge on your left, cross it and bear diagonally left across the next field to paired stiles separating a carefully netted collapsing bridge over a stream. Bear diagonally left across this final field to a gate in the far corner beside the Rest and Welcome Inn. Kay-Robinson postulates this as the 'little inn' of 'Interlopers at the Knap'; it is an old hostelry on this former Roman road and a good point to stop for refreshment.

From the pub, cross the road and, still heading north, turn left over a stile in the hedge at the footpath signpost. Follow along the left-hand hedge until you cross a line of oak trees, signifying an old field boundary. From this point bear very slightly right across this long field to a gate beside a cottage garden at its farthest right corner. From here turn right onto a concrete track and then left along the lane, over the bridge and uphill, past thatched cottages, towards the church. Jemima Hardy was born in the thatched house on your left at the top of the hill (1 Barton Hill Cottages).

Past the cottage is an old red telephone box, beyond this turn left across the gravelled drive to enter the churchyard. This is the church of *Great Hintock*, 'standing at the upper part of the village, and which could be reached without passing through the street'. Here Grace and Fitzpiers were married to the sound of 'the three thin-toned Hintock bells', here Melbury visited the grave of John Winterbourne, and subsequently Marty and Grace made regular pilgrimages to the grave of his son Giles, until eventually Grace deserted the dead for the living and Marty was left to eulogize alone:

> 'Now, my own, own love,' she whispered, 'you are mine, and on'y mine; for she has forgot 'ee at last, although for her you died. But I – whenever I get up I'll think of 'ee, and whenever I lie down I'll think of 'ee. Whenever I plant the young larches I'll think that none can plant as you planted; and whenever I split a gad, and whenever I turn the cider-wring, I'll say none could do it like you. If ever I forget your name, let me forget home and Heaven! – But no, no, my love, I never can forget 'ee; for you was a GOOD man, and did good things!'

On the wall to your left as you enter the church is a copy of Hardy's parents' marriage certificate with an accompanying notice stating that his grandmother, Elizabeth Swetman, was married there also. Note the adjoining Roll of Honour, headed by the Earl of Ilchester. As you leave the churchyard by the southern gate, observe the Childs grave on your right; Hardy's maternal great-grandmother was a Childs, another long-established Melbury family.

Follow the street straight ahead. It is composed of a series of delightful stone houses, many with thatched roofs set at irregular angles, and it curves gently down to a causeway beside the water-splash. On your right you pass Manor Farm Cottage, which equates with 'The Knap' (its sycamore replaced by a linden), the home of Sally Hall and her mother in the story loosely based upon Hardy's father's journey to Melbury Osmund to marry Jemima, 'Interlopers at the Knap'. **Ascend the hill and follow the lane as it curves into the hamlet of Townsend.** A fine thatched house with 'windows mullioned in the Elizabethan manner' appears on your left; it is now known as Monmouth's Cottage in recognition of Hardy's 'The Duke's Reappearance', which was set here and based on a Hardy family tradition involving a real ancestor, Christopher Swetman.

In the more recent past, his descendant, John Swetman, disowned his daughter Betty (Hardy's maternal grandmother) on her marrying a labourer from Affpiddle, George Hand, 'a wight often weak at the knee / From taking o' sommat more cheerful than tea' (CP 48). Having sired seven children by Betty, George 'died of his convivialities', leaving his family to seek poor relief; thus giving Jemima and her siblings a very tough start in life. Her brothers, as they grew up, went the same way as their father, and Jemima may well have passed this genetic propensity onto her son Thomas, in whom it re-emerged as a creative cyclothymic tendency. Betty's insistence that George be buried alongside his mistress is the source of the poem 'Her Late Husband' (CP 134).

Don't take the hedge-enshrouded path beside the cottage but follow the lane round to Clammers Gate – the north entrance to Felice Charmond's estate. The route now lies straight ahead through undulating parkland, containing many magnificent specimen trees. The wood to your right as you approach the second cattle grid is Great High Wood, within which is 'The Circle', the place where Melbury had the appointment with Mrs Charmond's steward that prevented him from fetching Grace from *Sherton* on the day of her much anticipated return home in *The Woodlanders*.

Before long you are confronted by the grand façade of *Hintock House*. The presenting late seventeenth-century front has the feel of a French chateau, but this is overtopped by a magnificent Tudor hexagonal tower, which was the original core of the house (plate 7.2). The fifth Earl (who disapproved of Hardy) constructed a massive Victorian extension to the west, the presenting

7.2 Hintock House

battlements, turrets and archway of which are of a stone now beautifully mellowed by time to match the rest of this palatial residence. Melbury House has been the home of the Strangways family, the Earls of Ilchester, since 1500. Here dwelt Betty Dornell, 'The First Countess of Wessex', and 'the little figured frock in which she had been married at the tender age of thirteen' is still preserved at the house, just as described by Hardy. The cruciform church of Melbury Sampford to the east of the house lost its parishioners with the enclosure of the deer park in 1546 and is accessible only by permission; within it is a memorial to Stephen Fox, the Stephen Reynard of Hardy's story.

Follow the drive to the right of the house and into the deer park. The small lake on your right is fed from the marshy wood beyond known as Stutcombe Bottom. This is *Tutcombe Bottom*, from where George Melbury carried home a pollard 'unassisted', resulting in a pain in his 'left shoulder'. This is also the scene of the barking operations and subsequent story-telling round the fire 'of white witches and black witches; and of the spirits of the two brothers who had fought and fallen, and had haunted *Hintock House* till they were exorcised by the priest, and compelled to retreat to a swamp in this very wood, whence they were returning to their old quarters at the rate of a cock's stride every New-year's Day, old style'. On the near edge of this wood grows a massive ancient oak tree 'Billy Wilkins', believed to be 400 years old, and described in *The Woodlanders* as 'Great Willy, the largest oak in the wood'.

Over the hill beyond Stutcombe are the small villages of East and West Chelborough. Hardy gives an accurate description of Grace's flight over the hilltop, across the park and through the woods beyond – a distance of 'between three and four miles' (five and seven kilometres) – to reach Giles's one-storey cot, 'formerly the home of a charcoal-burner' at *Delborough*, and of her return journey to fetch Dr Fitzpiers, passing back 'over Rubdon Hill' to descend to *Little Hintock. Delborough* (East Chelborough) is less wooded than in Hardy's time and there is no evidence that a 'One-Chimney Hut' ever existed, so there is little point in pursuing Grace westward.

Climb the hill through the deer park. Pause to look at the view behind you of Melbury Lake and the church (from here also the house is set in a depression), and perhaps to read 'Autumn in King's Hintock Park' (CP 163). As you leave by the magnificent Lion Gate, you have just traversed in reverse the route taken by the enigmatic stranger in 'The Duke's Reappearance'. **A short walk downhill brings you back to the common at Evershead (Evershot).**

Flintcomb-Ash

Prior to Lea's *Thomas Hardy's Wessex*, Flintcomb-Ash in *Tess of the D'Urbervilles* was generally understood to be Dole's Ash Farm on the ridge to the east of Piddletrenthide. Dole's Hill itself, at the further end of Puddletown Down, overlooks Bathsheba's farm and therefore nicely fits my theory about the centripetal tendency of Hardy's topography. But this is his later fiction: he is expanding northward. Dole's Ash is not in the 'middle of the cretaceous table-land', it is not a village and no-way can it then or now have been properly described as 'a starve-acre place' – the soil is far too rich, the trees lush and the slopes gentle.

Hardy's description of Tess's nocturnal journeys suggest that *Flintcomb-Ash* is Plush, a hamlet wedged in a crevice between steep downs. Although impoverished in the nineteenth century, if visited today in summer sunshine 'Plush' seems the most appropriate epithet, with its brace of pheasants on display over the door of the pub beneath a green wooded hillside with buzzards cruising lazily overhead. But explore the farm in winter, by following the Wessex Ridgeway from Ball Hill to Barcombe, and 300 feet (ninety metres) above the village on the crest of the arid open down, muddy treeless plough as far as the

7.3 'That starve-acre place' – *Flintcomb-Ash*

eye can see, you are exposed to driving rain and biting wind which takes your breath away. You will see 'a stretch of a hundred odd acres, in one patch, on the highest ground of the farm, rising above stony lanchets or lynchets'; this is 'the swede-field in which Tess and her companion were set hacking' (plate 7.3). This is Alton Pancras Parish, known for its immense fields which are a rarity in Dorset, and called *Alton-Ash* by Hardy in the serial version of *Tess of the D'Urbervilles*. Here, as Marian observes, 'you can see a gleam of a hill within a few miles o' Froom Valley – when 'tis fine'.

On first arriving at *Flintcomb-Ash*, Tess shelters against the wall of a cottage 'whose gable jutted into the road'. 'The wall felt warm to her back and shoulders, and she found that immediately within the gable was the cottage fireplace, the heat of which came through the bricks.' Entering Plush, you first encounter the pub, from where the through road turns down to the stream, beside which a cottage projects awkwardly into the road, its fireplace still against that outer wall. Here at Corner Cottage, Tess found lodgings.

From *Flintcomb-Ash* (Plush) to *Emminster* (Beaminster)

Tess on Foot

By foot, bicycle or car (eighteen miles/twenty-nine kilometres)

Hardy gives a clear and detailed account of Tess's walk to *Emminster* (Beaminster) and back so that it is possible to follow her route with certainty. Tess rose at 3 a.m. because the distance was 'fifteen miles each way'; in reality it is nearly eighteen miles (twenty-nine kilometres), so if you fancy a (rewarding) thirty-six mile (fifty-eight kilometres) round trip start early, take your mountain bike, or, I concede, this is a route which can mainly be followed by car.

From *Flintcomb-Ash* (Plush), take the bridleway straight up to the 'Wessex Ridgeway' above, cross Barcombe Down to turn right beside the B3143, then left along Barnes Lane. At the next road crossing, take the northward track along Little Minterne Hill to emerge at Dogbury Gate. Here Tess kept straight ahead 'skirting Dogbury Hill and High-Stoy, with the dell between them called "The Devil's Kitchen"', that is, **circling to the north of High-Stoy and turning sharp left up the bridleway at the end of the wood.** High-Stoy was reputedly one of Hardy's favourite viewpoints; today, surrounding trees and woodland to the south preclude views from the top and the best views, north over Blackmoor, are obtained from the route taken by Tess. **At the end of the bridleway Tess turned right and from here on, it is road all the way to Beaminster.** Follow the description given in chapter XLIV of *Tess of the D'Urbervilles* for something of a rollercoaster ride over the humpbacked downs with many fine views northward.

To reach this point (west of High-Stoy) by car from Plush is a far more complex journey but it passes several places of interest. Take the road through Alton Pancras to Buckland Newton. Here turn left past the church, whose clock struck twelve whilst Fitzpiers watered his horse at *Lydden Spring* on his return from a clandestine visit to *Middleton* Abbey. **Head up Ridge Hill to turn sharp right downhill passing Revel's Farm on your right,** once Reveller's Inn, where Giles encountered the wandering Fitzpiers. **On reaching the main road at Middlemarsh, turn left up to High-Stoy via Lyons-Gate and Dogbury Hill.** Middlemarsh is one of the villages which Hardy mentions as a possible *Little Hintock*; there is plentiful woodland to the west of the village but it lacks all other qualifications, it is too big, too flat, too readily accessible (on the A352) and quite intensively farmed. 'The Horse on Hintock Green' from 'A Trampwoman's Tragedy' (CP 153) flourishes here still, under a new alias: 'Hunter's Moon'. Another nearby 'lone inn' favoured by the Trampwoman, the 'King's Stag', on the road north of Buckland Newton, has disappeared without trace. To the east of the Middlemarsh woods, below High Stoy – although the wrong side of it to fit the text – lies Hermitage, another village on Hardy's list of possible *Little Hintock's*. Tranquil, remote from the woodlands, too flat, too open and the site of intensive dairy farming; it is a non-starter.

Just beyond Hillfield woods (now a car park and official viewpoint), Tess 'reached Cross-in-Hand, where the stone pillar stands desolate and silent, to mark the site of a miracle, or murder, or both'; it is now neatly fenced off in the grass on your right. The site remains desolate and the purpose of the monolith obscure, notwithstanding Hardy's explanation in 'The Lost Pyx' (CP 140), that it commemorates a medieval miracle, and the several alternatives which he offers on Tess's return journey. Certainly it has long been considered a mystical monument, used for the swearing of solemn oaths (Tess on Alec's insistence) or as a wishing stone – note the oblatory coins (plate 7.4). In a footnote to the poem, Hardy states that this spot commands 'in clear weather views that extend from the English to the Bristol Channel'; Blackmoor is indeed laid out before you to the north but a degree of poetic licence must be acknowledged regarding the southern aspect!

A short diversion north from here down one of two very steep narrow lanes takes you to Batcombe, the *Owlscombe* home of 'Conjuror Mynterne', that 'genuine' man whose advice was sought by Dairyman Crick's grandfather.

7.4 *Cross-in-Hand*

Minterne's extraordinary half-tomb stands in the graveyard just south of the nave of this isolated church.

Tess's route along Haydon Lane then dips down to cut across the straight and (sadly no longer) deserted Roman road called Long-Ash Lane at Holywell, soon passing the common, where *The Woodlanders* Walk began, to reach 'the small town or village of Evershead' (Evershot). As you climb Fore Street, little changed since the nineteenth century, you pass on your right firstly the Tanyard, where the remains of the barn in which Tess discovered Alec in his new role as 'Methodist Ranter' can be seen, then 'the Sow-and-Acorn' inn, avoided by Tess but used by Tupcombe in 'The First Countess of Wessex' and Philip Hall in 'Interlopers'. Beyond the inn, a footpath leads to St John's Well: the spring which is the source of the Frome. You then come to the church and, immediately beyond it, Tess's Cottage, where she 'breakfasted a second time, heartily enough', before heading up West Hill to then descend Horsey Knap to Benville Bridge and Lane (plate 7.5). Although Hardy correctly describes 'the

7.5 Tess cottage, *Evershead*

second half of her journey' as being 'through a more gentle country' the route itself is a switchback over undulating downland as opposed to the more gentle and level earlier route along the ridge.

Benville Lane climbs to Toller Down Gate, where it crosses Crimmercrock Lane, the scene of the unnamed 'maiden-no-more's' encounter with 'The Dark-Eyed Gentleman' (CP 201). The downland and valley due south of here – Westcombe Hill and Hooke – are Hardy's *Norcombe*, where the opening scenes of *Far From the Madding Crowd* are set. **Beyond Toller Down, Benville Lane becomes the B3163**; consequently there is an increase in traffic volume and less verge (though replaced at times by a glorious tunnel of beeches), making this a somewhat hazardous walk. **At the first field boundary below Toller Down Gate, a bridleway, ominously named Dark Dale, branches off to the left**, across the land farmed by Gabriel, **passing through Westcombe Wood and down Burnt Bottom to the millpond at Hooke**, at the far end of which can be found the Mill House (*Tewnell Mill*).

From here another bridlepath returns you to Crimmercrock Lane, passing the remains of chalk pits on the way but nothing to match the scene of the tragic loss of Gabriel Oak's flock in *Far From the Madding Crowd*. It is an unspoilt area of tranquil downland where the sky at night is still 'remarkably clear' and where it is easy to envisage Gabriel standing alone on

Norcombe Ewelease, not only telling the time by the stars but sensing that 'poetry of motion' – 'the roll of the world eastward' in an 'almost palpable movement' – with the proviso that you keep your back towards the Rampisham Down transmitting station.

The bridleway ends opposite Linnet Lane which leads down the eastern slope of the hill to Rampisham Church, where Pugin's chancel abuts the nave restored by Hicks in 1858–9 during Hardy's architectural apprenticeship. Within the church is a fourteenth-century stone carving of a kneeling (probable) ox, captured in reverent pose on a distant Christmas Eve; a tradition recorded by Hardy both in 'The Oxen' (CP 403) and in Crick's tale of William Dewy's lucky escape from the pious bull. The church is kept locked so viewing has to be by appointment.

Tess's walk continues its switchback descent from Toller Down, thence up to Dirty Gate, then down and up to Storridge Hill. Here was the gate where Tess paused to survey 'the basin in which *Emminster* and its Vicarage lay'. The gate is not readily identifiable but the hedge remains, in which she stowed her thick walking boots. **The road descends to the River Brit and the Bridport Road; here turn right up to the centre of Beaminster – the market square. From here Church Lane leads down to the delightful mellow-sandstone St Mary's with its prominent tower**. Today, the main point of interest here is a memorial plaque to Gertrude Bugler, Hardy's adored Tess, to be found in the raised grass at the south-east corner of the churchyard. Beyond the church, in Barnes Lane, the vicarage has lost its uninviting chill; now smartly refurbished as 'The Beauty Room', it offers to 'relax, indulge, pamper and transform' the descendants of Parson Clare's parishioners!

A Walk Around *Stourcastle* (Sturminster Newton)

Idyllic Riverside

By foot (one-and-a-half miles/two-and-a-half kilometres)

Hardy's *Stourcastle* (Sturminster Newton) is 'the capital of Blackmoor Vale'. On 3 July 1876, Hardy and Emma moved into Riverside Villa, a new semi-detached house overlooking the water meadows to the south-west of the town. Here they enjoyed 'A Two-Years' Idyll' (CP 587), the 'happiest time' in their marriage. **Stourcastle is easily explored on foot, the best starting point being Sturminster Mill, clearly signposted off the A357.** It is indeed an idyllic and beautiful spot, an ideal place to lay back in the warmth of the sun, serenaded by the quiver of the wind through the trees, the whirl of water round the millpond and the idle splash of the waterfowl. **Cross the footbridges over the mill race and follow the Stour downstream to reach the road at the medieval Town Bridge. Bear left uphill towards the market square. The first turning on your right leads to the church.** This was the setting of the poem 'The To-Be-Forgotten' (CP 110), his first published Sturminster poem, the idyll having retrospectively turned morbid. **The next right, Ricketts Lane, leads to the recreation ground. Follow the path along the top border and after it bends right; the house behind the wall is Riverside Villa.**

The Hardys lived in the northern half, currently painted cream and bearing a blue plaque. Here he wrote *The Return of the Native*, whilst enjoying splendid views of the water meadows, commemorated in 'Overlooking the River Stour' (CP 424). 'The Musical Box' (CP 425) indicates retrospective regret at his neglect of Emma as he walked alone beside the river, his mind preoccupied by the *Egdon* of the formative novel. **Follow the path on beyond his home, bearing left after 200 yards (180 metres) to Colber Bridge,** the setting of the next poem, 'On Sturminster Foot-Bridge' (CP 426). **From here retrace your steps downstream,** past the villa and the spot where Hardy 'rowed on the Stour in the evening', gathering water-lilies, which is fortunately unchanged. **Then take the path across the meadows back to the mill,** where flour is still ground in the traditional way. Stourside Mill is the setting of that wonderful little poem about an experience that comes to many of us with time, 'The Second Visit' (CP 880). In the poem Emma was the woman on the bridge and it recalls when Hardy returned to the scene with Florence and his sister Kate in 1916, forty years after that 'happiest time'. Whilst living at Riverside Villa, Hardy walked the three miles (five kilometres) due north to Marnhull. **Today you can retrace his route up the road, or alternatively continue through the water meadows along the clearly waymarked 'Stour Valley Way'.**

A Walk Around *Marlott* (Marnhull)

The Home of the Durbeyfields

By foot (one-and-a-half miles/two-and-a-half kilometres)

Desmond Hawkins questioned why Hardy decided upon Marnhull as Tess's birthplace, *Marlott*, since it was a completely atypical village, the largest in Dorset and 'nearer a federation of detached wards than an organic entity'. (2) **Approached from Sturminster,** the first ward one encounters is Walton Elm. This hamlet, as close as one can guess, was the home of the Durbeyfields. **If you turn left at the staggered crossroads at the south end of Walton Elm,** the third house on your right, 'Lamb Inn House', is believed to have been the site of 'Rolliver's inn, the single alehouse at this end of the long and broken village, which could only boast of an off-licence'. **A short distance further ahead on the main road, turn left (on foot) up the un-named no through road (there is a lay-by just opposite beyond the post box). Follow this 'crooked lane or street' straight ahead and you are soon confronted by a five-bar gate labelled Tess's Cottage with the thatched building itself beyond. Walk up the drive (it is a public footpath) and admire the cottage. You will unfortunately then have to retrace your steps because at present the far end of the path is obstructed (plate 7.6).**

From the cottage, there are fine views to the north towards the village church and eastward over the *Vale of the White Hart*. **Half a mile (800 metres) further on by road or footpath**, one reaches the crossroads in the village centre. Here stands the church of St Gregory, its graveyard well tended; there is no sign today of Sorrow's grave, 'that shabby corner of God's allotment where He lets the nettles grow, and where all unbaptized infants, notorious drunkards, suicides, and others of the conjecturally damned are laid'. On the other side of the crossroads stands the expensively restored Crown Inn, which confirms its connection with the novel by maintaining a 'Pure Drop' bar (map 7.1).

7.6 Tess' cottage, *Marlott*

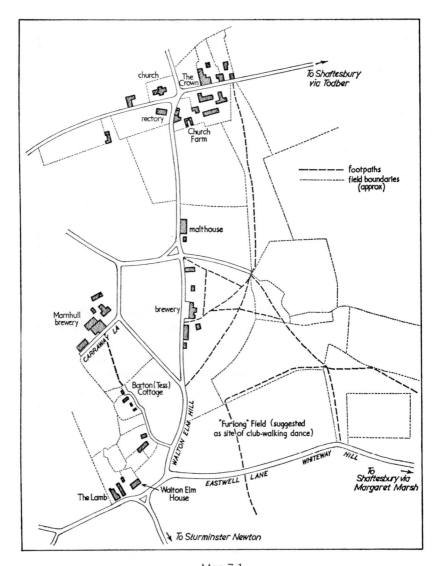

Map 7.1

The Slopes

Kay-Robinson attempted to confirm his identification of *Trantridge* with
Pentridge by following Tess on her two journeys to *The Slopes* and back but,
despite 'a comprehensive study of maps, guides and directories of the period,
supplemented by an exhaustive study of the terrain', he had to admit defeat.
Whilst I agree that it is impossible to map Alec's journey with Tess 'on that day

in June', the incline 'down which D'Urberville had driven her so wildly' was undoubtedly one of the roads leading into *The Chase* from Win Green, for Alec counters Tess's fearful protestations by retorting that 'when people find them- selves on one of the highest points in the county, they must get down again'. Win Green, at 910 feet (280 metres) above sea level, is just in Wiltshire, but the adjoining highway forms the county boundary. On a clear day, the views are magnificent: the Isle of Wight extant to the south-east; the Jurassic coast straight ahead; and Shaftesbury nestling on its hilltop to the south-west. The 'incline down which the road stretched in a long straight descent of nearly a mile' is the road from Win Green down to Tollard Royal and beyond; a total descent of over 600 feet (180 metres), although not entirely straight because it skirts round the boundaries of the Rushmore Estate and adjoining Larmer Tree Gardens (where Hardy danced on the greensward with Agnes Groves ('Concerning Agnes' CP 862).

Kay-Robinson's problems are caused by his perpetuation of Lea's original error that Hardy had Pentridge in mind as *Trantridge*. Nobody has ever been able to identify a property matching *The Slopes* at *Trantridge*, nor have they been able to match Hardy's descriptions of journeys to and from *Trantridge* with the geography in the neighbourhood of Pentridge. In particular the junc- tion which Hardy calls *Trantridge Cross*, generally identified as the intersection of the A354 and B3081 (now a roundabout), is situated on Handley Down, a hill from which all roads slope downward rather than uphill as described repeatedly in the text. To solve this conundrum, let us forget Lea and return to an earlier authority, Windle (1902), who identifies the hamlet of Boveridge as the place where Georgy Crookhill lost his clothes ('A Few Crusted Characters'), continuing, 'near here is a house, which may be looked upon as corresponding in situation with that in which the Stoke D'Urbervilles lived'. On Hardy's original map of Wessex, he marked in this order and in this exact relationship to each other:

> **The Slopes**
> **Chaseborough**
> **Trantridge Cross +**

These positions correspond exactly to Boveridge, Cranborne and the cross- roads south of Cranborne where the road from Edmondsham crosses the B3078. Boveridge House is a nineteenth-century brick-built mansion on the slopes above Cranborne village on the edge of *The Chase*.

> Every village has its idiosyncrasy, its constitution, often its own code of morality. The levity of some of the younger women in and about Trantridge

was marked, and was perhaps symptomatic of the choice spirit who ruled The
Slopes in that vicinity. The place had also a more abiding defect; it drank
hard. The staple conversation on the farms around was on the uselessness of
saving money; The chief pleasure of these philosophers lay in going every
Saturday night, when work was done, to Chaseborough, a decayed market-
town two or three miles distant …

Hardy gives a detailed description of Tess's return journey from the *Flower-de-
Luce*, still readily identifiable as the heavily ivy-clad Fleur-de-Lys near the
church in Cranborne, on that fateful Saturday night. Boveridge lies two-and-
a-half miles (four kilometres) by road or two miles (three-and-a-quarter
kilometres) by footpath from the Fleur-de-Lys. Pentridge, which lies in a valley
not on a slope, is just under four miles (six-and-a-half kilometres) distant by
the most direct route, which is entirely by bridleway over the downs.

Tess's unfortunate altercation with Dark Car occurred as the party had left
the open highway and passed through a field-gate. There is no possible such
route between Cranborne and Pentridge but the direct route from Cranborne
to Boveridge starts on the public highway and then branches off by footpath,
Boveridge being situated on the hill to the north of Cranborne with
Boveridge House to the eastern end of the hamlet (map 7.2). A walk of about
one hour from Cranborne allows a full exploration of this area.

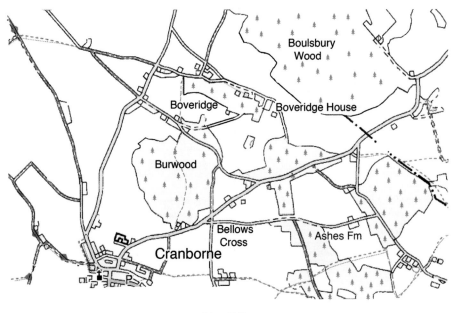

Map 7.2

A Walk from Cranborne to Boveridge

The Home of the D'Urbervilles

By foot (three miles/five kilometres)

From the Fleur-de-Lys in Cranborne head down towards the village square, turn right, then first left, then right again into Penny's Lane and follow this straight on as it becomes a pleasant footpath rising between hedges. Turn left at the end of the first field. As you climb the edge of this second field Boveridge House can be seen in its commanding position on *The Slopes* through a gap in the trees to the half-right. On reaching the lane, turn right and then left through the gates and cross the yard into the wood. Follow the track, which is not waymarked, straight ahead up and down through Burwood, avoiding turnings – it is generally the most obvious forward path. You will soon encounter not only pheasants and other game birds but free-range hens in the forest: a 'community of fowls', most reminiscent of old Mrs D'Urberville.

Bear left on reaching the lane, then right up a signposted footpath through the trees beside a cottage. This track takes you straight up the hill to Boveridge Farm, which is really the centre of the hamlet. On emerging onto the road at Boveridge, note to your left 'the warm red brick lodge', no longer quite 'up to its eves in dense evergreens'. If you bear right and then left on the bridleway heading north from the farmyard, you will soon find yourself deep in the heart of:

> The Chase – a truly venerable tract of forest land, one of the few remaining woodlands in England of undoubted primaeval date, wherein Druidical mistletoe was still found on aged oaks, and where enormous yew-trees, not planted by the hand of man, grew as they had grown when they were pollarded for bows.

The extensive primaeval forest behind Boveridge straddles the boundary between Dorset and Hampshire. On that fateful night, Alec, riding 'quite at random for over an hour, taking any turning that came to hand', may well have entered Stone Hill Wood by this route. Alternatively, had he been riding along the road from Cranborne towards Tidpit and long ago 'passed the point at which the lane to *Trantridge* branched from the highway' he could have followed a track into the same part of *The Chase* from near Stone Hill Gate. It is an area of dense, tranquil, undisturbed woodland where:

Sycamore shoulders oak,
Bines the slim sapling yoke,
Ivy-spun halters choke
Elms stout and tall. ('In a Wood' CP 40)

Historically, a 'forest' was held directly by the king but a 'chase was in the hands of a subject' – in this case the Earls of Salisbury, who own Boveridge to this day, the wider Chase being now the property of the Pitt-Rivers family. *The Chase* had a reputation as 'a nursery for all kinds of vice, profligacy and immorality' and was thus an appropriate setting for Alec's violation of 'that beautiful feminine tissue, sensitive as gossamer'. Indeed, an old Dorset proverb runs, 'When Cranborne is whore-less, Wimborne poor-less and Harley Wood hare-less, the world will be at an end'; small wonder that Saturday night in Cranborne generated that floating 'vegeto-human pollen', whose perpetrators Tess rashly labelled a 'whorage'.

Boveridge House is a yellow-brick mansion dating from the 1820s but extended and refurbished in the 1880s. It nestles on the slopes above Cranborne, enclosed on all sides by *The Chase*, and is currently used as a school for young people with learning difficulties. **It is approached from Boveridge by woodland tracks, which are not designated public rights of way.** It is as near as one will ever get to identifying 'Mrs D'Urberville's seat, *The Slopes*, 'on the borders of

7.7 *The Slopes*

the district known as The Chase', 'not a manorial home in the ordinary sense', but 'a country-house built for enjoyment pure and simple' (plate 7.7).

The simplest way back to the square in Cranborne, that 'decayed market-town', is to retrace your steps through Burwood but, as the map shows, there are a variety of wooded alternatives (map 7.2).

A Walk Around *Melchester* (Salisbury)

Tess and Angel's Flight Northward

By foot (two miles/three kilometres)

By a Hardyan coincidence, Tess's final act of sexual fulfilment (and delayed marital consummation) was to occur only a short distance from the site of that initial abuse and also within the bounds of an ancient forest (pp.184–5). From *Bramshurst Manor*, Tess and Angel fled to *Melchester* (Salisbury).

Kay-Robinson lived in Salisbury and it is hard to improve on his very detailed description of Hardyan sites in this, his home city, where fortunately things have changed little in the intervening forty years. The cathedral close remains tranquil and unspoilt; the cathedral itself usually draped in scaffolding in one aspect or another – providing work for Jude's professional successors. On the western side the teacher training college remains as a museum, its garden still stretching down to the Avon, through which Sue waded in desperate flight from the oppressive regime in *Jude the Obscure*, better tolerated by Hardy's sisters. This is the setting of 'The High-School Lawn' (CP 794), whilst the cathedral itself, surely the most beautiful in England, is the scene of that important early poem 'The Impercipient' (CP 44) and one of Hardy's many moon poems 'A Cathedral Façade at Midnight' (CP 667), deriving from a visit in August 1897. 'In a Cathedral City' (CP 171) is addressed to an unknown woman, possibly Tryphena Sparks, who is thought to have been a model for Sue Bridehead. In *The Hand of Ethelberta*, Christopher practised the organ whilst Ethelberta wandered through the cathedral.

A short walk north from the cathedral takes you through the ancient gateway, near which Jude had lodgings, **to the Church of St Thomas Becket,** where Sue and Phillotson were married; **thence bear right into the market square.** The most likely surviving candidate for Edith Harman's house ('On the Western Circuit') is the cream-painted Georgian house on the diagonally opposite (north-eastern) corner of the square (the ground floor of which is currently a Bathstore). On the south-eastern corner the Guildhall, the scene of Christopher Julian's concert, survives unscathed. A short distance from

here are to be found both the Red Lion (in Milford Street), visited by
Ethelberta and Phillotson and where 'The First Countess of Wessex' held
clandestine meetings with her own husband, and the White Hart (in nearby
St John Street), favoured by Lord Mountclere and Madam V in 'A
Committee Man of the Terror'. The White Hart is adorned by a beast which
matches its forlorn cousin on the now abandoned Dorchester Inn (see
pp.101–2). **A ten-minute walk south from the White Hart, past the cathedral walls, brings you to the New Bridge over the Avon,** from the western
parapet of which you obtain a rewarding and unspoilt view of the old St
Nicholas Bridge (plate 7.8). Here remember Tess and Angel:

> The intercepting city, ancient Melchester, they were obliged to pass through
> in order to take advantage of the town bridge for crossing a large river that
> obstructed them. It was about midnight when they went along the deserted
> streets, lighted fitfully by the few lamps, keeping off the pavement that it
> might not echo their footsteps. The graceful pile of cathedral architecture
> rose dimly on their left hand, but it was lost upon them now.

**As you retrace your steps to the market square you will be following this
pair in their final flight northward.** From here they groped their way through

7.8 St Nicholas Bridge, *Melchester*

that 'night as dark as a cave' the 'two or three miles' (three or five kilometres) (in reality eight or nine miles/thirteen or fifteen kilometres) to Stonehenge, a temple 'so solemn and lonely', upon which they stumbled without let or hindrance, freely open to the wayfarer as it had been for millennia until it was fenced off around the turn of the nineteenth century in defiance of undoubted public rights of way, a circumstance with which we sadly seem to be indefinitely lumbered.

Wintonchester (Winchester)

Wintonchester, where 'the President of the Immortals ... ended his sport with Tess', is Hardy's resurrection of the Saxon name for Winchester. Tess was executed here because Bournemouth until 1974 was in Hampshire. 'From the western gate' the highway still climbs the Roman (Sarum) road, past 'Winchester Community Prison' and the hospital, but 'the top of the great West Hill' does not afford the panorama of the city enjoyed by Angel and Liza-Lu and it is unlikely that it ever did. Their visit, however, is recorded in a hilltop development named Marnhull Rise!

Hardy gives a detailed description of *Wintonchester* Cathedral at the start of the tale of his fourth Noble Dame, Lady Mottisfont. On 8 August 1893 he attended evensong here with Florence Henniker as the culmination of a day which had not gone at all as he had planned, for Florence had made it clear to him that she was neither Sue nor Arabella (*vide Jude the Obscure*), merely a conventional wife, fully committed in Christian duty to remain faithful to her husband. He recorded his frustration with that day, for both Mrs Henniker and posterity, in the poem 'At an Inn' (CP 45); they had lunched at the George Inn, which alas does not survive.

Weydon-Priors (Weyhill)

Midway between Stonehenge and Winchester, at the junction of the modern A303 and A342, on a hilltop which marks the point of convergence of eight ancient trackways, stands the site of Weyhill Fair, *Weydon-Priors*, where Henchard auctions off his wife Susan in the first chapter of *The Mayor of Casterbridge*. A Michaelmas Fair, once described as 'the greatest fair in the kingdom', had been held on this hilltop from at least the eleventh century and continued as an annual event until 1957. The Weyhill Fair Register for 1832 records that a farmer named Joseph Thomson offered his 'tormentor' of a wife for sale at a price of 50 shillings, but takers were thin on the ground;

eventually, however, he struck a successful bargain for 20 shillings, plus a Newfoundland dog in part exchange! Sadly, in recent years much of the original fairground has been built over, but the central core near the church has been retained, the old booths converted into a craft centre. After fifty years in abeyance, the Michaelmas Fair has recently been revived with 'old tyme fairground attractions' and country craft demonstrations but alas, as yet, no furmity on sale! A notice in the adjoining thirteenth-century church informs visitors that here Michael Henchard swore his solemn oath to 'avoid all strong liquors for the space of twenty-one years to come'. Unfortunately this cannot be the case for the text clearly states that Henchard walked away from the fairground, stopping at a church in a village 'three or four miles' (five or seven kilometres) distant.

Shaston (Shaftesbury)

Shaftesbury, that ancient borough created by King Alfred on the flat top of a spur of Greensand over 700 feet (210 metres) high was abbreviated by Hardy to *Shaston*, the name used on milestones. This was the town from which Durbeyfield was returning at the start of *Tess of the D'Urbervilles*. To the young Tess it seemed a fairytale city 'standing majestically on its height; its windows shining like lamps in the evening sun' (like *Christminster* to the young Jude) unknown to her until she walks there to take the carrier's van to *Trantridge*. Part Four of *Jude the Obscure*, which is entitled 'At Shaston', begins with a detailed description and potted history of 'the ancient British Palladour', which Hardy claims will 'throw the visitor, even against his will, into a pensive melancholy'. Jude enters the town 'after a toilsome climb' up Gold Hill (originally called Cold Hill), that cobbled street bounded by the old Abbey wall on one side and irregular cottages on the other, beloved by tourist brochures and immortalized (for one generation at least) by the Hovis advertisement. At the top of the incline, Jude turned left into Park Walk, from where there are still wonderful views south over Blackmoor Vale and then right along Abbey Walk to Bimport.

The then new 'extensive and stone-built' schools where Sue and Phillotson taught have rather more rapidly gone the way of the abbey itself. Halfway along Bimport on the northern side, with its front door projecting into the street, is 'Ox House', the original *Old-Grove Place* with its ground floor sunk below street level, somewhat mitigating the damage which Sue inflicted upon herself in her leap from the bedroom window. A new development to the right of Ox House has been quite appropriately named 'Jude Court' (caught?)! To the left of Ox House a path leads into Castle Hill

Gardens from where there are fine northward views towards Gillingham (*Leddenton*) where Phillotson's friend Gillingham was Schoolmaster.

Sherton Abbas (Sherborne)

Approaching Sherborne (*Sherton Abbas*), the road from Dorchester (A352) climbs a wooded hill, near the peak of which it is joined by the road from Sturminster Newton (A3030). The dark stone cottage in the fork (West Hill Lodge) was the home of 'Dan Randall', the sleepy keeper of the Sherton Turnpike, where Oak and Coggan caught up with Bathsheba on her nocturnal flight to Bath in *Far From the Madding Crowd*. Sherborne itself retains the air of an old-world market town; here it is easy to imagine the grand front of Percomb's shop, with a 'waxen woman in the window', on Sheep Street with his tuppenny barber's premises tucked away in the yard behind. The market place where Winterbourne stood with 'his specimen apple-tree', its boughs rising above 'the heads of the farmers', was at the junction of Long Street and Cheap Street. This is just to the east of the town's tranquil centrepiece, the magnificent Abbey Church, which Taylor justly describes as 'the finest building in the County'. In *The Woodlanders*, Grace and Giles 'walk about the abbey aisles' and ponder the sorry circumstances 'to which a cruel fate has consigned' them. This church was originally the cathedral for the see of the Bishop of Wessex until this was moved to Salisbury (Old Sarum) in 1075. Wander through its glorious perpendicular interior, admiring in particular the breathtaking fan tracery of the vault of the nave. Sherborne is 'the Abbey north of Blackmoor Vale' in the poem 'The Lost Pyx' (CP 140) just as Cerne is 'the Abbey south thereof'.

At the end of her eight-week honeymoon tour, Grace is resting in 'the chief hotel in Sherton Abbas, the Earl of Wessex' when she spies Giles making cider in the yard outside her window. Hardy gives a detailed description of this 'substantial inn of Ham-hill stone with a yawning backyard' at the midpoint in the novel, but in the final chapter concedes that it has been demolished 'having been rebuilt contemporaneously with the construction of the railway'. His initial description was of the New Inn, demolished in 1860 to make way for the station. Its replacement, 'the building that offered the best accommodation in *Sherton*', the Digby Arms, stands nearby – the first building on the left as you head from the station up towards the Abbey – no longer a hotel but a boarding house for Sherborne School. Grace also visited Sherborne Castle, a short walk to the east of the town, down Long Street. This was the home of Lady Baxby, Hardy's Seventh Noble Dame, reduced to its current ruined state on Cromwell's orders. The Digby family (Baxby) still live in the adjoining (new) castle, built by Sir Walter Raleigh in 1594. Both buildings and their grounds are open to the public throughout the summer.

Review: For the three principal novels of his mature fiction, Hardy moved north to the Vale of Blackmoor and thence, with the increasing use of the railway, Wessex rapidly expanded across Wiltshire and Hampshire into Berkshire and Oxfordshire. The umbilical cord, however, still stretched back to *Egdon*, for Tess spent her happiest time on the edge of the heath at *Talbothays* and even Jude was a native of *Lower Mellstock*, transported to an alien northern landscape. The territory of *The Woodlanders* alone remains isolated and compact, distant from *Egdon*, the action occurring within the visual field of an observer on Bubb Down, thus paralleling the role of Rainbarrow with woodland substituted for heath. The confused and mobile geography of progressive editions of *The Woodlanders* is the direct result of Hardy's attempts to placate the wrath of the fifth Earl of Ilchester, within whose ancestral home the fictional Felice Charmond had taken up residence. The landscape around Melbury Bubb is the landscape of Jemima Hardy's childhood, well known to young Hardy and hence requiring no tie back to *Egdon*. A single seven-mile (eleven-kilometre) walk from Evershot, through tranquil woodlands, returning across the glorious Melbury Sampford estate, replete with lakes and deer park, allows the reader to fully savour the land-scape of *The Woodlanders*, encountering en route 'Interlopers at the Knap', 'The Duke's Reappearance' and 'The First Countess of Wessex'.

More ambitious, is to follow in Tess's footsteps from that starve-acre place, *Flintcomb-Ash*, via High Stoy, *Cross-in-hand* and Evershot, to *Benville Lane* and ultimately *Emminster*, passing en route *Norcombe Hill*, where Gabriel Oak could detect the nocturnal 'roll of the world eastward'. From Sturminster Newton, where Hardy and Emma spent their 'happiest time', it is but a short walk to *Marlott* and Tess's Cottage. Returning to early sources and by careful study of local geography, I argue that *Trantridge* should be correctly identified with Boveridge rather than the generally accepted Pentridge. A short walk from Cranborne, retracing the steps of Tess and her inebriated companions, leads readily to *The Slopes* at Boveridge, surrounded by the primeval woodland of *The Chase* where Tess's guardian angel deserted her. The text then follows Tess's final flight from *Sandbourne* via Salisbury to Stonehenge and on to *Wintonchester*, to conclude by visiting *Weydon-Priors*, *Shaston* and *Sherton Abbas*.

CHAPTER EIGHT

Wessex Heights

B Y THE SUMMER of 1893 Hardy had met and fallen in love with the 'charming intuitive' thirty-seven-year-old literary lady, Florence Henniker, and had courted her relentlessly until a frigid denouement in 'the railway carriage when we met at Eastleigh'. She was just not that kind of girl. Meanwhile he was renewing his experience as a hands on stonemason by working as architect and site manager on the restoration of West Knighton Church, where his brother Henry was the contractor. Simultaneously he was beginning to write the text which was eventually to emerge as that troubled novel *Jude the Obscure*, conducting research by revisiting the Berkshire home of his paternal grandmother, Mary Head, and the nearby Midland city of Oxford which:

> ... stood within hail of the Wessex border, and almost with the tip of one small toe within it, at the northernmost point of the crinkled line along which the leisurely Thames strokes the fields of that ancient kingdom.

Whilst *Jude the Obscure* contains much that can be seen as autobiographical, it is in truth an amalgam of many disparate influences and individual tragedies as well as Hardy's personal frustrations. It is a restless, peripatetic novel of the modern age, ripe with forebodings of the coming *fin-de-siècle*: the action is driven by the railway timetable as the itinerant participants relentlessly pursue their fate, travelling by train from station to station around North Wessex in ever-accelerating and ever-decreasing circles. In *Jude the Obscure* Hardy pulled out all the stops; he was finished with fiction and determined to go out with a bang rather than a whimper: Damn marriage! Damn the Church! Damn the education system! Damn the universities! Damn Society! Damn human relationships! It was great fun while it lasted, but the rebound when it came was harsh and severe and nearly cost him his life, the deep, dark sorrow of 1896, of the *In Tenebris* poems and Wessex Heights, and that is where the final part of this chapter will take us.

A Walk Around Fawley

Part First: At *Marygreen*

By foot (six miles/nine-and-a-half kilometres)

Marygreen is based upon the village of Fawley, from which Jude derives his surname. It remains a sleepy agricultural community nestling in the north Berkshire Downs on the edge of an area renowned for its racehorses. Both Sue and Jude journeyed to *Marygreen* by taking the train to *Alfredston* (Wantage) Road Station, the tram into the town and then climbing the five miles (eight kilometres) up and over the Ridgeway. Wantage Station was yet another Wessex victim of Dr Beeching's cuts so **the modern traveller has little option other than to approach the area by car, taking the A338 north through Hungerford from the A4/M4**. Little in Fawley appears to have changed from the major upheavals which Hardy decried following his visit in 1893:

> It was as old-fashioned as it was small, and it rested in the lap of an undulating upland adjoining the North Wessex downs. Old as it was, however, the well-shaft was probably the only relic of the local history that remained absolutely unchanged. Many of the thatched and dormered dwelling-houses had been pulled down of late years, and many trees felled on the green. Above all, the original church, hump-backed, wood-turreted, and quaintly hipped, had been taken down, and either cracked up into heaps of road-metal in the lane, or utilized as pig-sty walls, garden seats, guard-stones to fences, and rockeries in the flower-beds of the neighbourhood. In place of it a tall new building of modern Gothic design, unfamiliar to English eyes, had been erected on a new piece of ground by a certain obliterator of historic records who had run down from London and back in a day.

The neo-Gothic church and its enclosing graveyard have mellowed with time but still appear alien and peripheral to the village. From here, the rectory house is still to be found 'round the corner', as described in the opening sentence of *Jude the Obscure*, and beside it the tiny school, well preserved and set in a beautiful garden – although neither of these buildings serves the purpose for which it was originally constructed. The wooded village green also remains unsullied, but beyond this positive identifications become more difficult. Several sites have been suggested for the well, the most likely of which is marked by some stones beside a beech tree at the eastern end of the green. Behind this tree is a terrace of cottages which mark the site of the old thatched cottage, once the village bakery and thus the model for Aunt Drusilla's home and shop. In the village it is believed that this honour falls to Straw Cottage, a neatly thatched and extended nineteenth-century dwelling opposite the church.

Across the lane from these cottages, steps lead up into the old church-yard; this has recently undergone a transformation and is now carefully restored and marked out in an environmentally sensitive way. It is a beautiful and peaceful place to sit, pause and reflect. After more than a century of neglect, someone listened to Hardy's complaint that 'the site whereon so long had stood the ancient temple to the Christian divinities was not even recorded on the green and level grass-plot that had immemorially been the churchyard'. Hardy notes that 'the obliterated graves' were 'commemorated by eighteen-penny cast-iron crosses warranted to last five years'. These crosses – no doubt of stout Victorian construction – are still very much in evidence in the revivified churchyard and look set to last five hundred years (plate 8.1).

Continue down the street from the churchyard past the village club to turn left up a tarmaced lane. This is the original 'northward path' leading to

8.1 *Marygreen* – the old churchyard

Farmer Troutham's field and providing access to the Ridgeway, *Christminster* and the whole world beyond (plate 8.2). Today the bridleway is metalled as far as the farm buildings at Winterdown Bottom – the nexus of that 'wide and lonely depression' 'sown as a cornfield' – to Jude a lonely, ugly, utilitarian workplace where the 'puny and sorry' lives of the rooks so much resembled his own. On a wet, muddy winter's day, it is indeed a forlorn spot, but in the summer sunshine with sky-larking, poppy-dashed wheat fields it is easy to envisage the 'groups of gleaners squatting in the sun' and share Hardy's poetic view that:

> Every inch of ground had been the site, first or last, of energy, gaiety, horseplay, bickering, weariness ... Love-matches that had populated the adjoining hamlet had been made up there between reaping and carrying. Under the hedge which divided the field from a distant plantation girls had given themselves to lovers who would not turn their heads to look at them by the next harvest; and in that ancient cornfield many a man had made love-promises to a woman at whose voice he had trembled by the next seed-time after fulfilling them in the church adjoining.

The track soon curves to join the *Alfredston* road, the site of the pig-killing in the snow. Thirty years ago the outline of the garden was still visible but

8.2 Farmer Troutham's field

now it has been completely obliterated and absorbed into the surrounding productive arable land. Just north of this junction stood the isolated cottage, where Jude and Arabella acted out their brief marital cohabitation. Three hundred-and-fifty yards (320 metres) due west of here a depression in the prairie marks the site of the 'large round pond'; it was here the ice cracked under Jude, but would not give way, leading him to surmise that 'he was not a sufficiently dignified person for suicide'.

Carefully follow the road uphill to the bend just beyond the summit. The Brown House, onto the roof of which Jude climbed for a view of distant *Christminster*, stood on the apex of the slope to your right, just before the turning to Letcombe Regis (highlighted by Hardy in red crayon on his map of Berkshire). Here, from the ground, where all that remains of the barn is some hard-standing amongst a rabbit-warren, 'the whole northern semicircle between east and west, to a distance of forty or fifty miles' (sixty-five or eighty kilometres) is still spread before you. Sadly in the twenty-first century, even on the darkest night, there is no hope of catching sight of those 'points of light like topaz' which unquestionably signify *Christminster*. By day the view to the north is obstructed by the massive towers of Didcot Power Station (plate 8.3), and by night the collective illuminations of Wantage, Didcot and Abingdon prevent even the faintest glimmer of Jude's 'city of light' from percolating

8.3 The view from the Brown House

through. At the edge of the main road on your right, fifty yards (forty-five metres) below the Court Hill Road turning, stood Jude's 'Thither JF' milestone, removed in 1939, restored during the 1970s, but now lost once more, hopefully just buried under brambles and awaiting rediscovery. Opposite this stood the gibbet 'not unconnected' with Jude's family history.

To return on foot to Fawley, retrace your steps to the Ridgeway. Head west here past Segsbury Camp, that 'circular British earthbank' explored by Jude and Arabella during their courtship, **200 yards (180 metres) beyond which a bridleway leads to the left over Segsbury Down back towards the rectory end of** *Marygreen*. **Alternatively, to visit Arabella's Cottage at Letcombe Bassett, continue along the Ridgeway a further 200 yards (180 metres), then turn right onto a footpath which descends across a field and beside a wood to join the road at Gramp's Hill. At the T-junction in the village turn left.** On your right you soon encounter a brick chapel ('Wesleyan Mission Room 1902'), a reminder of Arabella's non-conformist heritage, attached to a timbered thatched cottage. Set back immediately beyond this unusual pairing is an immaculate, large thatched house with stream-frontage boldly labelled 'Arabella's Cottage'. There is not a pig's pistle in sight, though the property would undoubtedly have met with Arabella's approval. Lea first made this identification, and although it seems far removed from the detailed descriptions given in *Jude the Obscure*, it is all that is on offer. Bassett Road, which takes you on to Letcombe Regis, affords some fine views of the watercress beds, no longer in commercial production.

Beyond Letcombe lies *Alfredston* (Wantage), where Jude was apprenticed as a stonemason: the route from *Marygreen* still passes 'the old almshouses in the first street of the town' and continues as the Roman road (A338) straight on to *Christminster*. *Alfredston* was the birthplace of King Alfred, whose statue dominates the market square. The only other building identifiable from the text can also be found here, the sixteenth-century Bear Hotel, where Sue hired a car to drive her to *Marygreen* for her final reconciliation with Phillotson.

A Walk Around Oxford

Part Second: At *Christminster*

By foot (four-and-a-half miles/seven kilometres)

Jude, approaching *Christminster* (Oxford) with all the hesitant tenderness of a lover, 'paused at the top of a crooked and gentle declivity, and obtained his first near view of the city. Grey-stoned and dun-roofed ... the buildings now lay quiet in the sunset, a vane here and there on their many spires and domes giving sparkle to a picture of sober secondary and tertiary hues.' The text implies that this 'species of Dick Whittington' entered the city via Cumnor and Botley, requiring a near two-mile (three-kilometre) diversion to Boars Hill, the only such viewpoint to the south-west. Before following Jude into Christminster, bear west into the village of Cumnor (*Lumsdon*) to where the church stands and beyond it the old school and school house at which Phillotson taught and lived. The attractive whitewashed thatched cottage opposite is identified as Sue's lodging during her time as Phillotson's pupil teacher.

Start from Carfax, the central crossroads in Oxford. A climb up the adjoining tower, all that remains of St Martin's Church, demolished to improve traffic-flow in the year in which *Jude the Obscure* was published, affords an initial panorama of the city. This is Hardy's *Fourways*, where:

> ... men had stood and talked of Napoleon, the loss of America, the execution of King Charles, the burning of the Martyrs, the Crusades, the Norman Conquest, possibly of the arrival of Caesar. Here the two sexes had met for loving, hating, coupling, parting; had waited, had suffered, for each other; had triumphed over each other; cursed each other in jealousy, blessed each other in forgiveness.

Head south down St Aldates. On your left you soon reach the magnificent façade of Christchurch College, the entrance of which is through Tom Tower, designed by an alumnus, Sir Christopher Wren. Here hangs the bell which sounded the 101-stroke curfew, carefully counted by Jude on his first evening in *Christminster*. Christchurch College was founded in 1524 by Cardinal Wolsey as Cardinal's College. Hardy, as was often his habit, reverted to this earlier name for the Wessex translation. *Cardinal* is one of the largest Oxford colleges and at the same time the Cathedral Church of the Diocese of Oxford. During his early days in *Christminster*, Jude frequently attended services at the cathedral in the hope of catching a glimpse of his admired but as yet unknown cousin, Sue. In his later disillusioned days, Jude mocks 'Cardinal with its long front, and its windows with lifted eyebrows, representing the polite surprise of the university at the efforts of such as I.' In addition to Wren, other alumni include John Locke, John Wesley, W.H. Auden, David Dimbleby and Rowan Williams.

Beyond Christchurch, turn left into Floyd's Row, then right down New Walk to reach the banks of the Isis. Continue to bear left along the path beside the stream (the Cherwell) around the periphery of Christ Church Meadow – in winter this affords fine views of *Cardinal* College and of *Christminster's* dreaming spires, in summer the perspective is limited by trees. When the Cherwell turns right, bear left into Broad Walk, then right up Merton Grove and left into **Merton Street to reach Oriel Square**; in doing so you pass round Corpus Christi, named by Jude as *Tudor College*. Oriel itself, founded in 1326, is Hardy's *Crozier College*; it was here in *Old Time Street* that Jude, whilst helping to haul 'a block of worked free-stone from a wagon' to the parapet he was repairing, encounters Sue, who looks 'right into his face with liquid untranslatable eyes'.

Return to the High Street and turn left. On the north side of *Chief Street*, you encounter first 'the church with the Italian porch, whose helical columns' are no longer 'heavily draped with creepers', noted by Jude and family on their arrival by train on that fateful 'Remembrance Day'. The next building is Brasenose (*Rubric*) College and beyond this, on the corner of Turl Street, the Mitre, the *Crozier Hotel* of the novel.

Retrace your steps down Chief Street. The first college beyond the University Church of St Mary the Virgin is All Souls (*Sarcophagus*). From the 'uncurtained window' of the lodging 'where she was not welcome' Sue contemplates 'the outer walls of *Sarcophagus College* – silent, black, and windowless' which 'threw their four centuries of gloom, bigotry, and decay into the little room she occupied, shutting out the moonlight by night and the sun by day' (plate 8.4). Past *Sarcophagus* is Queen's College which Hardy visited in June 1923 to receive an honorary fellowship from the university which sixty-five years previously would not consider him as an undergraduate.

8.4 The outer walls – 'silent, black, and windowless'

Turn left up the meandering Queen's Lane, which with its continuation New College Lane form the model for *Mildew Lane*, 'a spot which to Jude was irresistible – though to Sue it was not so fascinating – a narrow lane close to the back of a college, but having no communication with it'. *Mildew Lane* opens out to be spanned by the so-called 'Bridge of Sighs' – of doubtful resemblance to its Venetian counterpart – built in 1913 to link the two halves of Hertford College. Immediately before the bridge, a narrow alleyway on your right, originally named Hell Passage, leads to the fourteenth-century Turf Tavern tucked below the city walls; this is the 'obscure tavern' where Jude lodged on the night his children died.

The strikingly beautiful building straight ahead under the bridge is Christopher Wren's Sheldonian Theatre. The young Jude climbed to the octagonal chamber in the lantern of the theatre to obtain a (disillusioned) view 'over the whole town and its edifices' (plate 8.5). On his final return to *Christminster*, 'a crowd of expectant people' stood 'in the open space stretching between this building and the nearest college' watching the Commemoration ceremonials. Here Jude, the 'Tutor of St Slums', entertained the spectators with his knowledge of the university, describing the carved frieze on the front of Hertford College – just to your left – and translating the inscription *Ad fonts aquarum sicut cervus anhelat*: 'As pants the hart for cooling streams' (plate 8.6). Opposite here is the Bodleian.

8.5 The Sheldonian Theatre

8.6 Hertford College

Turn left from the Sheldonian down Broad Street, passing Balliol (*Biblioll*) College, whose Master offered Jude the 'terribly sensible advice' of 'remaining in your own sphere and sticking to your trade'. In exasperated response, Jude scrawled in chalk on the *Biblioll* wall, 'I have understanding as well as you; I am not inferior to you: Yea, who knoweth not such things as these? – Job XII, 3.' In the centre of Broad Street is a cobbled cross in the road surface; this is 'the cross in the pavement which marked the spot of the Martyrdoms' where Jude arranges to first meet Sue. A plaque on the wall of Balliol College gives the details of this 'gloomy and inauspicious place'.

From Broad Street, turn right up Magdalen Street East into St Giles. Pass the front of St John's College, whose twentieth-century alumni include Phillip Larkin, much influenced by Hardy, **to reach the adjoining Lamb and Flag.** This is the 'obscure and low-ceiled tavern up a court' where Jude, his academic hopes frustrated, drowned his sorrows 'long and slowly' in liquor before reciting the Nicene Creed in Latin. Later, Jude's amatory hopes frustrated by Sue's marriage to Phillotson, he again resorts to the same inn 'one of the great palpitating centres in Christminster life', 'now a popular tavern … entirely renovated and refitted in modern style', replete with Arabella as barmaid. In the twenty-first century, the profits from the Lamb and Flag are used to fund graduate scholarships at the adjoining St John's College and thus enables modern-day Judes the fulfilment which he was denied. From the Lamb and Flag it is but a short walk to the 'suburb nicknamed Beersheba' where Jude found 'on inexpensive terms the modest type of accommodation he demanded'.

Cross over St Giles and as it forks into the Woodstock Road, turn left down Little Clarendon Street and continue straight on down Walton Crescent and along Nelson Street to bear right into Canal Street. Note the typical late nineteenth-century two-storey terraced housing: slate roofed, solid-brick walls, some unpainted with beautifully surviving salt-glazed headers, a few stone fronted. This is Jericho, originally developed to house the workers of the nearby Oxford University Press and now being jealously preserved in its working-class authenticity by Oxford City Council. The houses resemble Hardy's description of Spring Street in *Aldbrickham* (Reading), for which an exact local original cannot be found.

A short way down Canal Street, it intersects with St Barnabas. Here stands the 'Church of ceremonies – St Silas', built in 1868–9 to the design of Hardy's former employer A.W. Blomfield, then, as now, 'the premier Anglo-Catholic Church in Oxford'. Sue betrays her attendance here by returning home smelling of incense. Subsequently failing to return home, Jude seeks her out in the church, which he has never previously visited:

> High overhead, above the chancel steps, Jude could discern a huge, solidly constructed Latin cross – as large, probably, as the original it was designed to commemorate. It seemed to be suspended in the air by invisible wires; it was set with large jewels, which faintly glimmered in some weak ray caught from outside, as the cross swayed to and fro in a silent and scarcely perceptible motion. Underneath, upon the floor, lay what appeared to be a heap of black clothes ... it was his Sue's form, prostrate on the paving.

The church remains ornate and beautifully decorated with a large gilt cross suspended over the altar steps.

From the church return via Victor Street and Jericho Street to Walton Street, where on your right you will find a pub named Jude the Obscure. Turn left down Walton Street and, beyond Juxton Street, a short leftward extension of Walton Street leads to the gatehouse of St Sepulchre's Cemetery. Here Jude's children were buried (plate 8.7). Closed to new business for the last fifty years, St Sepulchre's forms a leafy and tranquil wilderness amidst the noisy bustle of the city, although overlooked on two sides by tall apartment terraces, which have replaced the factories which were its original nineteenth-century neighbours. This is a place to pause and reflect, catch up on Jude or 'The Complete Poems'. The only poem relating directly to Oxford is 'Evelyn G. of Christminster' (CP 578), written in

8.7 The cemetery,
Beersheba

memory of Emma's cousin, Evelyn Gifford, the daughter of Canon Gifford, who had married Hardy and Emma.

From St Sepulchre's it is only a ten-minute walk down Walton Street back to Oxford Station. Although Jude initially enters *Christminster* on foot, the increasingly frenetic journeys of the main characters as the novel accelerates through its last three parts are made by train. Oxford Station is now an entirely late twentieth-century reconstruction and offers little succour to the imagination of the Hardyan tourist.

Melchester, Shaston, Aldbrickham and Elsewhere

Part Third: Great Railway Journeys

'Shall we go and sit in the cathedral?' he asked, when their meal was finished.

'Cathedral? Yes. Though I think I'd rather sit in the railway station,' she answered, a remnant of vexation still in her voice. 'That's the centre of the town life now. The cathedral has had its day!'

When Jude re-encounters Arabella in the Lamb and Flag, they head for the railway station. But instead of catching the train to *Alfredston* Road, as intended to meet Sue, he adopts Arabella's suggestion 'of the nine-forty to Aldbrickham' but a 'half-hour's journey', then as now, from Oxford to Reading. For their one-night stand they check in at 'a third-rate inn near the station in time for a late supper'; by an unfortunate coincidence Jude takes Sue to the same inn on the first night of their unconsummated elopement a month or so later. On this occasion Hardy names it the George – which today claims to be the oldest building in Reading (1423) and the town's premier hotel, perhaps never 'a third-rate inn' – in King Street, only five minutes' walk from the station. Spring Street, where Jude and Sue lived as an unmarried couple and raised their small children, cannot positively be identified; I can add nothing to Kay-Robinson's valiant attempts to do so. Similarly, 'the church which was only two miles off', where Jude is commissioned to restore the Decalogue – being the impetus for the story of the Devil and the Ten Commandments in a 'church out by Gaymead' – and *Gaymead* itself, 'the pretty village' of 'The Son's Veto', remain completely elusive. Kay-Robinson's argument that Sulhamstead is the most likely original for *Gaymead* has not been strengthened by the recent demolition of the village church. If forced to name an original for *Gaymead*, I would go for Theale, which is exactly where Hardy placed the village on his Wessex map.

To return to the railways, 'In the down-train that was timed to reach Aldbrickham station about ten o'clock ... a small, pale child's face could be seen in the gloom of a third-class carriage. He had large, frightened eyes, and wore a white woollen cravat, over which a key was suspended round his neck by a piece of common string ... in the band of his hat his half-ticket was stuck.' His sombre eyes 'seemed mutely to say: "All laughing comes from misapprehension. Rightly looked at there is no laughable thing under the sun."' Thus Little Father Time, conceived near *Marygreen* but born in Australia, travels to *Aldbrickham* from Lambeth, seen by some critics as a self-portrait of Hardy as a child; he subsequently recreated this image in the magical poem 'Midnight on the Great Western' (CP 465).

Like Jude, his father, before him, the child is 'deposited' on an alien landscape 'from a railway station southward'. The railway becomes not only the strongest metaphor for the restless displaced mobility of the modern age but the railway map and the railway timetable become the very framework around which the novel is constructed. From the boy Jude's first deportation northward from Dorset to the man Jude's final suicidal journey from Oxford to

Alfredston Road and back, the text contains descriptions of no less than twenty-three railway journeys. When Jude and Sue take a day trip to Wardour Castle (now divided into apartments), Hardy is briefly captivated by the romance of the age of steam; the trains may 'scream' but the guard thinks they are lovers and 'everything formed a beautiful crystallization'. Otherwise the railway merely represents the structuring conveyance of modern life: 'he would meet her at *Alfredston* Road, the following evening … if she could come by the up-train which crossed his down-train at that station'. Travel by train is inexpensive, for the generally impecunious Sue and Jude have no compunctions about such repeated arrangements. Indeed when they take Little Father Time to the Great Wessex Agricultural Show, it is for 'a day's excursion at small expense'.

Here at *Stoke-Barehills* (Basingstoke), where 'the fast arriving excursion trains two from different directions enter the two contiguous railway stations at almost the same minute', the 'picturesque mediaeval ruins' still exist beside the railway in the now disused and tranquil cemetery. To the south the ancient parish church of St Michael exudes a melancholy charm absent from its 'gaunt unattractive' modern neighbours, and beyond it the showground survives as May's Bounty Cricket Ground.

Although many Wessex Railway lines did not survive the twentieth century, the remaining routes still provide a wonderful way of exploring Hardy's landscape, particularly the main line from Southampton to *Budmouth* (Weymouth); this passes through the heart of Hardy's Wessex, offering unrivalled views of the *Valley of the Great Dairies, Egdon* Heath and *Mellstock*.

Wessex Heights

'I think I am one born out of due time, who has no calling here' (CP 137)

In the 1890s Hardy underwent a difficult period: in 1892 his father died; in 1893 he fell in love with Florence Henniker but his advances were rejected; 1894 marked his twentieth wedding anniversary to the barren, uncompanionable, 'inconsequential' Emma; in 1895 he celebrated his fifty-fifth birthday and *Jude the Obscure* was published; but in 1896 *Jude the Obscure* was reviled by critics, burnt by the Bishop of Wakefield and withdrawn by WHSmith. As a consequence, Hardy sunk into a deep, dark depression, which found creative expression in such poems as 'The Dead Man Walking' (CP 166) and the *In Tenebris* sequence where 'death will not appal / One who, past doubtings all, / Waits in unhope' (CP 136–8), and culminating in that cathartic piece of writing, frequently regarded as his finest poem, 'Wessex Heights' (CP 261), completed on 14 December 1896.

> There are some heights in Wessex, shaped as if by a kindly hand
> For thinking, dreaming, dying on, and at crises when I stand,
> Say, on Ingpen Beacon eastward, or on Wylls-Neck westwardly,
> I seem where I was before my birth, and after death may be.

Hardy, whose narrative technique is often described as cinematic and depends so much upon the distant observation of a person or scene from an isolated viewpoint, was a lover of barren hilltops. They were a final citadel against 'the devices and desires of this world', a place of retreat and a place of communion with both nature and the inner self; the expression of an instinctual need to escape to a place where 'mind-chains do not clank' because 'one's next neighbour is the sky'; a place where in Wordsworthian phrase 'the heavy and weary weight / Of all this unintelligible world / Is lightened'.

Inkpen Beacon stands at the highest point on the ridge of hills running parallel to but twelve miles (nineteen kilometres) south of Jude's North Wessex Ridgeway, separated by the valley of the River Kennet (plate 8.8). At Inkpen the boundaries of Berkshire, Hampshire and Wiltshire converge; from

8.8 *Ingpen Beacon*

the long barrow, surmounted by Coombe Gibbet, the views extend north-wards into Oxfordshire and south across a series of Wessex Heights to the New Forest and the Isle of Wight beyond. The adjoining Walbury Hill at 970 feet (295 metres) is the highest point in Southern England, east of the Quantocks.

Westwardly, in the Quantocks, stands *Wylls-Neck*; at 1261 feet (385 metres) above sea level, this is Hardy's wildest Wessex Height and the one with which he had least personal involvement. This is Coleridge and Wordsworth Country. Footpaths converge on this moorland peak from all directions, including Nether Stowey, although the most direct route is from the village of West Bagborough onto the Macmillan Way. By car, the me-andering road through the forest from Plainsfield to the car park at Triscombe is closest. On a clear day *Wylls-Neck* commands outstanding views: north across the Bristol Channel to Wales, east over the Somerset Levels, west to Exmoor and, especially, north-west towards Dunster, Minehead and the land-scape of *A Laodicean*.

> In the lowlands I have no comrade, not even the lone man's friend –
> Her who suffereth long and is kind; accepts what he is too weak to mend:
> Down there they are dubious and askance; there nobody thinks as I,
> But mind-chains do not clank where one's next neighbour is the sky.

'Her who suffereth long and is kind' is most probably Emma Hardy.

> In the towns I am tracked by phantoms having weird detective ways –
> Shadows of beings who fellowed with myself of earlier days:
> They hang about at places, and they say harsh heavy things –
> Men with a wintry sneer, and women with tart disparagings.

> Down there I seem to be false to myself, my simple self that was,
> And is not now, and I see him watching, wondering what crass cause
> Can have merged him into such a strange continuator as this,
> Who yet has something in common with himself, my chrysalis.

> I cannot go to the great grey Plain; there's a figure against the moon,
> Nobody sees it but I, and it makes my breast beat out of tune;
> I cannot go to the tall-spired town, being barred by the forms now passed
> For everybody but me, in whose long vision they stand there fast.

The 'great grey Plain' has been interpreted by some authorities as being *Egdon Heath* and the figure as Jemima Hardy. Both these interpretations seem improbable: the Plain conjoined with the 'tall-spired town' suggest Salisbury and the figure possibly Tryphena Sparks or Eliza Nicholls.

> There's a ghost at Yell'ham Bottom chiding loud at the fall of the night,
> There's a ghost in Froom-side Vale, thin-lipped and vague, in a shroud of white,
> There is one in the railway train whenever I do not want it near,
> I see its profile against the pane, saying what I would not hear.

'Yell'ham Bottom' is the point where the path called Snail Creep ('Dick Goes Nutting') crosses the old main road (A35). 'Froom-side Vale' could be applied to the water meadows either side of Stinsford. The ghosts are either Tryphena, Fanny Hurd (both by then dead and buried, the latter in Stinsford) or Cassie Pole. The ghost in the railway train 'saying what I would not hear' is most probably Florence Henniker who did exactly this on their fateful journey by train from Eastleigh to Winchester on Tuesday 8 August 1893. Mrs Henniker is without doubt the 'rare fair woman' of the following stanza:

> As for one rare fair woman, I am now but a thought of hers,
> I enter her mind and another thought succeeds me that she prefers;
> Yet my love for her in its fullness she herself even did not know;
> Well, time cures hearts of tenderness, and now I can let her go.

This is a wonderfully succinct summary of the fate of all unrequited lovers.

> So I am found on Ingpen Beacon, or on Wylls-Neck to the west,
> Or else on homely Bulbarrow, or little Pilsdon Crest,
> Where men have never cared to haunt, nor women have walked with me,
> And ghosts then keep their distance; and I know some liberty.

Bulbarrow Hill is indeed the most 'homely', being only ten miles (sixteen kilometres) north of Dorchester on a stretch of the Dorset Ridgeway, due south of Sturminster Newton. Surprisingly, it is also the least accessible, being guarded east and west by radio transmitting masts, complete with barbed wire fencing and MOD 'Keep Out' signs (plate 8.9). Although at 902 feet (275 metres) it is the third highest point in Dorset, the views (southerly only) are limited by hedging, all, sadly, twentieth-century despoliation. A far more spectacular panorama can be obtained from its eastern extremity, Woolland Hill, where Blackmoor Vale stretches out beneath your feet, and from its western outpost, Rawlsbury Camp, an Iron Age hill fort from where most of Hardy's Wessex and five geographical counties can be seen. Nearby Hambledon Hill, the first in

8.9 View towards Bulbarrow

8.10 View across Marshwood Vale

Hardy's litany of Wessex Heights at the start of *Tess of the D'Urbervilles*, makes up for what it lacks in height (623 feet (190 metres)) by its spectacular appearance – a mile-long vertical wall of chalk downland, dividing Blackmoor from *The Chase*, with superb views to match.

'Little Pilsdon Crest' is Pilsdon Pen, tucked away near the Somerset and Devon borders, west of Beaminster and due north of Golden Cap. At 909 feet (275 metres) it was long believed to be the highest point in Dorset, but a recent reassessment has given this accolade to Lewesdon, its wooded neighbour to the east (now 915 feet (280 metres) high). In the care of the National Trust, Pilsdon offers unspoilt views southward across Marshwood Vale to the sea (plate 8.10).

Review: In the summer of 1893 Hardy fell in love with Florence Henniker, resulting in a literary friendship which was to last her lifetime, rather than the passionate affair for which his heart was yearning. Between their meetings, he occupied his mind with the restoration of West Knighton Church and research in Berkshire and Oxfordshire for the book which was to become his final novel, *Jude the Obscure* – a restless, peripatetic story of the modern age, situated far from his *Egdon* heartland. This account explores the landscape of *Jude the Obscure*. Beginning at *Marygreen*, recognizable still from Hardy's description, it follows Jude's footsteps across Farmer Troutham's field to reach the *Alfredston* road and the site of the Brown House; this was identified by Hardy as being on the eastern escarpment, not beside the Ridgeway to the west, where all recent Hardy topographers have placed it. Beyond lies Arabella's Cottage, *Alfredston* and *Christminster*, where a two-hour walk encompasses the urban landscape of the novel. Beyond *Christminster*, the train leads Jude to 'Melchester, Shaston, Aldbrickham and elsewhere'; the railway is not only the strongest metaphor for the restless, displaced mobility of the modern age but the railway map and the railway timetable are the very framework around which the novel is constructed.

Wessex Heights, the major poem which arose (along with the *In Tenebris* sequence and 'The Dead Man Walking') out of the deep depression which followed the publication of *Jude the Obscure*, contains the distilled essence of Hardy's creative genius and tentative philosophy. The poet has become the archetypal Hardyan protagonist, alone on a series of hilltops, a spectator rather than an active participant in the world around him, the landscape beneath his feet populated by phantoms 'saying what I would not hear', but here unobserved but observing: the 'ghosts then keep their distance; and I know some liberty'.

CHAPTER NINE

Beyond Wessex

'THE HORIZONS AND landscapes' of Hardy's 'partly real, partly dream country' extend far beyond his neatly delineated Wessex. In four out of his fourteen novels, considerable parts of the story are set in London, two involve lengthy expeditions to the continent, and in a further five novels significant plot events occur – off-stage, so to speak – in different parts of the globe. London was Hardy's home from February 1862 to August 1867 and intermittently thereafter. When early critics tried to dismiss him as a naive young man from a rural backwater, he pointed out that he was equally a Londoner, fully acquainted with all that the metropolis had to offer, both in terms of culture and popular entertainment. He made full use of the capital city, stating, as an example, that he had heard Palmerston speak in the House of Commons and subsequently attended his funeral in Westminster Abbey. London, certainly, exercised a profound influence upon the man of Wessex.

Thomas Hardy's London

Reminiscences of a Dancing Man

By foot and underground train (seven miles/eleven kilometres)

This walk is not a definitive guide to Hardy's London but rather an introduction to those buildings or places in London most associated with him and which survive in a form evocative enough of his life, work and times to be worth visiting. As an established writer, with a substantial home in Dorchester, he made an annual pilgrimage to mix with the titled and fashionable in London, a habit which started in the 1880s and continued up until the First World War; however, I have excluded many of the hotels, flats and houses where he stayed temporarily during the London season, as well as Covent Garden, where he made his stage debut on Boxing Day 1866.

The walk starts at Waterloo Station because this is where Hardy first arrived in London courtesy of the London and South Western Railway; the line had been extended from Southampton to Dorchester in 1847, where it officially opened on 1 June, the eve of Hardy's seventh birthday. Hardy first came to London in 1849 when he accompanied his mother on a visit to her sister in Hertfordshire. On their return journey they stayed at the Cross-Keys in Clerkenwell where 'Shelley and Mary Godwin had been accustomed to meet at weekends not two-score years before'. The walk ends at Westminster Abbey where Hardy's ashes were interred in Poets' Corner on Monday 16 January 1928.

Leave Waterloo Station down the steps of the main entrance. This war memorial is a piece of prehistoric Dorset, being made from Portland Stone – as are the British Museum, St Paul's Cathedral and County Hall. In August 1914, the wounded from Mons, the first major battle of the First World War, were brought from France to this station. The station is, of course, named after the concluding battle of the Napoleonic Wars, the history of which had held a lifelong fascination for Hardy, culminating in his magnum opus *The Dynasts*. Hardy, who twice visited the field of Waterloo, was deeply disturbed by the harsh realities of the Boer War and even more distressed and depressed by the First World War, which destroyed his 'melioristic' views of the gradual bettering of human nature. Hardy's greatest war poetry was however his poetry of the Boer war, poetry which was to strongly influence the younger generation of poets, who flowered briefly in the trenches of Northern France. Beside this memorial, read 'Drummer Hodge' (CP 60).

From Waterloo, head west past the Festival Hall and cross Hungerford Bridge. Descend the steps to Victoria Embankment Gardens and cut diagonally across these, then turn left along the road and up the steps (before Adelphi Parking) to 8 Adelphi Terrace (note the stone plaque), facing the river. Hardy came to London aged twenty-one on Thursday 17 April 1862. He arrived at Waterloo after a four-hour journey from Dorchester where he had purchased a return ticket, for he had no prior arrangements for either work or accommodation. He had a letter of introduction from Hicks, his Dorchester employer, to two London architects, the second of whom, Arthur Blomfield, offered Hardy immediate work as a 'Gothic draughtsman who could restore and design churches and rectory houses'. Hardy first worked for Blomfield at 9 St Martins Place but moved into the building which stood here in February 1863; he wrote to his sister Mary, saying, 'the new office is a capital place – on the first floor overlooking the river. On a clear day every bridge is visible.' But Hardy worked here before the Embankment had been constructed, at a time when the

Thames was little more than a 'tidal sewer'. In summer the stench from the Thames was so intense that all windows in their offices had to be kept tight shut despite the heat; Hardy's health deteriorated to the point where he was too weak 'to hold the pencil and square' and was forced to return to Dorset in July 1867, thus ending his longest continuous period of residence in London.

Royston Pike records how both Parliament and the law courts were at times disrupted by 'a sudden outbreak of stench from the river'. This was a particular problem in the 1860s because the major mid nineteenth-century drive to improve sanitation had provided clean piped water and promoted the widespread use of water closets without there being any change in the sewerage system; this could not cope with the increased demand and, as a result, discharged untreated sewage straight into the Thames, which was unenclosed and tidal. In *The Hand of Ethelberta*, Picotee:

> ... arrived in town late on a cold February afternoon, bearing a small bag in her hand. She crossed Westminster Bridge on foot, just after dusk, and saw a luminous haze hanging over each well-lighted street as it withdrew into distance behind the nearer houses, showing its direction as a train of morning mist shows the course of a distant stream when the stream itself is hidden. The lights along the riverside towards Charing Cross sent an inverted palisade of gleaming swords down into the shaking water, and the pavement ticked to the touch of the pedestrians' feet, most of whom tripped along as if walking only to practise a favourite quick step and held handkerchiefs to their mouths to strain off the river mist from their lungs.

In Hardy's day there was a toll on Waterloo Bridge, so the normal route across the Thames from Waterloo Station, for Hardy as for Picotee, was via Westminster Bridge. On Hardy's last visit to London (21 April 1920), to attend Harold Macmillan's wedding, he stayed at J.M. Barrie's flat very near here. As a young man about town, Hardy lived life to the full, as he records in the poem 'Reminiscences of a Dancing Man' (CP 165).

Retrace your steps to the corner, then turn left up Adam Street to the Strand. Cross diagonally left to Bedford Street. This is where Hardy worked in 1872 for T. Roger Smith, designing new school buildings. **Turn left into Chandos Place.** Note the Dickens blue plaque on the wall to your left. Hardy regularly attended Dickens's readings at the Hanover Square Rooms.

Keep straight onto St Martin's Place. Here, on your right, at No. 9, Hardy started work for Blomfield. The Alpine Club shared the same building; thus Hardy met Leslie Stephen, the editor of the *Cornhill Magazine*, who subsequently published *Far From the Madding Crowd* and *The Hand of Ethelberta*.

From 1885, when he moved into Max Gate, Hardy regularly spent a month or so during 'the season' in London, initially in lodgings but subsequently renting a house or flat. At least seventeen such temporary homes can be identified, but visiting them offers little reward. The next part of the walk takes in the British Museum and five of Hardy's early lodgings. **It can, however, be excluded by taking the Piccadilly Line from Leicester Square to King's Cross.** Hardy generally used his feet to cross London but did try the 'underground railway' which he described as 'excellently arranged'!

Otherwise, head from St Martin's Place to Great Russell Street and the British Museum. Here Hardy spent a considerable amount of time over many years conducting research in the British Library – in the process courting his amanuensis, Florence Dugdale, who was to become his second wife. The British Museum is the setting for Florence Henniker's admonition in 'A Broken Appointment' (CP 99). Hardy lodged at No. 56 Great Russell Street, opposite the magnificent South Front of the museum.

First left, immediately beyond the museum, is Montague Street where Hardy stayed at both 29 and 23 (now the Ruskin Hotel). Just past this, at 74–77 Great Russell Street, are the offices of Faber & Faber, publishers of many poets influenced by Hardy. **Take the next left into Bedford Place,** where Hardy lodged at No. 14, **and continue across Russell Square into Bedford Way,** where Hardy stayed at 28 – sadly neither of these buildings is the original. **On reaching Euston Road, bear right past the new British Library and the gleamingly restored St Pancras Hotel to turn left into Pancras Road – use the paired pedestrian crossings by the corner of Nature Reserve – then under the railway to turn right into St Pancras Old Churchyard.** On the left behind the church, you will find 'The Hardy Tree' (plate 9.1).

This hillock is the site of an old Roman encampment and legend has it that a church has stood on this site since AD 313. The construction of the Midland Railway out of St Pancras Station in 1865 required 'the removal of many hundreds of coffins and bones in huge quantities'. The architect Arthur Blomfield, for whom Hardy was working, was the son of a former Bishop of London and therefore considered a proper man for the removal of graveyards. Blomfield gave Hardy the job of supervising this process which took place during the night behind high hoardings to the light of flare-lamps. It was a gruesome job; Hardy records how one coffin fell apart and was found to contain a single skeleton with two skulls. The poet in Hardy responded to these macabre activities: see 'The Levelled Churchyard' (CP 127):

> We late-lamented, resting here,
>   Are mixed to human jam,
> And each of us exclaims in fear,
>   'I know not which I am!' (plate 9.2)

9.1 The Hardy Society paying homage at the Hardy Tree

9.2 Human jam

Hardy was aware that it was in this graveyard that Shelley first saw and fell in love with Mary Godwin, whilst she was visiting the tomb of her mother, Mary Wollstonecraft, and made love to her on her mother's grave. Hearing of forthcoming railway works, Shelley's son had his grandparents' bodies exhumed to be buried in Bournemouth beside their daughter, Mary. The churchyard still forms an oasis in the centre of this febrile city. It is an appropriate point to pause and read:

This hum of the wheel – the roar of London! What is it composed of? Hurry, speech, laughters, moans, cries of little children. The people in this tragedy laugh, sing, smoke, toss off wines, etc., make love to girls in drawing-rooms and areas; and yet are playing their parts in the tragedy just the same. Some wear jewels and feathers, some wear rags. All are caged birds; the only difference lies in the size of the cage. This too is part of the tragedy ... How pathetic it all is! (*The Life*, 28 May 1885).

By way of contrast, and also from *The Life*:

May 1894: A Party at the Countess of Yarborough's: On coming away there were no cabs to be got [on account of a strike, it seems], and I returned to SK on the top of a 'bus. No sooner was I up there than the rain began again. A girl who had scrambled up after me asked for the shelter of my umbrella, and I gave it – when she startled me by holding on tight to my arm and bestowing on me many kisses for the trivial kindness. She told me she had been to 'The Pav', and was tired and was going home. She had not been drinking. I descended at South Kensington Station and watched the 'bus bearing her away. An affectionate nature wasted on the streets! It was a strange contrast to the scene I had just left.

The party most likely bore a close resemblance to Lady Iris's crush, detailed in Part Second of *The Well-Beloved*. Also consider some of his London poems, particularly 'An East-End Curate' (CP 679), 'In St Paul's a While Ago' (CP 683) and 'Coming up Oxford Street; Evening' (CP 684).

Retrace your steps to King's Cross Station and take the Hammersmith and City Line to Royal Oak. Turn left over the bridge out of Royal Oak, then right over the pedestrian crossing and straight ahead into Westbourne Park Villas. Hardy lived at No. 16 from the summer of 1863 until July 1867 (not the dates on the blue plaque). Apart from an initial stay in Kilburn, all Hardy's London lodgings prior to his marriage were in the area just west of Paddington station. This appears to have been something of a West Country enclave since Paddington was the London terminus for most trains from the

West of England. Amongst the Dorset people here was Eliza Bright Nicholls (p.180), in service in Orsett Terrace, a short distance from Westbourne Park Villas. Millgate considers that they were 'more or less engaged from 1863–67' when Hardy probably lost his heart to her younger sister Mary. At least twenty-eight of Hardy's surviving poems were written at Westbourne Park Villas; many arising from his relationship with Eliza, including the 'She, to Him' sequence and his most-renowned early poem, 'Neutral Tones' (CP 9: p.187).

Hardy's room, at the rear on the second floor, looked towards St Stephen's Church, where he regularly attended worship; he sketched the view of the church from his room. In Hardy's time there were houses opposite, subsequently demolished as the railway expanded. The view across the railway from here is towards Elgin Avenue where on 17 September 1874 Hardy married Emma at St Peter's Church (now demolished), with her brother Walter, with whom she was staying in nearby Chippenham Road, and Sarah Williams, the daughter of Hardy's Cellbridge Place landlady, as the only witnesses.

Further down Westbourne Park Villas, turn left into Westbourne Park Passage to reach St Stephen's Church. Continue straight across to Kildare Terrace and Gardens, then left into Newton Road. Hardy and Emma lived at No. 18 from March to July 1875 (it is now part of the Medical Centre).

Follow this into Westbourne Grove, turn left and cross at the pedestrian crossing. Stop to admire the façade of Westbourne Hall, where Hardy attended lectures and concerts. **Walk on, then turn left up Queensway to Porchester Leisure Centre (the old Public Baths), then left up Porchester Road.** Hardy lived at No. 50 – then No. 4 Cellbridge Place – intermittently from March 1872 until his marriage. **Retrace your steps to turn left through Porchester Square, then right and soon left into Orsett Terrace.** Eliza lived at the elegant No. 40 – then No. 2 Orsett Place. **Turn right into Westbourne Terrace, left into Bishop's Bridge Road and right into Eastbourne Terrace to reach Paddington Station.**

From Paddington, take the Circle Line to Victoria and thence the train to Wandsworth Common. From the station, follow the path across the Common to St James's Drive. Turn left, then right into Nottingham Road, then right down Trinity Road. At the corner of Brodrick Road, you will find 172 Trinity Road (blue plaque) (plate 9.3). In this house, known then as The Larches, 1 Arundel Terrace, Tooting, Hardy and Emma lived from 22 March 1878 to 22 June 1881 and Hardy completed *The Return of the Native* and wrote *The Trumpet-Major.* On 19 May 1878, Hardy could not sleep, partly on account of an eerie feeling that sometimes haunted him – a horror at lying down in close proximity to 'a monster whose body had four million heads and eight million eyes'. He wrote: 'In the upper back bedroom at daybreak: just past three. A golden light behind the horizon; within it are the

9.3 The author
outside 172 Trinity
Road, Tooting

four million. The roofs are damp grey: the streets are filled with night as with
a dark stagnant flood.'

It was here, whilst writing the early chapters of *A Laodicean*, that Hardy
fell seriously ill. Overcome by 'an indescribable physical weariness', he
took to his bed on 24 October and was visited first by Dr Beck, who lived
nearby, and then Dr Arthur Shears, who was recommended by Hardy's
neighbour, Alexander Macmillan, of the publishing house. Both doctors
diagnosed 'internal bleeding'. Hardy, who described himself as 'in considerable pain', accepted the recommended treatment of being 'compelled to
lie on an inclined plane with the lower part of his body higher than his
head', rather than submit himself to 'a dangerous operation'. From this
awkward position, with his 'feet on the mantelpiece', he dictated *A
Laodicean* to Emma. This illness confined Hardy to the house for six
months, at the end of which time the Hardys decided to move back to
Dorset for good.

A graphic account of his sufferings is recorded in 'A Wasted Illness' (CP
122). Here he also wrote 'Beyond the Last Lamp' (CP 257), 'A January Night'

(CP 400), 'Snow in the Suburbs' (CP 701) and 'A Light Snowfall after Frost' (CP 702).

Turn back up Trinity Road, past the church where Hardy worshipped, to Bellevue Road and right beside the common to catch the train back to Victoria. Follow Victoria Street (or take the underground) to Westminster Abbey; if you walk you will pass Ashley Gardens (beside Westminster Cathedral), where Hardy took a flat in 1895. To enter the abbey, except for 'divine worship', costs £15, so you may prefer to **head for the garden by the South Transept,** on the outside of Poets' Corner, where Hardy's ashes are buried.

Hardy attended funerals at Westminster Abbey including Palmerston's (1865), Tennyson's (1893) and Meredith's memorial service (1909). In 1893, he became infatuated with Florence Henniker and offered to teach her about architecture, starting with Westminster Abbey – read 'A Thunderstorm in Town' (CP 255). Dickens and Tennyson are actually buried in Poets' Corner but abbey authorities would not allow Hardy the space, insisting that his body be cremated. Internment in Westminster Abbey was directly contrary to Hardy's express wish to be buried at Stinsford in the grave of his once-more-beloved Emma and beside the graves of his parents and grandparents. The Vicar of Stinsford suggested a somewhat bizarre compromise, which was then carried out; a local surgeon removed his heart, his body was taken to Woking for cremation, and in simultaneous services his heart was buried beside Emma whilst his ashes were interred here in Poets' Corner. Here read 'The Impercipient' (CP 44) and 'Afterwards' (CP 511).

This walk gives a feel of Hardy's personal London. Many of the sights of his descriptive passages can no longer be relived: the Swancourts in Rotten Row, Knight's chambers at *Bede's* (Clement's) Inn, the setting of 'To a Tree in London' (CP 852), or the mud-splashed wharves along the Thames, described in both *A Pair of Blue Eyes* and *The Well-Beloved*. Also gone for good are 'those crowded rooms of old yclept', 'The Argyle', Willis's (Almack's) balls and 'Gay Cremorne' Gardens, which so thrilled the heart of the young man up from the West Country.

'Dear Abroad ...'

Hardy: 'Our experiences were much like those of other people visiting for the first time the buildings, pictures and historic sites of the continent.'

Tom and Emma made six trips abroad together; their first was their honeymoon in 1874, which was the first time either of them had left England, and their last was their 'pilgrimage' to Switzerland in June 1897, timed to escape 'the racket of the coming Diamond Jubilee'. In matters of travel, as in matters of housing, the Hardys behaved like a conventional Victorian middle-class couple. Their itineraries were carefully planned in advance from Baedeker; Hardy's copies can still be inspected with careful pencil markings against hotels, places of interest and points of travel advice plus annotations against targets achieved in the form of 'T.H. E.L.H. 1887'. Emma's diaries survive covering four of the six holidays.

France

Knight's adventures abroad in *A Pair of Blue Eyes* can be ascribed to textbook knowledge. Ethelberta travels from *Knollsea* to Cherbourg (unlikely the Hardys who preferred Dover but once used Southampton) and thence by train to Rouen in *The Hand of Ethelberta*, thus partly re-enacting the Hardys' honeymoon – the detailed descriptions being presumably first-hand, with Baedeker as backup. A significant amount of the action of *A Laodicean* takes place on the continent in the form of a protracted chase between the various participants, who continually just miss each other. The detailed description of the cruise up the Rhine is a reversal of the Hardys' own itinerary from June 1876. When Somerset returns to Normandy, pursued this time by Paula, they re-enact, once more in reverse, the Hardys' itinerary from their July 1880 holiday. To follow in their footsteps is not especially rewarding: Le Havre has grown exponentially; Trouville would appeal even less to Hardy now than it did then; only the medieval heart of Honfleur remains beautiful and unscathed.

Étretat, however, is still well worth visiting. The heavily scored chalk cliffs with their dramatic arches and stacks strongly resemble Purbeck – the local drink is *cidre* and the cottages are frequently thatched. The town remains modest and despite two world wars still retains its medieval core. Sadly the Hotel Blanquet in which both the Hardys and Monet (1883) stayed has been demolished to make way for an apartment block, but there are still fishing boats on the beach outside, as painted by Monet. Hardy's description of Étretat as 'the village between the cliffs' parallels his description of *Knollsea*. This is the beach from which Hardy swam for so long that he developed the chill which, he believed, contributed to his severe illness of 1880–1 during which he had to dictate *A Laodicean* to Emma with his feet on the mantelpiece; small wonder then that the novel contained much recycled holiday experience. This is the beach on which Paula finally catches up with Somerset and the terrible misunderstandings of the past are cast aside so that they become re-engaged both professionally and personally and 'there was friendly intercourse all round'.

The final illustration in A *Laodicean* shows Paula greeting Somerset on the beach at Étretat against a background of the arched 'door' with cliff-top chapel – a view unchanged to this day (plates 9.4 and 9.5).

9.4 Étretat, where Paula and Somerset are reconciled

9.5 Étretat

248

Waterloo

The Battlefield of Waterloo was Hardy's major objective on his travels abroad of both 1876 and 1896. Since childhood, he had been fascinated by the Napoleonic Wars, a preoccupation which resurfaced throughout his fiction and finally culminated in *The Dynasts*. He bought a new Baedeker on both occasions and pencilled in additional details, especially regarding the battle of Quatre Bras and the Duchess of Richmond's Ball, recording 'Rue de la Blanchisserie, 40 & 42 Coachmaker's Depot (now V. Vangenderachter, Brasseur)' in both copies. See 'The Eve of Waterloo' (CP 392). Hardy and Emma travelled by train to Waterloo station, walked the two miles (three kilometres) from there to the battlefield, and then walked around the entire site – a distance of about six miles (nine-and-a-half kilometres). It is small wonder that Emma complained the next day of 'being greatly fatigued and Tom cross about it'. Today the battlefield is well preserved and carefully managed. The *Butte-du-Lion* memorial gives a bird's-eye view over the site, as described by Emma. The farmhouses still exist, relatively unchanged, although the skulls are confined to the museum (the site of the hotel where the Hardys lunched), not available under the bread basket, as Emma experienced (plate 9.6). A battlefield tour in an open-sided lorry takes the pressure

9.6 Skulls at Waterloo – as seen by Emma

off the feet and the film of children playing over the battlefield *est très émou-vant*. Overall, to visit the fields where 10,000 men died and over 30,000 were wounded is a poignant experience which enhances one's understanding of both Hardy and *The Dynasts*.

Poems of Pilgrimage: Rome and Switzerland

Baedeker at the ready, the Hardys toured Italy in the spring of 1887 and Switzerland ten years later. The Italian trip was part standard tourist itinerary, with an emphasis on the pagan aspects, part pilgrimage to Keats and Shelley. The Swiss journey was almost entirely a pilgrimage in the footsteps of Byron (and Shelley), who in turn had followed the ghosts of Gibbon and Goethe. Wording from Baedeker can be detected in the first three of Hardy's Roman poems (CPs 68–70) and 'Genoa and the Mediterranean' (CP 66) is an angry lament that the reality fell far short of the guidebook description. 'Shelley's Skylark' (CP 67) soars far above these limitations but is based more on Hardy's lifelong love affair with the poet than on any Italian experience. Similarly, 'Rome: At the Pyramid of Cestius' (CP 71) is a beautiful poem, reflecting Hardy's admiration for 'those matchless singers'. The *Cimitero Acattolico*, in Rome, overshadowed by the Pyramid of Cestius, remains in Shelley's words 'beautiful and solemn' and worth visiting as the last resting place of Keats, who died in Rome from consumption, and of the ashes of Shelley, who was cremated on the shore near Viareggio where he drowned. Shelley's heart is buried in Bournemouth beside Mary Shelley (p.243). Emma's diary from the Venetian leg of the Hardys' trip found its way directly into 'Alicia's Diary'.

    With Napoleon's final defeat, the longstanding embargo on continental travel was lifted and, in the summer of 1816, many Englishmen, Byron and Shelley included, made haste to the Alps. En route, Byron visited Waterloo, purchasing relics from the battle, before settling at the Villa Diodati on the shores of Lac Leman, where Shelley joined him. During the course of the summer they met up with Monk Lewis and Madame de Stael and made Rousseau pilgrimages. Their subsequent itinerary reads like Hardy's trip of 1897 in reverse: Geneva, Ouchy, Vevey, Clarens, Chillon, Lausanne, Lauterbrunnen, Wengernalp, Interlaken, Brienz. On 27 June 1816, the twenty-ninth anniversary of the completion of *Decline and Fall*, they visited Gibbon's summerhouse, by then a ruin. Following in Goethe's footsteps they continued to the Staubbach Falls in Lauterbrunnen, then rode on horseback over Wengernalp to Grindelwald, passing 'the majestic Yungfrau and the two Eigers' – an experience subsequently reproduced by Byron in *Manfred*.

The Hardys' Swiss pilgrimage was therefore more Byron than Baedeker and since they travelled by train, and in Switzerland railways remain an effective means of transport, it is rewarding to retrace their path. **Interlaken is easily reached by train from England. Change here for Grindelwald and thence catch the train from Grund to Kleine Scheidegg, although I would strongly recommend walking up. If you walk, take the path first overshadowed by 'The Schreckhorn'** (CP 264) – Hardy's tribute to Leslie Stephen who first conquered this mountain in 1861 (interestingly each of Hardy's Swiss poems is about an Englishman at a particular place and time) – **and then by the enormous gloomy north face of the Eiger (plate 9.7). From Kleine Scheidegg walk down to Wengernalp in the footsteps of Tom and Emma,** the path dominated by the magnificent trilogy of Eiger, Mönch and Jungfrau with the more delicate Schneehorn and Silberhorn beyond. It is still possible to sit on the terrace outside the Hotel Jungfrau at Wengernalp and have tea facing these wonderful mountains but sadly only in the winter months, for in the twenty-first century the hotel only opens during the skiing season. The onward walk to Lauterbrunnen via Wengen is most rewarding – for the flowers, the scenery and the pure joy of the Alpine air – or the train is at hand (plate 9.8). In Lauterbrunnen the Staubbach Falls, admired by Goethe, Byron and Hardy, are only a short distance from the station.

9.7 The Schreckhorn with the Eiger Nordwand in the foreground

9.8 Wengernalp 1895 with Eiger and Monch dominant

9.9 The Matterhorn as seen from Zermatt

The Hardys followed Byron to Lausanne, staying at the Hotel Gibbon. Hardy sat up in the garden to midnight on 27 June to catch Byron's passing spirit, see 'Lausanne: In Gibbon's Old Garden: 11–12 p.m.' (CP 72); this poem adds Milton to the list of Hardy's literary antecedents. Today both hotel and garden have been redeveloped, the spirits of romanticism long-since vacating the spot. A short train journey from Lausanne brings you to Montreux and the Chateau de Chillon, which remains Switzerland's most visited historic monument. The train continues down the Rhone Valley, where the avenues of Lombardy Poplars were planted by Napoleon, to Brig. The connecting railway here takes you up the wild steep-sided Mattertal to Zermatt, which, like Wengen, has refused to surrender to the internal combustion engine.

Zermatt, a small village in 1897, is now a sprawling urban resort, but this does not detract from the beauty, splendour and wonder of the mountains, especially that of the amazing, dominant Matterhorn. It is still possible to stay at the Hotel Mt Cervin as the Hardys did although it now has five stars with prices to match. The path to Riffelalp is easy to find, steep, of course, as Emma said, but yields fine views of the Matterhorn, once the alp is reached. It can be approached much more lazily by the Gornergrat Railway, which was under construction in 1897. Here read Hardy's sonnet tribute to Whymper 'Zermatt: to the Matterhorn' (CP 73) (plate 9.9). There are a thousand wonderful things to experience in Zermatt, but a visit to the museum, with its displays strongly evocative of the world of Whymper and Victorian Alpinism, is well worthwhile. Call also at St Peters, the English church, where the Benedicite Omnia Opera is displayed in a frieze around the tops of the walls – just as recited by Tess on Rainbarrow as she first looks over the *Valley of the Great Dairies*.

Review: 'The horizons and landscapes' of Hardy's 'partly real, partly dream country' extend far beyond his neatly delineated Wessex. In four out of his fourteen novels, considerable parts of the story are set in London, two involve lengthy expeditions to the continent and in a further five novels significant plot events occur in different parts of the globe. London was Hardy's home from February 1862 to August 1867 and intermittently thereafter. This chapter follows a meandering route from Hardy's first point of arrival in the capital city, Waterloo Station, past various places of work and residence, to the final resting place of his ashes in Poets' Corner at Westminster Abbey. One of the high-points of this pilgrimage is the Hardy Tree, a magnificent ash forcing its way out through a palisade of compacted headstones in the tranquil oasis of St Pancras Old Churchyard. Abroad, we follow Hardy's literary and Romantic pilgrimages to Étretat, Waterloo, Rome and Switzerland, where he followed in the footsteps of Byron and Shelley, who in their turn had followed Goethe and Rousseau. The account ends at St Peter's Church in Zermatt where the Benedicite Omnia Opera is displayed in a frieze around the tops of the walls as recited by Tess on Rainbarrow in a typically Hardyan scene; the solitary observer surveying the landscape from a hidden vantage point.

CHAPTER TEN

Landscapes of the Mind

'... the essential energy of a Hardy novel is to be found in the descriptive detail, especially in his depiction of landscape' (1)

ABOVE ALL, HARDY was a landscape novelist and poet, who painted enduring pictures of a natural world – a real outdoor world – which formed the stage upon which his dream characters live out their tragic lives. Throughout his works, the landscape offers a tacit commentary on the mutability and brevity of existence, not just for his human protagonists but for all living creatures, from the maggoty ephemera 'heaving and wallowing with enjoyment' in the *Egdon* mud to the combatant trees locked in a perpetual struggle for survival 'In a Wood' (CP 40). These are the landscapes of Darwin – the voice of Wordsworth which echoed through his earliest writings (CP 1) long-since suppressed – there is no grand design; random chance and subconscious instinct are the governing forces which 'lure life on' (CP 388).

Egdon Heath forms the centre of Hardy's creative universe and *The Return of the Native*, the archetypal Hardyan text, in which the landscape is the main protagonist, of greater significance than the human beings who crawl over its face like 'ants on a great plain' or 'flies on a billiard table'. *The Return of the Native* opens with a detailed description, verging on the anthropomorphic, of the appearance of *Egdon* at different times and seasons expressed in terms of its moods and emotions. The chapter indeed is entitled 'A *Face* on Which Time Makes But Little Impression'. The title of the following chapter confirms the author's Darwinian view of the role of man in this world: 'Humanity Appears Upon the Scene, Hand in Hand with Trouble'. Not only do landscapes express mood but their emotions correlate directly with the feelings of the human flies upon the billiard table. As in *King Lear*, the storm without stands for the storm within.

For Hardy, man's behaviour is also driven by a kind of environmental determinism: the landscape which you occupy affects your outlook on the world at large; human affairs are determined by the context in which people live and work. Thus *Egdon* directly influences the state of mind of the heathmen, and the woodlands the conduct of *The Woodlanders*. In Wessex, character and environment thus meld together in a complex expressive metaphor as Hardy emphasizes and enlarges the differences between different landscapes to reflect the character and fate of their inhabitants.

Although this book is constructed around a series of walks through still identifiable landmarks and landscapes in Hardy's Wessex, it must not be forgotten that this is 'a partly real, partly dream country'. The first chapter of Book III of *The Return of the Native* is entitled 'My Mind To Me a Kingdom Is', an important signpost on the route to a full understanding of Wessex as a territory where the author's imagination reigns supreme. Although Hardy's characters inhabit a seemingly real landscape, it is not twenty-first century Wessex nor even nineteenth-century Dorset. His novels are not guidebooks; merely 'tales worth the telling' enacted upon a stage which bears a passing resemblance to the outside world in which he lived his material life.

The re-creation of the Kingdom of Wessex gave Hardy the freedom to 'select, invent and imagine' just as we can 'select, invent and imagine' as we read his fiction and poetry and explore his landscapes. Wessex was therefore for Hardy both 'a disclaimer and a trademark: "This is my perception of how things are, but because it is personal, it is not to be taken as impartial or objective."' (2) Life and the landscape could be no more than 'a series of seemings', a canvas upon which to express his view that 'If way to the Better there be, it exacts a full look at the Worst' (CP 137), his 'tentative philosophy' derived from a childhood at large on the *Egdon* wilderness, reinforced by his readings of Darwin and an innate pessimism inherited from the fatalistic Jemima.

The cottage at Higher Bockhampton and the surrounding heathland formed the centre of Hardy's poetic universe. Although the Wessex delineated on the map which accompanied all later editions of his novels covered half of southern England, from Tintagel (and the Isles of Scilly) in the south-west to Oxford in the north, the essence of Hardy's Wessex lay within a few square miles surrounding his 'Domicilium'. His fictional Wessex is the outward extension of a very narrow landscape, an attempt to resist that constant centripetal poetic force which draws all locations back towards their heart on *Egdon*. Careful examination of the effects of Hardy's contracting kaleidoscope calls into question some of the previously accepted identifications of his Wessex locations; generally, and specifically, the originals are to be found significantly closer to Higher Bockhampton than the text implies.

Hardy described himself as 'a man who used to notice such things' (CP 511). His heightened powers of poetic observation not only utilize the landscape to express emotion through all the conflicting moods and modes of nature, but frequently focus upon the 'immediately recoverable past', recording human history through interpretation of the multiple little marks which man has left upon the environment. This typical example refers to the cottage at Bockhampton: 'Here is the ancient floor, / Footworn hollowed and thin' (CP 135). Such autobiographical references are common in Hardy's landscape descriptions as evidenced in the exploration of *Casterbridge* where it rapidly becomes apparent that this territory is more real than imagined, for Hardy has placed his personal stamp on so many of the places visited. In *Lyonnesse*, autobiography combines with the magical scenery of 'that wild weird western shore' to enhance emotion as music does in opera, intensifying the sense of love, loss and betrayal.

The archetypal Hardyan protagonist is to be found alone on a hilltop, a detached solitary spectator rather than an active participant in the world beneath him. All of the action of *The Return of the Native* can be observed from Rainbarrow as can that of *The Woodlanders* from Bubb Down and *Tower on a Tower* from Rings-hill Speer (although in the latter the vision is more often directed up towards the heavens). These Wessex Heights facilitate Hardy's cinematic technique; descriptions start with a bird's-eye view panning out over the landscape, then focus sharply in upon a particular scene and a particular character within that scene. He employs this method repeatedly throughout his fiction, resurfacing in *The Dynasts* as the ant-like opposing armies crawl across Europe.

The poet himself seeks safety in the solitude of Wessex Heights, places 'for thinking, dreaming, dying on' away from the harsh reality of the 'crass clanging town' where he seems to be 'false to myself, my simple self that was' (CP 261): a 'green' man communing with nature on his chosen hilltop. 'Where one's next neighbour is the sky' it becomes easier to understand our place on this planet and our responsibility not just to our fellow human beings but to all other living creatures on the face of the earth. Hardy's interpretation of Darwin led him to believe that all species have an equal right to exist, to be protected and have their environment preserved. Hardy saw man as a species with an almost unending destructive capability, a unique capacity to cause unlimited suffering, but linked to this an ability to comprehend his position and thus a responsibility to protect and conserve this Earth for 'God's Humblest':

An August Midnight

A shaded lamp and a waving blind,
And the beat of a clock from a distant floor:
On this scene enter – winged, horned, and spined –
A longlegs, a moth, and a dumbledore;
While 'mid my page there idly stands
A sleepy fly, that rubs its hands …

Thus meet we five, in this still place,
At this point of time, at this point in space.
– My guests besmear my new-penned line,
Or bang at the lamp and fall supine.
'God's humblest, they!' I muse. Yet why?
They know Earth-secrets that know not I.

Max Gate 1899 (CP 113)

Notes

Introduction
1. Fowles, John, and Draper, Jo, *Thomas Hardy's England* (Jonathan Cape, London 1984), p.9
2. Irwin, p.4

Chapter One
1. Hawkins, p.24
2. Furzeacker is the *Egdon* name for the Dartford Warbler
3. Lea, p.67
4. Lea, p.75
5. Lea, p.75
6. Millgate, p.199
7. *The Return of the Native*, Penguin Classics (1998), p.442
8. *The Life* pp.309–10

Chapter Two
1. Butler, Lance St John (ed.), *Alternative Hardy* (Palgrave Macmillan, Basingstoke, 1989), p.104
2. *Brewer's Dictionary of Phrase and Fable*, 1999 edition

Chapter Four
1. Harper, p.63
2. Harper, p.70

Chapter Six
1. Legg, Rodney, *The Jurassic Coast* (Halsgrove, Wellington, 2007), p.5
2. Proust, Marcel, and Clark, Carol (trans.), *The Prisoner* (Penguin, Harmondsworth 2002), p.348
3. Pevsner, p.341

Chapter Seven
1. Lea, p.107
2. Hawkins, p.67

Chapter Ten
1. Irwin, p.143
2. Gattrell, Simon, *Thomas Hardy's Vision of Wessex* (Palgrave Macmillan, Basingstoke 2003), p.88

A Hardy Glossary

Wessex Name	Geographical Equivalent
Abbot's Cernel	Cerne Abbas
Abbotsea	Abbotsbury
Aldbrickham	Reading
Alderworth	Cottages near Cull-peppers Dish
Alfredston	Wantage
Anglebury	Wareham
Aquae Sulis	Bath
Athelhall	Athelhampton Hall
Barwith Strand	Trebarwith Strand
Beal, The	Portland Bill
Bede's Inn	Clement's Inn, London
Beersheba	Jericho district of Oxford
Biblioll College	Balliol College
Blackbarrow	Rainbarrows
Blackon	Blackdown
Blooms-End	The Hardys' Cottage
Bollard Head	Ballard Point
Bramshurst Manor	Moyles Court, Hants
Budmouth	Weymouth
Budmouth Regis	Melcombe Regis
Bull-Stake Square	North Square
Camelton	Camelford
Cardinal College	Christchurch College, Oxford
Cardinal Street	St Aldate's Street
Carriford	West Stafford/Lower Bockhampton
Carriford Road Station	Moreton Station
Casterbridge	Dorchester
Castle Boterel	Boscastle
Castle Royal	Windsor Castle
Catknoll	Chetnole
Chalk Newton	Maiden Newton
Chalk Walk	Colliton Walk
Charmley	Charminster

Wessex Name	Geographical Equivalent
Chase, The	Cranborne Chase
Chaseborough	Cranborne
Chief Street	The High, Oxford
Chillington	Killerton, Devon
Christminster	Oxford
Cirque of the Gladiators	Maumbury Rings
Cliff Martin	Coombe Martin, Devon
Clyffe-Hill Clump	Pallington Clump
Corvsgate	Corfe
Cresscombe	Letcombe Bassett, Oxon
Creston	Preston, Dorset
Cross-in-Hand	Cross and Hand
Crozier College	Oriel College
Crimmercrock Lane	A356 NW of Maiden Newton
Damer's Wood	Came Wood
Deadman's Bay	West Bay, Portland and Lyme Bay
Delborough	East Chelborough
Downstaple	Barnstaple
Dundagel	Tintagel
Durnover	Fordington
East Egdon	Affpuddle
East Endelstow	Lesnewth
East Mellstock	Lower Bockhampton
East Quarriers	Easton, Portland
Egdon Heath	Heathland between Dorchester and Bournemouth
Elsenford	Islington, Puddletown
Emminster	Beaminster
Endelstow	St Juliot
Endelstow House	Lanhydrock
Enkworth Court	Encombe House
Evershead	Evershot
Exonbury	Exeter
Flintcomb-Ash	Plush
Flychett	Lychett Minster
Forest of the White Hart	Blackmoor Vale
Fountall	Wells
Fourways	Carfax, Oxford
Froom-Everard	Stafford House
Froom-side Vale	Frome Valley

Wessex Name	Geographical Equivalent
Gaymead	Theale
Giant's Town	Hugh Town, Scilly Isles
Glaston	Glastonbury
Great Forest	New Forest
Great Grey Plain	Salisbury Plain
Great Hintock	Melbury Osmund
Great Pool	Islington Weir
Greenhill	Woodbury Hill, Bere Regis
Haggardon Hill	Eggardon Hill
Havenpool	Poole
Henry VIII's Castle	Sandsfoot Castle
Higher Crowstairs	Fiddler's Green, Stinsford
Hintock House	Melbury House
Holmstoke	East Stoke
Hope Church	St Andrew's, Church Ope
Hope Cove	Church Ope Cove
Idmouth	Sidmouth
Ingpen	Inkpen
Island, The	Isle of Wight
Isle of Slingers	Portland
Ivel(l)	Yeovil
Ivelchester	Ilchester
Kennetbridge	Newbury
Kingsbere (-sub-Greenhill)	Bere Regis
Kingscreech	Steeple
King's Hintock	Melbury Osmund
King's Hintock Court	Melbury House
Knapwater House	Kingston Maurward
Knollingwood Hall	Wimborne St Giles House
Knollsea	Swanage
Leddenton	Gillingham
Lew-Everard	West Stafford
Lewgate	Higher Bockhampton
Little Enckworth	Kingston, near Corfe
Little Hintock	Melbury Bubb
Little Weatherbury Farm	Druce Farm
Little Welland	Winterborne Zelston/Milborne St Andrew
Longpuddle	Piddletrenthide and Piddlehinton
Longpuddle Church	All Saints, Piddletrenthide

Wessex Name	Geographical Equivalent
Lorton Inn	Horton Inn
Lower Longpuddle	Piddlehinton
Lower Mellstock	Lower Bockhampton
Lulwind/Lulstead Cove	Lulworth Cove
Lumsdon	Cumnor, Berks
Maidon/Mai-Dun	Maiden Castle
Markton	Corfe and/or Dunster
Marlott	Marnhull
Marshwood	Middlemarsh
Marygreen	Fawley, Berks
Melchester	Salisbury
Mellstock	Stinsford (Parish)
Mellstock Cross	Bockhampton Cross
Middleton Abbey	Milton Abbas
Mildew Lane	Queen's Lane and New College Lane
Millpond St Jude	Milborne St Andrew
Mistover Knap	near Green Hill, Puddletown Heath
Mixen Lane	Mill Street, Fordington
Mount Lodge	Killerton House, Devon
Narrobourne	Hollywell, West Coker, Somerset
Nest Cottage	Chine Hill Cottage, Druce
Nether-Moynton	Owermoigne
Newland Buckton	Buckton Newton
Norcombe Hill	Toller Down
Nuttlebury/Nuzzlebury	Hazelbury Bryan
Oakbury Fitzpiers	Okeford Fitzpaine
Old-Grove Place	Ox House
Old Melchester	Old Sarum
Old Time Street	Oriel Lane, Oxford
Oldgate College	New College
Oozewood	Ringwood
Overcombe	Sutton Poyntz
Owlscombe	Batcombe
Oxwell Hall	Poxwell Hall
Peakhill Cottage	Manor Gardens Cottage
Pebble Bank	Chesil Beach
Pen-Zephyr	Penzance
Peter's Finger	King's Head, Mill Street
Pilsdon Crest	Pilsdon Pen
Port Bredy	Bridport/West Bay

Wessex Name	Geographical Equivalent
Po'sham	Portesham
Prospect Hotel	Hunter's Inn, Devon
Pummery	Poundbury Hill Fort (not Charleville)
Pure Drop Inn	The Crown at Marnhull
Pydel Vale	Valley of the Piddle
Quartershot	Aldershot
Quiet Woman Inn	Wild Duck/Traveller's Rest – now Duck Dairy Farm
Red King's Castle	Rufus Castle
Ring, The	Maumbury Rings
Ringsworth Shore	Ringstead Bay
Rou'tor Town	Bodmin
Roy Town	Troy Town
Rubdon Hill	Bubb Down
Rubric College	Brasenose College
St Launce's	Launceston
St Silas	St Barnabas, Jericho
Sandbourne	Bournemouth
Sarcophagus College	All Soul's College
Scrimpton	Frampton
Shaston	Shaftesbury
Shadwater Weir	Nine Hatches Weir, Ilsington
Sherton Abbas	Sherborne
Shottsford Forum	Blandford Forum
Silverthorn Dairy	Upexe Farm, near Silverton, Devon
Sleeping Green	Slepe and/or Carhampton
Slopes, The	Boveridge House
Solentsea	Southsea, Hants
Springham	Warmwell
Stagfoot Lane	Hartfoot Lane, Bingham's Melcombe
Stancy Castle	Corfe Castle and/or Dunster Castle
Stapleford	Stalbridge
Stoke-Barehills	Basingstoke
Stourcastle	Sturminster Newton
Street of the Wells	Fortuneswell and Chiswell
Sylvania Castle	Pennsylvania Castle
Talbothays	Norris Mill Farm
Targan Bay	Pentargon Bay
Tolchurch	Tolpuddle
Toneborough	Taunton

Wessex Name	Geographical Equivalent
Tor-upon Sea	Torquay
Trantridge	Boveridge
Tudor College	Corpus Christi
Tutcombe Bottom	Stutcombe Bottom
Upper Longpuddle	Piddletrenthide
Upper Mellstock	Higher Bockhampton
Valley of the Great Dairies	Frome Valley
Vale of the Little Dairies	Blackmoor Vale
Vale of the White Hart	Blackmoor Vale
Vindilia	Portland
Warborne	Wimborne
Weatherbury	Puddletown
Weatherbury Upper Farm	Waterston Manor
Welland Bottom	Ashley Bottom
Welland House	Charborough House and/or Manor House, Milborne
Welland Tower	Charborough Tower and/or Rings Hill Speer
Wellbridge	Wool
Wellbridge Abbey	Bindon Abbey
Wellbridge Manor	Woolbridge Manor, Wool
West Endelstow	St Juliot
West Mellstock	Stinsford
West Shaldon	West Chaldon
Western Moor	Exmoor
Weydon-Priors	Weyhill, Hants
Windy Beak	Cambeak
Wintonchester	Winchester
Wylls-Neck	Wills Neck
Yalbury	Yellowham

Bibliography

Gibson, James (ed.), *The Complete Poems of Thomas Hardy* (Macmillan, London, 1976)

Hands, Timothy, *Thomas Hardy: Distracted Preacher?* (Macmillan, Basingstoke, 1989)

Harper, C.G., *The Hardy Country* (A & C Black, London, 1925)

Hawkins, Desmond, *Hardy's Wessex* (Macmillan, Basingstoke, 1983)

Irwin, Michael, *Reading Hardy's Landscapes* (Macmillan, Basingstoke, 2000)

Kay-Robinson, Denys, *Hardy's Wessex Re-appraised* (David & Charles, Newton Abbot, 1972)

Lea, Hermann, *Thomas Hardy's Wessex* (Macmillan, London, 1913)

Millgate, Michael, *Thomas Hardy: A Biography* (Oxford University Press, Oxford, 1982)

Millgate, Michael (ed.), *The Life and Work of Thomas Hardy by Thomas Hardy* (Macmillan, London, 1984)

Pevsner, Nikolaus, and Newman, John, *Dorset: Pevsner Architectural Guide* (Yale University Press, London, 1991)

Phelps, Kenneth, *The Wormwood Cup: Thomas Hardy in Cornwall* (Lodenek, Padstow, 1975)

Pite, Ralph, *Thomas Hardy: The Guarded Life* (Picador, London, 2007)

Pitfield, F.P., *Hardy's Wessex Locations* (Dorset Publishing, Wincanton, 1992)

Taylor, Christopher, *The Making of the English Landscape: Dorset* (Dovecote Press, Wimborne, 2004)

Windle, Bertram, *The Wessex of Thomas Hardy* (John Lane, London, 1902)

Index